Into the Mêlée

Francis Mulhern comes from Enniskillen in Northern Ireland. His other books include *The Moment of 'Scrutiny'*, *Figures of Catastrophe*, *Culture/Metaculture* and most recently *What Is Cultural Criticism?* with Stefan Collini. He lives in London and is associate editor at *New Left Review*.

Into the Mêlée

Culture/Politics/Intellectuals

Francis Mulhern

VERSO

London • New York

First published by Verso 2024
© Francis Mulhern 2024
Author and publisher express their gratitude to the publications
where the following essays originally appeared.

1 3 5 7 9 10 8 6 4 2

Verso
UK: 6 Meard Street, London W1F 0EG
US: 388 Atlantic Avenue, Brooklyn, NY 11217
versobooks.com

Verso is the imprint of New Left Books

ISBN-13: 978-1-80429-334-8
ISBN-13: 978-1-80429-336-2 (US EBK)
ISBN-13: 978-1-80429-335-5 (UK EBK)

British Library Cataloguing in Publication Data
A catalogue record for this book is available from the British Library

Library of Congress Cataloging-in-Publication Data

Names: Mulhern, Francis, author.
Title: Into the mêlée : culture/politics/intellectuals / Francis Mulhern.
 Description: First edition paperback. | London ; New York : Verso, 2024. |
 Includes bibliographical references.
Identifiers: LCCN 2023046001 (print) | LCCN 2023046002 (ebook) | ISBN
 9781804293348 (paperback) | ISBN 9781804293362 (ebk)
Subjects: LCSH: Fiction—History and criticism—Theory, etc. | LCGFT:
 Essays. | Literary criticism.
Classification: LCC PN3331 .M84 2024 (print) | LCC PN3331 (ebook) | DDC
 809/.3—dc23/eng/20240102
LC record available at https://lccn.loc.gov/2023046001
LC ebook record available at https://lccn.loc.gov/2023046002

Typeset in Minion by Biblichor Ltd, Scotland
Printed and bound by CPI Group (UK) Ltd, Croydon, CR0 4YY

Contents

Preface   vii

English Reading   1
Some Irish Questions   21
Society as Nation as Culture   36
Britain after Nairn   53

Conradian Histories   69
   i.   *Telling Tales, or Hyperphasia*   73
   ii. *Figures of Disavowal*   88
   iii. *Fascinations*   107

Intellectual Identities   120
   i.   *Teachers, Writers, Celebrities*   121
   ii. *Into the Mêlée*   143

Burke's Way   155
Afterlives of the Commune   170
Forever Orwell   183
Good Sense and Sensibility   198
William Empson, Nonesuch   210
About Roberto Schwarz   222
Hobsbawm's End Times   232
Caution, Metaphors at Work   247
A Party of Latecomers   258

Preface

The 'mêlée' or fray that the writer Romain Rolland wrote to deplore in the *Journal de Genève* was the Great War of 1914, then in its early weeks. The phrase from which the word comes—a title made final only at proof stage—has outlived the conflict by more than a century, over the years losing much of its specific reference and gaining a measure of general authority as a call to cultural service beyond the deforming pressures of everyday political and social strife, a vocation 'au-dessus de la mêlée'. I have taken issue with positions of this kind in previous contexts of discussion—most relevantly *Culture/Metaculture* and the exchanges it provoked—and will not rehearse the arguments here, except to say, in sum, that all the texts now gathered in this volume have been written in the contrary belief that there is in reality no social location corresponding to this desire, strong and appealing though it may be, that 'above' or 'beyond' the mêlée there is, finally, nothing in the relevant sense.[1] Of course, the cultural dimension of our social being is none the less real for that, and its relation to politics is intrinsically discrepant. Yet they inhabit one another, if only in permanent tension, each, in regard to the other, at once too broad and too narrow, both ecumenical and sectarian, and unavoidably so.[2]

---

1   See now Stefan Collini and Francis Mulhern, *What Is Cultural Criticism?*, London and New York 2024.
2   See Francis Mulhern, ed., *Contemporary Marxist Literary Criticism*, London and New York 1982, pp. 26–9.

These texts are diverse in provenance and date, and it is not superfluous to say a word about their general character, as they were written and first published, and about the shape in which they appear now. The most obvious change is contextual: the texts appear here together for the first time, arranged in clusters about which it may be useful to offer some elucidation. The shared interest in the first cluster is nationality, and within this conceptual space the accent of critical discussion varies from the predominantly cultural—the Leavisian effort to assert a normatively English literary subject—to the directly political, as Tom Nairn projects his vision of England and Scotland 'after Britain'. A retrospect of Raymond Williams's *Culture and Society* after fifty years leads into a critique of the nation as society-as-culture, while Joe Cleary's inquiries attend to the promise and the problems of implementing Marxist schemes of literary history on the terrain of a once-colonized culture such as Ireland's.

A second cluster concerns the antithetical valuations of knowledge in the culture of modernity, first in a single three-part investigation of Joseph Conrad as a novelist of the modern world, his alienation from the novelistic as such and compulsive recourse to a rhetoric of disavowal as his central narrative strategy. This study in literary fascination develops into a comparative analysis of fetishism in Freud and Marx, returning finally to the novelist's most ambitious attempt to capture the unthinkable world system of capital, in *Nostromo*.

What then can be said about that exemplary bearer of critical knowledge, 'the intellectual'? A pair of conjectural essays present differently angled attempts to clarify the question through the idea of intellectual corporatism. The last of these three clusters is devoted to particular intellectuals—intellectuals in politics and in the greater number of cases, in one way or another, the politics of revolution and counter-revolution. Burke on the American and French Revolutions; Morris and Kropotkin as advocates for the Paris Commune; Orwell in Barcelona and Empson in China; Schwarz in São Paulo, the unblinking analyst of Brazilian 'neo-backwardness'; and Hobsbawm, the outstanding synopticist of modern times and the short twentieth century. The writings of the liberal Tory Ferdinand Mount offer a contrasting way into consideration of this question. The book closes with treatments of two notable legatees of the Anglophone twentieth century's critical revolutions, James Wood's charismatic literary journalism and, in an altogether different vein, the record of the magazine *n+1*, as a self-conscious renewal of the leftist traditions of *Partisan Review*.

Some of these pieces were commissioned as introductions to books or as chapters in edited collections, while others began as invited lectures; the rest, just over half the total, belong to the hybrid form that Bagehot described as 'the review-like essay and the essay-like review'. As such, they are more or less explicitly occasional in character—in reference and more often in address, that whole set of assumptions we make about our audience every time we speak, and as a condition of speaking at all. It follows too that in preparing a diverse set of originals for republication, there can't be a simple editorial formula, even where the core substance of the text remains essentially unchanged. Some demands were constant, such as the need to manage the temporal shifters, the intimate markers of the writer-reader relationship in time (*since, recent, now, then* and the rest), which changes inexorably, though in no fixed rhythm or pace. Others were called upon according to perceived need: here a new opening or concluding paragraph, there a postscript, elsewhere a new title or additional material to take account of a changed situation. There were repetitions to cut, inevitably, but not according to a mechanical rule, for these remain relatively autonomous essays to be read in variable order, not as if simulating a chapter sequence in a through-written book. None of them has passed unrevised.

For all kinds of support in this work over the years I have to thank Perry Anderson, Rachel Malik, Peter Osborne and Susan Watkins. I owe particular thanks to Tom Hazeldine for his editorial oversight of this collection and to Simon Hammond for some detailed advice.

I have also to acknowledge the editors and publishers of the books and journals in which these essays first appeared:

'English Reading', Homi K. Bhabha, ed., *Nation and Narration*, London: Routledge, 1990.

'Some Irish Questions' (as 'Just Another Island?'), *Field Day Review*, 5, 2009.

'Society as Nation as Culture' (as '*Culture and Society*, Then and Now'), *NLR*, 55, 2009.

'Britain after Nairn', *NLR*, 5, 2000.

'Conradian Histories' parts 1 and 2 together (as 'Storia inconcepibile'), Franco Moretti, ed., *Il Romanzo*, vol. 2: *Le Forme*, Torino: Einaudi, 2002, and trans. 'Conrad's Inconceivable History', *NLR*, 38, 2006; part 3 (as 'Critical Considerations on the Fetishism of Commodities'), *ELH* (Johns Hopkins University Press), 74.2, 2007.

'Intellectual Identities' part 1 as the introduction to Régis Debray, *Teachers, Writers, Celebrities*, London: Verso, 1981; part 2 (as 'Intellectual Corporatism and Socialism: The Twenties and After'), *News from Nowhere*, 5, 1988.

'Burke's Way', *NLR*, 102, 2016.

'Afterlives of the Commune', *NLR*, 96, 2015.

'Forever Orwell', *NLR*, 87, 2014.

'Good Sense and Sensibility' (as 'A Tory Tribune?'), *NLR*, 105, 2017.

'William Empson, Nonesuch', *NLR*, 2017.

'About Roberto Schwarz', as the editor's introduction to Schwarz, *Two Girls and Other Essays*, London and New York: Verso, 2012.

'Hobsbawm's End Times' (as 'End Times'), *NLR*, 81, 2013.

'Caution, Metaphors at Work', *NLR*, 127, 2021.

'A Party of Latecomers', *NLR*, 93, 2015.

English Reading

My task which I am trying to achieve is, by the power of the written word to make you hear, to make you feel—it is, before all else, to make you see. That—and no more, and it is everything.

Joseph Conrad

English ought to be kept up.

John Keats

What should we read, how should we read it, and why? Such questions are staple elements of any politics of reading. But they remain less than critical if they are put without consciousness of the un-avowed answer they already insinuate. Issues of selection, procedure, and purpose are often settled in advance by the meanings assigned to the collective pronoun. So there is a further question: as whom, as what, do 'we' read? Asked or not, this question is always answered, and my purpose here is to consider the answer given in an especially forceful practice of reading: the English literary criticism chiefly represented by F. R. and Q. D. Leavis.

1

Pressed by René Wellek for a philosophical defence of his criticism, F. R. Leavis offered a narrative:

The cogency I hoped to achieve was to be for other readers of poetry—readers of poetry as such. I hoped, by putting in front of them, in a criticism that should keep as close to the concrete as possible, my own developed 'coherence of response', to get them to agree (with, no doubt, critical qualifications) that the map, the essential order, of English poetry seen as a whole did, when they interrogated their experience, look like that to them also . . . My whole effort was to work in terms of concrete judgements and particular analyses: 'This—doesn't it?—bears such a relation to that; this kind of thing—don't you find it so?—wears better than that', etc.[1]

In this way, Leavis sought to elude the very terms of Wellek's demand. There would be no 'explicit' and 'systematic' account of principles, no 'abstract' evaluation of 'choices': only reading, and dialogue with other readers.

The upshot was paradoxical. Apparently unforthcoming, Leavis's countermove was perhaps more revealing than a more compliant response would have been. The founding assumption of Leavisian criticism, it turned out, was a rigorous humanism: the experiential merging of critic and poem, and of both with the experience of 'other readers', was scarcely thinkable without the 'philosophical' guarantee of a human essence—something constant, universal, and, like the Arnoldian 'best self', potentially decisive.[2] However, there is a logical strain in the notion of an essence whose efficacy is contingent, and this is evident in Leavis's narrative of 'the common pursuit'. The imagined scene is ideal: critic and interlocutor in informal, even intimate exchange. But the very informality of the critic-narrator's questions betrays the imposture of openness: negatively phrased, they presume assent—or what is imagined at another moment as corroborative self-'interrogation'. The interlocutor, meanwhile, is silent; the expected 'critical qualifications', never uttered, remain parenthetical concessions in the discourse of the critic. Lacking this

---

1   F. R. Leavis, 'Literary Criticism and Philosophy', *Scrutiny*, 5, 4 (March 1936), repr. F. R. Leavis, *The Common Pursuit*, Harmondsworth 1972, pp. 214, 215.

2   My critical use of the term 'humanist' bears only on this kind of essentialism.

interlocutor, the situation and its justifying event are jeopardized, and Leavis seems almost resigned to the loss: 'I hoped . . . I hoped . . . my whole effort was . . .', he writes, as if telling a story of what might have been.

Leavis's half-realized character—present, presumably assenting, yet silent—embodies a compromise between two incommensurable entities: the ideal interlocutor whose active, confirming presence is the necessary ground of Leavisian criticism, and an actual, contingent readership that is neither present to the author nor predictable in the range and substance of its qualifications. This, abstractly speaking, is a logical dilemma: Leavisian criticism is a long-drawn-out fallacy, endlessly bent on establishing what it already assumes to exist. But practically, it is a problem of suasion. 'My task', wrote Conrad, in a declaration uncannily close to Leavis's, 'is, before all else, to make you *see*. That—and no more, and it is everything.'[3] If so little is everything, it is because there is indeed something more. The preferred reading of the passage is clearly signalled in its syntax and typography: the goal is shared vision. But these indications of emphasis are crossed by the counter-emphasis of repetition: the task is 'to make you . . . to make you . . . to make you . . .'. In a characteristic movement of disavowal, Conrad's words admit the moment of dictation in all writing. To represent the object is, measure for measure, to position the subject, the clarity of the one depending on the stability of the other. To 'make' is at once to compel and to compose: to compel the actual reader by composing an ideal one, to pre-scribe the subjective conditions of 'seeing'. No less than of Conrad's fiction, this is the rhetorical task of Leavisian criticism.

Leavis's task is to determine the object ('the map, the essential order') and, as a necessary part of this, to position the subject. His critical writing must work to reduce the discrepancy between its ideal interlocutor and real readers, to compose the *normal* subject of Leavisian reading-writing. In other words, the writing must complete the half-sketched second character in the exemplary narrative of

---

3 Joseph Conrad, preface, *The Nigger of the 'Narcissus', Typhoon, Falk and Other Stories*, London 1950, p. x.

criticism. And it really will be a 'character', not an ontological cypher. The sponsors of humanism are, dependably, rather more than generically 'human', and so equally are the normative images of their writing. As Perry Anderson once observed, 'the real solidarities of Leavisian humanism are quite specific in time and place.'[4] The character whose features emerge in Leavisian criticism is a fully historical being, and 'normal' in every way.

2

This normalizing drive is sometimes declared, as on those occasions when critical attention turns from the literary object to the (qualifying?) reader: 'Here a few illustrations [from *The Prelude*] must suffice, as indeed, to point the attention effectively, they should: that once done, the demonstration is the reading, as anyone who cares to open his Wordsworth may see; the facts, to the adverted eye, are obvious.'[5]

But conspicuous interventions of this kind are only the periodic excesses of an activity whose signs are everywhere in the ordinary workings of Leavisian analysis and judgement. For in this cultural zone nearly all seasons are bad ones. The imagined time of Leavisian criticism ('I hoped . . . I hoped . . . my whole effort was . . .') is that of impending loss. The ideal interlocutor is chronically prone to distraction by the spectacle of historical change. The meaning of modern history, for Leavis, was the dissolution of community. Emerging in the period of the English Revolution and gathering strength in the succeeding century, a whole array of social forces had worked to undermine a traditional, integrated way of life, and then unleashed the industrializing dynamic that shook it apart. Where once there had been an 'organic' community, there were now two mutually opposed and unequal realities: 'civilization', the world of means and quantities, which drove forward according to the

---

4   Perry Anderson, 'Components of the National Culture', in Robin Blackburn and Alexander Cockburn, eds, *Student Power*, Harmondsworth 1969, p. 271.

5   F. R. Leavis, *Revaluation*, Harmondsworth 1972, p. 146.

autonomous logic of industrial production, and 'culture', the world of qualities and ends, the memory of a human norm that could never again find general social acceptance, and the only resource of those who fought to avert a final breach in continuity. By the early twentieth century, the lot of 'culture' had so worsened that language, in its most demanding literary usage, was the only remaining element of continuity. Out of that history and that vital 'human' need came the cultural warrant of literary judgement and the objective responsibility borne by any who thought to exercise it.

Such representations of the past are not truly historical in mode. Processes of change are described and interpreted, but only as the corrosive, demoralizing environment of something that is held to be essentially changeless, and whose value is the decisive theme of the retrospect. This is the past not as history but as 'tradition'. Its characteristic mode is, so to say, transjunctive, its valued moments 'joined across' the objective order of what has been in the service of what now exists. Tradition, as Leavis himself noted, is akin to memory. And, as he did not add, their procedures and functions are the same. Tradition, usually said to be received, is in reality made, in an unceasing activity of selection, revision, and outright invention, whose function is to defend identity against the threat of heterogeneity, discontinuity and contradiction. Its purpose is to bind (and necessarily, therefore, to exclude). Tradition is prone to represent itself as custom, as the settled fact of continuity, but its real process is shot through with anxiety, as the history of Leavis's journal itself attests. *Scrutiny's* watchword, as it evaluated the claims of writing in its own day, was 'for continuity' (the title of Leavis's first collection of essays). But its retrospects were no less wary, and the last years of the journal witnessed a restless probing of the 'organic community' itself, in its putative seventeenth-century setting. The essential strengths of that period were found to be residues of pre-Reformation culture, which in its turn was discovered to run back into a pre-Christian past. And so the deepest continuities of English literature seemed to be with a society and a culture that were not in any reasonable sense 'English'.

The poignancy of this conclusion deserves emphasis, for the sovereign *topos* of Leavisian discourse was precisely the continuity of

Englishness. The basic categories of *Scrutiny*'s historiography were implicitly universal in application; as is manifest in the kindred sociological line descending from Tönnies's *Gemeinschaft und Gesellschaft*, they frame a certain interpretation of the transition to capitalism as such. But in Leavis's writing, their privileged reference is to England and the doom of English culture, and his key values are not so much 'culture' or 'literature' as a language and a people.

Shakespeare, Leavis affirms, is 'the pre-eminently (in his relation to the language) English poet',[6] and the decisive nuance of the adverbial is fixed in this tribute to Donne: 'This is the Shakespearian use of English: one might say that it is the English use—the use, in the essential spirit of the language, of its characteristic resources.'[7] The attributes of this essential spirit are celebrated again and again. Donne's poetry exhibits 'the sinew and living nerve', the 'strength of spoken English'.[8] Jonson evinces a 'native robustness', a 'rooted and racy Englishness'; his 'toughness is lively and English', going with his 'native good sense'.[9] In Jonson, these qualities are such as to subdue the external, 'classicizing' language of the Renaissance, his 'racy personal tone' turning 'erudition into native sinew'. Where classicism prevails, as in Milton, the outcome is 'rejection of English idiom', for which the critical penalty is exile.[10] The integrity that animates this English idiom has more than one specification. Leavis largely agrees with Gerard Manley Hopkins that Dryden's 'native English strength' is 'masculine' in its stress on 'the naked thew and sinew of the language', and compliments Crabbe on his 'generous masculine strength'.[11] The lapse from this idiom is a token of moral deficiency, as the case of Shelley shows. But Keats bears witness to the possibility of regeneration, finding at last 'a strength—a native English strength— lying beyond the scope of the poet who aimed to make English as like Italian as possible [and a] vigour such as is alien to the Tennysonian

---

6   Ibid., p. 12.
7   Ibid., p. 58.
8   Ibid., pp. 19, 21.
9   Ibid., pp. 26, 29.
10   Ibid., p. 55.
11   Ibid., pp. 35, 118.

habit, and such as a Tennysonian handling of the medium cannot breed.'[12]

The steady connotative pressure of Leavis's idiom is quite remarkable. The literal emphasis on the specificities of the English language is developed, across an unvarying range of metaphor, association and (scarcely intended) pun, into a positive characterization of 'Englishness'. By the later stages of *Revaluation* an elaborate order of solidarity and antagonism has been enforced: the native, racy, vigorous, strong, masculine, and against these the classicizing, Italianate, alien, corrupt, voluptuous, effeminate, impotent. In vouching for Wordsworth as 'normally and robustly human', Leavis summarizes a whole anthropology of virtue.[13] 'The facts, to the adverted eye, are obvious.'

The Great Tradition was to do for the English novel what *Revaluation* had done for English poetry. Like the earlier work, it is concerned not to construct a history (it is expressly pitched against 'the literary histories') but to ascertain the 'tradition', the 'line' of the English novel as it comes down through the heterogeneous mass of narrative fiction in prose. The nature of the operation approaches self-consciousness in this sentence from the opening pages of the work: 'One of the supreme debts one great writer can owe another is the realization of unlikeness (there is, of course, no significant unlikeness without the common concern—and the common seriousness of concern—with essential human issues).'[14] The movement of this passage epitomizes the activity of binding and exclusion in which Leavisian criticism is involved. Heterogeneity is at first acknowledged, but is then reduced to 'significant' unlikeness, which turns out to be the deceptive sign of an inner consonance whose bearing (cognitive and ethical) is the essentially human—in short, the self-identical. And the medium of the essentially human, it turns out, is English. The nativism of *Revaluation* is equally, if less euphorically, evident in *The Great Tradition*.

---

12   Ibid., p. 245.
13   Ibid., p. 160.
14   F. R. Leavis, *The Great Tradition*, Harmondsworth 1972, p. 19.

Of Leavis's three chosen novelists, only one (George Eliot) was English. James was Anglophone but American; the language of Conrad's novels was his third; and both learned significantly from other literatures. A key purpose of *The Great Tradition* was to reduce these complexities of formation to biographical accident and to naturalize James and Conrad as exponents of a transcendent language that must be understood as adequate, and finally as necessary, to the novelistic exploration of 'essential human values'. The story of the book is the victory of an English tradition over the circumstances of origin and, crucially, over the latter-day Renaissance, French realism. Thus, James may be located in 'a distinctively American' line, but this is as it were a ruse of tradition: Hawthorne emancipated James from the influence of Thackeray and from Flaubert, making possible an authentic, enabling connection with Eliot.[15] Conrad did indeed learn from 'the French masters': the stylism and exoticism of his weaker writing is derived from Chateaubriand, and *Nostromo* recalls Flaubert.[16] Yet Conrad's work, with its 'robust vigour of melodrama', is also 'Dickensian', 'Elizabethan' even.[17] And if he evinces that 'racy strength' it is because, his origins notwithstanding, his themes and interests actually called for the English language rather than any other. He is 'unquestionably a constitutive part of the tradition, belonging in the full sense'.[18]

A second major theme of *The Great Tradition* is the novel as such. It was in the course of writing this book that Leavis substantiated his conception of the novel as linguistic art. 'The differences between a lyric, a Shakespeare play, and a novel, for some purposes essential, are not in danger of being forgotten; what needs insisting on is the community', he wrote in the early 1930s, and the criticism that ensued was to be interested not in 'character' and 'incident' but in the 'pattern of moral significances' that novelistic art might yield, in 'the novel as dramatic poem'.[19] Much of the meaning of this

---

15 Ibid., pp. 148, 151.
16 Ibid., pp. 217, 218, 219.
17 Ibid., pp. 241, 225, 227.
18 Ibid., pp. 27, 29.
19 F. R. Leavis, *Towards Standards of Criticism* (1933), London 1976, pp. 19–20.

conception, and the polemical force with which Leavis promoted it, must be sought in the history of academic and lay literary criticism. Leavis, like others around him, was determined to redeem the novel from its common status as a cultivated or narcotic diversion and to establish its parity with the canonical arts of language. But his manner of doing so bears an interesting relation to his critical practice generally. His terminology disrupts the received classification of verbal art and redefines the novel (epic) as a combination of the two types from which it was usually distinguished, the lyric and the dramatic. The effect of this development—which reinforced an already well-established emphasis on the 'poetic' essence of verse drama—was to reorder the field of critical perception at the expense of narrative. All wider differences set aside, it can still be said that the greatest weakness of Leavisian criticism lay just here; and part of the sense of that weakness may be glimpsed in Leavis's reading of *Typhoon*. The 'elemental frenzy' (Leavis's phrase) that occupies most of Conrad's story is a literal event: a British merchant ship is exposed to a devastating tropical storm and only narrowly escapes destruction. But from the outset it is metaphorized as a psychic and political ordeal. The ship's captain, MacWhirr, is an obsessional. Locks and charts are the emblems of his life; his letters to his wife are phatic observances, without value as registrations of feeling or incident; his speech, which he enforces as a shipboard norm, is laconic, literal, and untouched by the smallest acquaintance with pidgin. However, the circumstances of this voyage are not wholly routine. The ship has been transferred from the British to the Siamese flag; and the cargo on this occasion is human—200 Chinese coolies returning from periods of labour in various colonies. Sailing under 'queer' colours, its crew outnumbered by their freight of alien bodies, the *Nan-Shan* heads into 'dirty' weather. The storm attacks every established social relationship of the vessel. Masculinity is abandoned for hysteria; linguistic order fails, as speech turns figural or obscene, is blocked by superstition or swept away by the gale. MacWhirr and his first mate, Jukes, reach for each other in encounters that mingle duty and desire, resolution and bewilderment, while in the hold the Chinese have apparently gone berserk. The lowering of the British ensign brings on a storm that unfixes identity ('He started shouting aimlessly to the man he could feel near him in that fiendish blackness, "Is it you, sir? Is it you, sir?" till his temples seemed ready to burst. And he heard in answer a voice, as if crying far away, as if screaming to him fretfully from a very great distance, the one word "Yes!"'), and *Homo Britannicus* is abandoned to a chaos of effeminacy, homoeroticism, and gibberish—the terrifying counter-order of the Chinese labourers below. The ship survives. But the restoration of order is understood as a furtive improvisation, the hurried winding-up of an incident better forgotten. It is related not by the main narrator but in a chattily complacent letter from Jukes, who, in his uncertain sexual orientation (his regular correspondent is male) and openness to linguistic transgression (metaphor, pidgin), is socially perverse. Worse, the protagonist himself is fatally ambiguous: MacWhirr, as we have learned from an early narrative recollection, is not British but Irish. The chief officers of the *Nan-Shan,* ultimate guarantors of imperial order, bear the typhoon within themselves.

Leavis's account discloses virtually nothing of this. Where he quotes passages whose manifest sense discourages any other reading, he confines himself to dubious technical observations on 'a novelist's art', and his wider commentary on *Typhoon* strikes a directly contrary emphasis. It is the 'ordinariness' and 'matter-of-factness' of the ship's captain and crew that hold his attention, 'the qualities which, in a triumph of discipline—a triumph of the spirit—have enabled a handful of ordinary men to impose sanity on a frantic mob'.[20] Leavis's language reveals his ideological relationship to *Typhoon* and, at the same time, the strategy of his reading. Identifying himself with the norms of the text, he sets out to rewrite its ending and to unwrite the greater part of the narrative. *Typhoon* works through a fearsome return of the repressed; Leavis's reading functions to assist repression, indeed to perfect it, simply silencing the anxieties that generated the story in the first instance.

Leavis's encounter with *Typhoon* may serve as a hyperbolic illustration of his critical relationship with narrative generally. Narratives

---

20   Leavis, *The Great Tradition*, p. 214.

vary, it need hardly be said; but the work of narrativity is always an opening and closing, a loosening and rebinding of sense. All but the most sedate or the most forensic narratives are in some degree unsettling, and *Typhoon* is neither. It may be ventured, then, that a criticism bent on affirming an essential human identity will be inhibited in the face of narrative, and will revise its object-texts (as the ego is said to revise dreams and memories) in that interest. It is apt that Leavis, confronted with a fictional dispersal of that identity, in a text of his own choosing by one of his canonical authors, should read with an averted eye.

3

The 'human' is a closely specified term in Leavisian discourse, as, in turn, is 'English': *Revaluation* makes this plain. They are normalizing terms that arrogate the common names of a species, a language and an ethnic formation as the honorific titles of particular social commitments and agencies. They are, in the necessary strict meaning of a slackened concept, ideological. The nature of these commitments and agencies is manifest in the social history of Leavis and his collaborators, and equally in their critical writing. The normal subject of Leavisian discourse is specified not only by nationality but also by class, gender, and sexual orientation.

The *Scrutiny* 'connection', as Leavis sometimes called it, was petty-bourgeois. Its leading members were generally such by provenance, as were its contributors and regular readers—teachers in the main— by occupation. The politics of the 'connection' were likewise suspended over the main national and international conflicts of the time. The anti-industrialism of the journal was inevitably shaded with anti-capitalism, sometimes markedly. But *Scrutiny*'s stand against Marxism is a legend; and notwithstanding social compassion and episodic political sympathy, Leavis and his collaborators rebuffed any suggestion that the industrial working class had the capacity to sustain or develop 'humane culture'. The class disposition of the journal was plainest in its constant attacks on the leisured academic rearguard of Oxford and Cambridge, and the part-rentier,

part-commercial intelligentsia of the capital. One among many nee-
dling allusions to the former can be discerned in Leavis's repeated
reference, in *Revaluation*, to 'the mob of gentlemen' who versified at
the court of Charles I; and a more striking index of this academic
class antagonism is the diction of Leavisian criticism, which characteristically qualifies the received idiom of cultivated leisure ('taste',
'sensibility', 'fineness') with a new and challenging idiom of effort
('strenuous', 'labour', 'collaboration', 'enactment'). The strategic prize
in *Scrutiny*'s contention with the metropolitan elites was the status of
'centrality', which Leavis and his collaborators sought to invest with a
strictly cultural rather than social meaning. Here too the polemical
idiom was telling: in a metaphorical economy of intellectual life, the
'inflated currencies' of the capital were to be regulated by authentic
'standards' and 'values', real measures of work and self-improvement.

Much of Q. D. Leavis's assault on Virginia Woolf can be read in
this light. The latter's *Three Guineas,* she charged, exemplified the
conceptions of a class-blinded 'social parasite'; Woolf's feminist critique of educational provision was 'a sort of chatty restatement of the
rights and wrongs' of propertied women intellectuals like herself,
designed to 'penalize specialists' in the interests of amateur 'boudoir
scholarship'. But there was more than righteous class hostility in a
passage like this, which duly places Leavis's occasional concessions to
feminism:

> 'Daughters of educated men have always done their thinking from
> hand to mouth . . . [Woolf had written]. They have thought while
> they stirred the pot, while they rocked the cradle'. I agree with
> someone who complained that to judge from the acquaintance
> with the realities of life displayed in this book there is no reason to
> suppose Mrs Woolf would know which end of the cradle to stir. I
> feel bound to disagree with Mrs Woolf's assumption that running
> a household and a family unaided necessarily hinders or weakens
> thinking. One's own kitchen and nursery, and not the drawing-
> room and dinner-table where tired professional men relax among
> the ladies (thus Mrs Woolf), is the realm where living takes place,
> and I see no profit in letting our servants live for us. The activities

Mrs Woolf wishes to free educated women from as wasteful not
only provide a valuable discipline, they serve as a sieve for determining which values are important and genuine and which are
conventional and contemptible. It is this order of experience that
often makes the conversation of an uncultivated charmless
woman who has merely worked hard and reared a family interesting and stimulating, while its absence renders a hypertrophied
conversation piece like *Three Guineas* tiresome and worthless.[21]

That Virginia Woolf was prone to rentier myopia is undeniable, and
Q. D. Leavis's attack would be sympathetic were not its terms
and tone those of a far more myopic, truculently conformist femi-
ninity. Not merely a self-pampering 'victim' of class privilege, the
suggestion went, Woolf was deficient as a woman. In such judgements the Leavises stood side by side. Corresponding assumptions
animate the language of *Revaluation,* with its ready gendering of
poetic idiom and associated imagery of virility and procreation (or
their vicious substitutes). Woolf did not lack male company either:
F. R. Leavis's summarizing review of E. M. Forster, in one way a
moving tribute, hesitated several times before the novelist's 'spin-
sterish' prose; and the most-lamented poetic wastrel of the 1930s,
W. H. Auden, was cast out in an article deploring his 'inverted'
development.[22] There were so many tests of what was 'normally and
robustly human'.

The evidence of these canonical works—the critical books and
essays—is supported by that of the apocrypha: the joint autobiography that occupied the Leavises (and those around them) all their
lives. This work was never written, in the ordinary sense, but as
Raymond Williams observed, it might as well have been: 'Most of
those who have heard [the story] will know how compellingly it was
told. It was a sustained structure of feeling through the only apparently random episodes. It was essentially composed, in a literary

---

21   Q. D. Leavis, 'Caterpillars of the Commonwealth Unite', *Scrutiny,* 7, 2
(September 1938), pp. 210–11.
22   F. R. Leavis, *Scrutiny,* 7, 2 and 13, 2 (September 1945) respectively.

sense.'[23] Williams was referring to the institutional history of
Cambridge, *Scrutiny*, the London 'literary racket', and so on. But the
volume of memoirs from which his words come extends their sense
to the sphere of the domestic and personal. What emerges from
Denys Thompson's gathering of 'recollections and impressions' is
how strongly, how theatrically, the Leavises emphasized the proprieties of gender and family, and with what impact on those who were
close to them. Frank was vain to the point of boasting about his ath-
letic prowess, as was Queenie about her domestic skills; his running
and her scones are staple topics of their memoirists. Their famous
intellectual 'collaboration' was subject to strict gender regulation and
a corresponding division of domestic labour. This was not a trouble-
free formula: Queenie, proudly a working woman intellectual but
just as proudly the wife and mother who never broke a cup, suffered
conflicts of identity and interest from which her husband was largely
exempt, and she knew it. But, in all, it seems that the drama of
Leavisian criticism was encoded also as a determined and conservative politics of 'mature', 'normal' gender and sexuality, whose ideal
scene was the family. It is not merely that the Leavises lived in a
certain way—that is of purely biographical interest. What is important is that they actively represented their life together as a further
specification of the 'human norm'.

The style of life, thus organized and projected, joined the critical
style in a discourse of formidable appeal, as grateful pupils soon
began to testify. 'Sanity and vigour and masculinity and Britishness'
were the qualities that compelled one early tribute—Martin Green's.
To him, F. R. Leavis seemed

> intensely and integrally British. Not Europeanized, not of the
> intelligentsia, not of the upper classes, not of Bloomsbury, not of
> any group or set. [He] comes to us from generations of decency
> and conscience and reasonableness and separateness, of private
> houses hidden behind hedges, along the road from Matthew

---

23 Denys Thompson, ed., *The Leavises: Recollections and Impressions*,
Cambridge 1984, pp. 119–20.

Arnold and John Stuart Mill . . . Alone in all Cambridge his voice
has echoes of the best things in my parents' England, makes
connections between all the parts of my experience.[24]

These are ingenuous words, but they are apt. Their structure of
feeling is manifestly Leavisian. In such terms, the ideal interlocutor
finds a social identity and begins to speak.

4

The governing values of Leavisian discourse are class-restrictive,
(hetero)sexist and ethnocentric. The 'human' image is caught in a
sepia print of family life in lower-middle-class England. In this composition of values, the fixing element, the guarantee of integrity, was
the notion of an abiding, self-evident Englishness. Ethnocentrism
did much to frame the perspective of *Scrutiny*'s literary criticism—
which in turn cannot fully be understood apart from its conditions
of formation in mid-century England.

'Ethnocentric' need not mean stay-at-home. If *Scrutiny* was less
cosmopolitan than some other literary journals of its time, it was not
insular. The literature of England was always its major concern, but
that was hardly an unreasonable option. French, German, and US literature were extensively discussed, and other national literatures
were surveyed or sampled. Neither was the journal in any ordinary
sense patriotic: on the contrary, opposition to British chauvinism was
a point of honour during the Second World War. The traces of
Scrutiny's ethnocentrism are to be found not in the range of its international coverage, which by the standards of the day was merely
unremarkable, but in its characteristic manner. *Scrutiny* was most
confident when dealing with native literatures: those emerging from
the home ground of their respective languages—English, French,
German, Italian. Inhibition and resistance became evident in the face
of 'rootless' diversity. 'More and more does human life depart from

---

24   Martin Green, 'British Decency', *Kenyon Review*, 21, 4 (Autumn 1959),
pp. 505–32.

the natural rhythms,' Leavis wrote, in an early, qualified reference to
Spengler; 'the cultures have mingled, and the forms have dissolved
into chaos.'[25] *Scrutiny*'s criticism—and more pointedly his own—
attempted to restore integrity and order. Thus, the Renaissance was
legitimate on its own territory, but not when it threatened to 'classi-
cize' English poetic idiom; and whatever might be said for the French
novel as a moment in the cultural history of France, it could not be
granted a formative role in the novelistic tradition of England.

Within Anglophone culture itself there were special problems, for
imperialism had made the metropolitan tongue a lingua franca
whose users were, in the majority, not ethnically English. The language
had won its international eminence at the cost of its native integrity.
The most salient foreign literary vernaculars in English at this date
were those of the United States and Ireland. America was always
important, and in many ways attractive, to *Scrutiny*. But attempts
to characterize its literature were unresolved. The journal's most sustained effort to describe a distinctive American literary tradition—the
work of an American contributor, Marius Bewley—ran a paradoxical
course. Bewley's purpose, openly opposed to Leavis's, was to establish
the 'essential Americanism' of Henry James. But this critical difference was not all its principals took it to be, for Bewley's thesis ended
in bathos: setting out from the example of Jane Austen and returning
to England in the person of James, the American 'line' turned out to
be a loop circuit of the great tradition.[26] *Scrutiny*'s coverage of Irish
writing, in contrast, was sparse and fragmentary. But its greatest
interwar representative, James Joyce, was rejected early and decisively,
and in telling terms. Joyce, for Leavis, was the anti-Shakespeare, his
work the destructive antithesis of an authentic, 'rooted' idiom.[27] The
charge was appropriate in a way, but the historical impetus of Joyce's
work was not one that Leavis, in his own pregnant word, could easily
'recognize'. What is lost in Joyce is indeed any sense of the English

25   F. R. Leavis, *For Continuity*, Cambridge 1933, p. 139.
26   Marius Bewley, *The Complex Fate*, London 1952.
27   F. R. Leavis, 'Joyce and "the Revolution of the Word"', *Scrutiny*, 2, 2
(September 1933), pp. 193–201.

language as second nature. Unlike James and Conrad, as *The Great Tradition* portrays them, Joyce was not relieved of his circumstantial beginnings by the language of Shakespeare. He was a product of colonial Ireland and wrote out of that formation. His writing is, in this respect, a dramatization of the 'native' as alien, the 'mother' language as another language. (Stephen, of the Dean of Studies: 'The language in which we are speaking is his before it is mine. How different are the words *home, Christ, ale, master,* on his lips and on mine! I cannot speak or write these words without unrest of spirit. His language, so familiar and so foreign, will always be for me an acquired speech. I have not made or accepted its words. My voice holds them at bay. My soul frets in the shadow of his language.') It is the writing of someone for whom 'English' could not be self-identical, a literary practice whose 'roots' lay in the history of colonialism.

That history sank just as deeply into the metropolitan culture, sparing none, not even the disinterested humanists of *Scrutiny*. Critical writing, like any other, proposes a subjective place of reading, but dictation is beyond its power. Many things may be written and read, but rather few are internalized, reiterated, elaborated, and applied. The ideal match of inscribed addressee and contingent reader cannot happen in the absence of favouring extra-textual conditions— whose shapes are, therefore, ultimately decisive for cultural history. The historical conditions of Leavisian discourse are those of Britain in the fifty-odd years between the Armistice and 'the end of empire'.

Scrutiny and its active audience emerged as part of a long re-formation of the dominant culture—its practices, orientation, and social equilibrium. One of the main constituent processes in this complex change was a recomposition of the intelligentsia. In the thirty years after the First World War, an established intellectual bloc was obliged to adapt or yield to an emergent formation of a quite distinct character. The old bloc was essentially Victorian. Lodged in the old universities and in the cultural centres of the capital, it cultivated a wide variety of interests without prejudice to its fundamental social unity. Even its most radical personalities tended to speak as if by right of inheritance, secure in the presumptions and licences of the class to which they directly or vicariously belonged. The post-war levies, in contrast, were not cohesive in much except their objective difference from this culture; both generational experience and typical class background estranged them. Drawn largely from the petty bourgeoisie, coming up through grammar rather than public schools and—more and more likely—the 'civic' universities rather than Oxford and Cambridge, they were perforce 'professionals', making livings and careers in a world still held by the mystique of effortless distinction. The forms and outcomes of this historical encounter were naturally various. There were stylistic accommodations on both sides, and mere generational turnover, reinforced by continuing educational reform, ensured the ultimate practical advantage of the new formation. But there were also passages of open conflict, of which the most acrimonious was the long affair of Leavis and *Scrutiny*. The new 'provincialism' of British intellectual life was widely observed, and celebrated or deplored, in the 1950s. Martin Green's sentiments are a vivid expression of it, and an index of the critical role of Leavis in its emergence.

'Provincial', as used then by both the exponents and the misfits of the new ethos, was the summary term for a whole social complex: tributary terms like 'ordinary', 'serious', and 'decent' (or 'lower-middle-class', 'earnest', and 'puritan') were seldom far away. However, Green's catalogue of virtue is a reminder of another sense of the term, and of the fact that these internal shifts in British culture occurred in the context of a fundamental alteration in its global position. Another difference between the old and the new intellectual dispensations is that they matured respectively before and after Britain's withdrawal from India. The old intellectual bloc was part of an *imperial* elite: its collective imagination, patrician and cosmopolitan in tone, was nourished by the international eminence of the British state. The successor formation came of age in a palpably shrinking country, in the years of imperial retreat and the rise of a new, American hegemony. 'Britain' and 'England', in Green's vocabulary, are exclusive terms: summarizing 'all the parts' of his experience yet surrounded by emphatic negatives, they are in effect diminutives.

In this sense Green was already 'post-Leavisian'—or, for it comes to the same thing, Leavis was not, as Green was, subjectively 'post-imperial'. There is nothing diminutive about the functioning of such terms in *Revaluation* or *The Great Tradition*. 'English', in these works, is both exclusive, socially and morally, and universalizing, systematically offered as the instance of a human norm. It was not a given: the most rigorous discriminations were necessary. But these were for the sake of its unquestioned claim to moral sovereignty. Here, as in much else, Leavis was critically disaffected from a world to which, however, he could imagine no alternative. He had inherited the humanism of 'the intellectual aristocracy' but not its patrician ease; he asserted a specific and normative Englishness but was still too much a cosmopolitan to settle for the gnawing, cheated resentments of Little England. Leavisian discourse in its high period—the *Scrutiny* years—cannot be assimilated either to the old, imperial literary culture or to its 'provincial' successor: its distinctive shape was that of the transition between them.

But transitions prolonged beyond their time are liable to decay. F. R. Leavis's 1967 Clark Lectures read in places like a desperate last struggle against silence. Rejecting all 'chauvinism' or 'patriotic nationalism', and any suggestion of a 'compensatory nostalgia for lost imperial greatness', he persisted nevertheless in his appeal to a reality that could and should be valued as England's 'national greatness'.[28] His affirmation was almost literally hollow: so many disavowals englobing an inexpressible faith. His partner's late conclusions, on the other hand, were typically forthright. In 1980, Q. D. Leavis gave her last public lecture. Her theme, appropriately synoptic, was 'the Englishness of the English novel'; the venue was Cheltenham. As she neared the end of her presentation, she turned to reflect on the plight of 'our run-down Britain', and the deep harmonies of the occasion became audible:

> The England that bore the classical English novel has gone forever, and we can't expect a country of high-rise flat-dwellers, office workers and factory robots and unassimilated multi-racial minorities, with

---

28   F. R. Leavis, *English Literature in Our Time and the University*, ed. G. Singh, London 1969, pp. 33–5.

a suburbanized countryside, factory farming, sexual emancipation
without responsibility, rising crime and violence, and the Trade
Union mentality, to give rise to a literature comparable with its
novel tradition of a so different past.[29]

Decadence, whose decadence? The 'humanism' that found words for
that noxious elegy had decayed into simple misanthropy.

Yet Q. D. Leavis was right in this at least: the cultural bases of
Leavisian discourse had weakened greatly in the thirty years since
Scrutiny's closure. This was so above all in schools, whose young
population—most of them children of the working class and of
settled minorities from the ex-colonial world—could not often be
made to adjust their intuitions to the normalizing imperative of her
kind of Englishness. Most English teachers were aware of this, and
many have positively asserted it as a premiss of their work, in schools
and, with predictable delays, in the higher, exclusive reaches of the
education system, where old traditions were more durable. Initiatives
of this kind have remained vulnerable or accident-prone, of course,
but they are indispensable for those of us who really believe that our
common humanity is less a heritage than a goal, and that it will be
defined, in its 'essential' diversity, by all or by none.

1990

---

29   Q. D. Leavis, *Collected Essays, Vol. 1: The Englishness of the English
Novel*, Cambridge 1983, p. 325.

Some Irish Questions

Culture and Capital in Modern Ireland is the admirably terse, plain subtitle of Joe Cleary's landmark contribution to debates in and about Irish culture, *Outrageous Fortune*.[1] The chronological range of 'modern' here extends from the later nineteenth century, though returns to earlier periods take an important part in the overall historical reasoning of the book and in one case form the substance of a whole essay. 'Culture' is for the greater part literature and drama, above all the novel and short story, but cinema features as well, and Cleary closes his book with a memorable discussion of the Pogues. The Ireland of the subtitle is, for most of the book, the South—the partitioned North gets one chapter to itself and otherwise features intermittently—and its critical constitutive social relation is capital. The eight studies that make up the book are in effect excerpts from a very ambitious undertaking, demanding in scale and in conceptual complexity, and no one can expect uncomplicated results. The complexities of method, focus and address present themselves before the book is even opened, on its cover, which displays three or even four titles altogether, each of them gesturing quite differently at the matters in hand.

The main title, *Outrageous Fortune*, is direct enough in its reference to the hyperbolic contrasts of Ireland's social and economic

---

1 Joe Cleary, *Outrageous Fortune: Culture and Capital in Modern Ireland*, Dublin 2006.

history since the Treaty, and in its silent borrowing from Shakespeare also takes the opportunity to signify Cleary's background in literary studies. Yet Hamlet has not often, if ever before, been collocated with Shane MacGowan, who stares from the cover photograph in his youthful capacity as editor of the punk fanzine *Bondage*, which he holds unemphatically but legibly to camera. There is grotesque irony in the reinscription of that title here, forty-odd years on, a stock feature of English punk style suddenly catching an echo of the high register of Irish literary-nationalist lamentation. And then, as if to mock this, there is the caption that dominates the front page of the magazine: 'just another country'. Cleary's cover is a theatre in itself, in which high and low, canonical and abjected meanings, and a range of national evaluations, extending from piteous identification through disenchanted realism to throwaway nihilism, are put into play.

'Just another country': where the phrase came from and what it refers to we cannot infer from the photograph alone. But if the claim is good, this cannot matter very much. The point is that it, whatever 'it' may be, is just another country. It is doubtful whether Joe Cleary would say this, just so plainly, about Ireland, but he could do worse. The other in 'another' signifies sameness as well as difference (and difference as well as sameness, to add the balancing counter-emphasis that the word ordinarily includes), and in this regard the phrase serves well enough as a provocative caption for the programme of historical reconstruction and cultural criticism he broaches in this book. Ireland is different, as nationalists of all kinds have always maintained. But to say so is not necessarily to reiterate an article of faith, let alone to reach a conclusion. What matters is how that difference is understood, in what it is taken to consist. Cleary pursues this understanding with considerable theoretical erudition and steady self-awareness and remarkable consistency. The consistency is in the first place that of purpose: what he adumbrates is a historical theory of Irish culture. It is remarkable given the varied beginnings of the essays that make up his book. These are strongly convergent, of course, and have been made more so in the editing. Still, the book remains a collection, not a single composition, and variations of formulation and emphasis remain. These circumstances are reinforced by another—Cleary's writing, combining range and thoroughness of argumentation, is characteristically dense—and suggest the preferable forms of a first response of the kind I offer here: a free generalizing account of Cleary's principal theses rather than forensic attention to textual particulars, and an associative series of counterpoints rather than a singular, linear statement.

1

Two basic concepts underpin Cleary's elucidation of southern Irish society and culture. The first is capitalism. His introductory pages are a striking illustration of how dramatically perspectives were revised in just a few years. Writing today, he would hardly feel the need for such emphatic reminders of the unabated misery attendant upon capitalist accumulation and of the insurmountable precariousness and ultimately illusory character of advanced consumerism. All that is more widely accepted now, and not least in Ireland, where the Tiger's leap ended in a most unfeline crash landing. In a longer time frame, these pages are striking also as a reminder of the long-drawn-out resistance among republican-inspired commentators to the idea of an Irish capitalism. It was a politico-cultural reflex. Capitalism was imperialism, in truth—a crucial domesticating trope even where there was good evidence for the identification. Irish capitalism, in so far as it existed, was dependent, comprador, an artificial thing sustained by tax breaks—as if to imply, with considerable casuistical resourcefulness, that one way or another, it really didn't matter which, there was a quasi-ontological mismatch between the Irish people and mere capitalism. There are times when Cleary seems vulnerable to the gravitational pull of that discourse. He is a little too insistent on the dependent character of capitalist development from the end of the 1950s, tacitly setting an unrealistic and perhaps anachronistic standard of autonomy for a small, late-coming economy with few special resources to speak of. He is tempted to overlook his own better judgement concerning the efficacy of 'choice' in the evolution of Irish capitalism, which, in so far as popular agency has been in question, has owed at least as much to inertia and pragmatic adjustment as to anything so momentous as a national decision. Contrary to Renan's stirring declaration, a nation is not a daily plebiscite. But the general thrust of Cleary's argumentation is unmistakable. Capitalism has been the governing economic reality of Irish life for a long time, and it is within the terms of the international capitalist system that its character and possibilities must be understood. If there is another social world, it lies beyond capitalism, not in some imaginary space outside it. The difference that is Ireland is a question not of otherness but of specificity. The search for specificity involves the effort to go beyond national nominalism, to clarify the individual configuration of elements that has made the Irish experience of capitalist development both normal and distinctive. The single most critical distinction in that experience was that for centuries it was mediated in a subordinate relation to one of the pioneer capitalist societies of the planet, Britain. The second of Cleary's grounding concepts is colonialism.

Here we are on canonical ground, but not quite. There is no reliance on customary verities in the long study 'Irish Studies, Colonial Questions: Locating Ireland in the Colonial World', which indeed offers one of the most illuminating general discussions in the book. Committed in this as in his understanding of capitalism to framing Irish historical experience comparatively, in international terms, Cleary returns colonial Ireland to its real conditions of formation in the early modern Atlantic. It is disconcerting, in a wholly positive way, to see England's interventions in Ireland thus classified together with Spain's proto-colonial initiative in the Canaries and Portugal's on the island of Madeira—even if a main effect of the comparison is to underline the unique and weighty military significance of Ireland's location just a handful of miles west of a big power with formidable, unsleeping enemies. The disposition of the country's effective rulers—be they indigenous or colonizing—was by this fact alone crucial for England's domestic security and maritime communications, and remained so until after the mid-point of the twentieth century. It is more disconcerting still to be shown the Irish colony in the company of the various imperial possessions in the Americas, and so to be prompted to ask the unsentimental question, what would—or could—have been the outcome if by some fluke of arms Ireland's creole revolutionaries, the United Irishmen, had succeeded too? The memory of the sweet equal republic-that-never-was hardly acknowledges the real balance of likelihood in the kind of colony Ireland had by then become.[2] Cleary proposes a valuable typology of colonial varieties, ranging from the administrative (as in the case of India, where the indigenous population, organized in largely inherited social structures, was the productive force of the colonial economy and the colonizing settlement was small and politically specialized) to cases such as Australia and New Zealand, where a 'pure' settler colonialism displaced the indigenous population and in effect created a substitute society through demographic restocking and expansion on seized lands. In this spectrum (which, Cleary insists, should not be reduced to a simplistic, disjunctive taxonomy) Ireland was one of an assorted class of hybrids, a 'mixed' settlement colony where the indigenous population remained in place but in transformed social relations based on extensive land seizures and a correspondingly substantial colonizing settlement. This is a very helpful complication of historical understanding, and it is all the odder then that it should quietly omit the most painful complication of them all. Ireland was not simply a mixed settlement colony. It was also one of a sub-set characterized by strong regional differentiation. (The United States furnished one of the outstanding cases of this, a pure settlement colony in the north coexisting with the southern plantation economy based on imported slave labour.) Ireland's colonial landlord class formed a homogeneous settler bloc of the 'mixed' variety, but the labouring population was crucially differentiated, a largely indigenous tenantry in most of the island with an alien counterpart in the settler population of north-east Ulster. In this corner, the settlement tended towards the 'pure' variety, aim-inhibited by comparison with the genocidal record of north America and the Anglo-Scottish Pacific but recognizable nonetheless in its generic tendencies, including its egalitarian 'frontier' ethos of inter-class bonding, or Orangeism.

---

2   'That sweet equal republic', from Tom Paulin, 'The Book of Juniper', *Selected Poems 1972–1990*, London 1993, p. 51.

2

Cleary's determination to elicit the specificities of Irish history from overweeningly generic accounts of capitalism and colonialism is matched in the critical procedures he adopts in his engagements with his core cultural material, literature. Now, in an essay on 'the national novel' that is the makings of a whole book in itself, received histories and fixed habits of comparison and generalization form the dialogic context of his reflections on the Irish novel and its critics. He challenges the normalizing grand narrative of 'the rise of the novel' for its Anglocentrism and unwarranted centring of realism, which, he maintains, has tended to function either as the standard by which the nineteenth-century Irish novel is found wanting (the missing *Middlemarch*) or as the pole against which the national culture is made to assert its virtuous alterity. This essay is a widely read and resourceful prospectus for an unwritten 'postcolonial history' of the novel in Ireland whose purpose would be 'to establish both the achievement of the colonial peripheries and the negative consequences that invariably attend such situations'. Another essay goes some way towards implementing that prospectus for the case of Irish modernism. Again, Cleary constructs his study in extended dialogue with the influential grand narratives associated with Georg Lukács and his intellectual posterity, notably Fredric Jameson. His critical point of departure is the observation that these Marxist cultural histories 'cannot easily be transposed onto the Irish situation', and this for reasons that illuminate the metropolitan narrowness of the intellectual construction rather than Irish cultural waywardness. (After all, as Lucio Colletti once wryly said, history can never be wrong.) Cleary takes pains to show that the Irish modernist interest in the past was neither as unvaried nor as conservative in general implication nor, come to that, as unusual in comparative perspective as many have been prone to say. The archaism of the Revival receded over time. The idea of modernity as catastrophe was potent in a culture only decades removed from the Great Hunger; and it surely made a difference to the balance of Irish modernist propensities that the country's most 'modern' region, the industrial enclave in the north-east, was by the early twentieth century locked in political reaction and historical pessimism. Folkish themes were common-place across the arts in modernism—even in Brecht, it might be added, with his *faux-naif* parables and sayings. In this too, Ireland occupied a historically intelligible place on a spectrum, not a zone apart. While defending Irish modernism in such terms, Cleary remains conscious of limitations of range and impact. Lacking the broad formal repertoire that the great centres of European innova-tion inherited from their royal court cultures, Irish modernism was a relatively private, minority affair. 'In the end', he writes, 'what distinguishes Irish modernism above all else from its European coun-terparts was that its literary modernism began so early and still managed to extend itself across several successive stages of modernist literary development, yet without reaching much beyond literature.' An essentially linguistic style of experimentation, prompted by a sense of national cultural alienation and loss, and capable of flourish-ing without large-scale institutional support systems, produced a brilliant but sequestered strain of modernism lacking the public pres-ence of 'music, architecture, public design or the performing arts'.

Given the substance of this case, the list of authors with which Cleary thinks to support it comes as a surprise: Wilde, Synge, Yeats, O'Casey, Joyce, Beckett and Ó Cadhain. What is unmissable in this 'literary' roll-call is the salience within it of *theatre*. Of these seven, four owe their reputations above all to their plays; a fifth, Yeats, was a playwright too and a publicly committed man of the theatre. Joyce likewise had his aspirations in that quarter, even if they came to little. It is not uncommon for scholars and teachers to assimilate drama, as play-text, to 'literature', but in the present context of argument, with its critical emphasis on the value of public presence and an explicit opposition between 'literature' and 'performing arts', this does not seem an adequate explanation.

It may be that the difficulty lies elsewhere, and closer to the heart of the issues of theory and method that Cleary tackles. It seems pos-sible that this lapse of logic has been induced by the attempt to answer an incorrectly framed question about reach and impact. And it is not, this time, that the Irish case is being held to an exaggerated standard, rather that the general concept of modernism is itself a faulty construction. Cleary has a tendency to assume, if only by default, that the historical schemes he considers are inadequate in so far as they are over-generalized, but probably sound on their native—metropolitan—terrain. But it need not be so, and the Anglo-American category of 'modernism' is a case in point.

It has often been said—and Cleary seems to agree—that the international array of movements and individuals grouped and putatively unified under the heading of modernism had little in common except their negations. There is a great deal of truth in this, and much of what was held in common was not historically distinctive. The great negations themselves—the disruptions of canonical forms, codes and expectations—were distinctive in their intensity, but not in kind. Negation is the constitutive gesture of the modern as such, across a historical range far more extensive than that of 'modernism'. Why bother with the category at all? The devil is in the suffix. Modern-*ism*, once so designated, must have its commonalities—which critics must then find, or not finding them, explain their absence—and the other appurtenances of a full-dress period in cultural history. There is no need for this, and good reason—not least in the empirical record—to look for an alternative construction. It is preferable, arguably, to abandon the notion of modernism, with its singularizing, unifying suggestions, and to refocus its referents as a plural, a proliferation of departures in the special conditions of their time. The time itself—say roughly 1890–1940—is better not seen as that of a cultural order such as neo-classicism—as Jameson proposed, with his tricyclic schema realism-modernism-postmodernism. This is the furthest implication of Perry Anderson's theses on modernism, in which Cleary finds his principal interlocutor for his discussion of modernism in Ireland. It is not merely that Anderson is far more closely attuned to the historical concrete, avoiding Jameson's schematism in a 'conjunctural' analysis of the specific conditions that prompted these dramatic European departures: a marmoreal high culture persisting amid the novelties of the second industrial revolution and excited or brooding expectations of fundamental social change. It is that his analysis calls into question the equivalence that Jameson assumes in his grand succession. In this alternative reading, we can pursue the idea that 'modernism' is not a historical order on categorically equal terms with its predecessor and putative successor, but, precisely, a conjuncture, however long-drawn-out, a phase of convulsions marking a transition in some respects, but at any rate a profound disturbance.

Re-viewing those decades of European culture in this modified perspective, we can more easily open up a question that the familiar schemes foreclose. In its broad terms, it is the question of realism in the twentieth century. Modernism and postmodernism are historically notable in the ways that Jameson and others before him have described. But what is less often remarked is the perdurance of a broadly realist narrative ethos, and not as an unsurmounted anachronism but as a vigorous, various tradition with a marked ability to renew its own repertoire by adapting resources from others both old and new. Gabriel García Márquez once observed of his metropolitan readers that they looked at so-called magic realism and saw only the magic. Something similar can be said about the varieties of novelistic realism after about 1930: what we are inclined to look for is the modernism (and post). T. S. Eliot's review of *Ulysses* and Virginia Woolf's essay on Arnold Bennett have long been stock references for literary modernism in English, no small achievement for such spectacular failures of historical expectation. The Joyce who entered the repertoire of the twentieth-century novel was not the contriver of the 'mythic method' but the pioneer of a new phase of big-city narrative. The moderns made their mark not in a new canon of storytelling such as Woolf envisaged but as contributors to a more versatile realism, a repertoire to which her own subjectivism now belonged. In this sense, the central modernist novelist was Proust: inheritor and refounder of the whole apparatus of realist narrative, he more than any had the future in his bones. We might say with Jameson, but perhaps with a stronger sense of consequences, that 'modernism' was 'the dominant', but just that, the element that dominates, and modifies what it subordinates, not a spirit suffusing the culture of the time. The traces of that moment are everywhere in the writing of later decades. But what

has survived more strongly is the modified subordinate, the continuing narrative culture of realism. The same kind of argument can be
made for the successor regime of postmodernism, prompting the
general thought that the history captured in that and its parent category have been passages in a continuing narrative order of realism.
And if that should be so, then Ireland's twentieth-century literary
culture is closer to the international norm than Cleary takes it to be.

3

The dominant in Irish writing over the past one hundred or so years
has been naturalism. This is Cleary's central cultural-historical
thesis, set out in 'This Thing of Darkness', another essay with more
than enough range and ambition for a book to itself. The understanding of naturalism he brings to his argument is not at all
formalist in the manner of the conventional histories or of Georg
Lukács, to whom, nevertheless, he gives full acknowledgement.
Naturalism is a variety (or cluster of varieties) in the broad history of
realism, but not only of the realist novel and drama, the usual ground
of reference: it includes poetry as well, most notably Patrick
Kavanagh's *The Great Hunger* (1942). It has its characteristic repertoire and occasions, of course, and like realism in general is socially
extended, oriented to the present, and secular (in narrative cosmology if not authorial conviction), but its basic unifying tendency is a
disposition and an expectation. Naturalism in this sense is an ethico-
ontological habitus not normally aligned with the more doctrinal
varieties of high Naturalism (to call it that) but nevertheless quite
settled in its vision of an overpowering world against which critical
will may not prevail, as a collective undertaking or even as a personal
bid for release. Schematically speaking, this is a prolonged rhetorical
agon between the great narrative modes of realism and romance,
each in its moment invalidating the other, without ever discovering a
productive union of criticism and desire. Cleary traces the workings-
out of this Irish naturalism from its self-conscious beginnings in the
Ibsenites George Bernard Shaw and James Joyce and the Francophile
George Moore, through the years of the Free State and the work of

Sean O'Casey (the Dublin plays), Sean O'Faoláin, Frank O'Connor
and Kavanagh; then, via the extremist case of Samuel Beckett, into
the fifties and onwards, in discussions of John McGahern, Edna
O'Brien and Tom Murphy. With this, we reach the present, where,
Cleary goes on to argue, the literary lease of naturalism has been
renewed even where it may appear to be ending. Ireland's novelistic
postmodern, conveyed in the ironies of Robert McLiam Wilson or
Patrick McCabe, is perhaps best thought of as 'neo-naturalism'.

Here, more emphatically than elsewhere in *Outrageous Fortune*,
Cleary's historical construction operates as a mode of politically
charged cultural criticism. Naturalism's historic vocation has been as
an art of exposure, in the name of reality or right or the good, and
thus as a critical resource for reform. But what it ends by exposing,
again and again, and as a part of its preferred kind of truth, is the
inadequacy or illusoriness of the right and the good, the preordained
failure of reform and the persistence of oppressive social or natural
order. The fatalist tendency of the naturalist imagination is a form of
conservatism that reinforces the conservatism it affects to expose.
This is a novelistic culture whose genius—to borrow a stoic formula
from Freud—is the conversion of suffering into pain. It is not a
socially innocent culture. In its terms, a literate middle class
acknowledges suffering, and with due sympathy but also due weigh-
ing of probabilities, agrees the imaginable forms of redress. And this
perhaps goes some way to explain in general terms a feature of Irish
naturalism that in one way is not characteristically naturalist at all, a
creeping anachronism of temporal range attendant upon a fixation
with the Ireland of Eamon de Valera.

There was in truth a lot to write about, but that does not quite deal
with Cleary's point. Sixty years after the official exit from national
autarky, the concentration of narrative energies in that thirty-year
mid-century span and the corresponding paucity of writing about
more recent periods seems disproportionate and suspect. The critical
construction of 'de Valera's Ireland', Cleary reminds us, was one of
the cultural conditions of the emergence of 'Lemass's Ireland' and all
that came from that, and, it may be, serves the new order still as a
displacement-object accommodating a ritual of critical exposure

while the new oppressions and inequalities of the last fifty years pass as the *faux frais* of historical deliverance.

Cleary is unsparing in his insistence on the depressive complicity of Ireland's naturalist tradition. He offers positive acknowledgements and concessions where he believes they are due; he is refreshingly lucid in his estimate of the extremely weak position from which any socialist cultural criticism must begin today; and he has no master-template to hand down, rather urging a bold, fallible elaboration of discoverable forms of a culture of liberation. For all that is discouraging in the present, he declares, 'no cultural moment is ever without either its structural conditions or utopian resources, and a radical Irish culture critically responsive to the demands of the new global conjuncture must always attend to these to discover its own project.'

4

Cleary's critique of naturalism as the Irish literary dominant is important in the simple sense that it makes a difference, in the politics of culture, whether it is substantially valid or not. And it matters, then, that it should be clearly distinguished from other considerations with which, at times, he associates it. His qualitative evaluation of naturalism as an ethico-ontological narrative disposition is not the same kind of thing as a conventional judgement of literary quality, and certainly not when the pole of comparison is the modernist canon. 'Works of some merit' appear in every current mode of Irish writing, he says, but there is no sign of a project 'charged with ambition sufficient to disturb and reconfigure the whole literary field itself'. Here, a familiar composed retrospect of European (including Irish) modernism is cited as the standard and type of literary achievement. The claim is debatable in both respects, and in any case not obviously relevant to a critique of naturalism as a way of seeing. Cleary makes a strong case, and the critical questions to put to him can be formulated without reference to modernism. They are, in the main, empirical.

The first thing to note is that the novelistic corpus on which he bases his claims is small. Even if it supports them, how representative is it of the archive as a whole? So far as I can tell, it does largely support the claims, though others with far greater knowledge may well find reasons to resist the onward march of the general thesis, as I do in the case of John McGahern's late novels. It seems to me something like a category mistake to assimilate *Amongst Women* (1990) and *That They May Face the Rising Sun* (2002) to the mainstream of his earlier work, pausing only to allow their '"autumnal" serenity'. The first of these is dominated by retrospect, and ends in release. The second, McGahern's last novel, is an elegy for a way of life that cannot be rejoined. Its title, transplanted from a sentence reporting an old burial custom, undergoes a change of grammatical mode, becoming a benediction, a pagan leave-taking. The point of Dev's Ireland, in all its characters good and bad, is that it has gone.

In one respect, to ask whether Cleary's corpus is representative is to miss a point. He is attempting to elucidate a literary dominant, not to generalize inclusively across the whole range of Irish writing in the twentieth century, whose overall plurality he acknowledges. In another respect, however, the question is necessary. This is also an ageing corpus. No writer born since 1948 receives more than a few sentences of particular attention, and the pattern of selectivity can be telling. Much of Roddy Doyle's work does indeed answer to Cleary's general naturalist thesis, but it is emphatically contemporary in focus, and there is only limited point in criticizing 'Northside realism' for its distance from the contrasting social worlds of the affluent middle class. Colm Tóibín's *The Blackwater Lightship* (1999) presents a more difficult case for Cleary's theses on all these counts and, further, for what it suggests for the kind of radical critical practice Cleary advocates. Set, again with emphasis, in the cultural conditions of Ireland in the 1990s, this is the story of three mutually estranged generations of middle-class women whose standoffs are unbalanced by the demands of a newly revealed AIDS crisis in the family. As the illness takes its course, friendship and family are tested as contrary versions of personal solidarity, in the one case active but transgressive (the gay friends), in the other conventional but blocked (the mother-daughters). The story closes on the prospect of a possible peace between the protagonist and her mother. *The Blackwater*

Lightship, an essentially private story, part drama, part comedy, part romance, is not many people's idea of a political novel. But the kind of story it tells and the kind of novel it is belong to the micro-politics of gender and sexuality which, on a state-wide scale, convulsed Irish society in the eighties and nineties of the last century, and it is in the nature of those orders of social relationship that their politics are always fought out *in parvo* as well as in the grand registers of the political. Such reflections have some bearing on the question of 'impact', which assumes an exaggerated scale in Cleary's criteriology of literary politics. The ripple effects of reading and reviews and conversations about reading are normally modest, lacking the sublimity of the modernist myth, with its giants and their signs taken for wonders, but they are effects nonetheless. The same reflections bear on the question of selection. Cleary urges critical attention to the 'utopian resources' that are to be found in any 'cultural moment' but confines himself, in the field of recent Irish writing, to a persisting naturalist dominant, with contrastive side-references to high postmodern practitioners such as John Banville and Paul Muldoon. Other kinds of writing, differently accented and surely not less promising, on the face of it, for his critical purposes, flicker on the radar, then disappear. 'Women's writing' and 'gay writing' appear just so, generically and in inverted commas, like two syllabus subheadings, in a non-committal statement beginning 'it might be argued' and ending 'and so forth'. A wholehearted search for utopian resources calls for greater exertion than this—for some of the energizing conviction that Cleary brings to his defence of *céilí*-punk.

5

After all that literary naturalism, Cleary turns to music, and Shane MacGowan's carnivalesque. Perhaps as a feedback effect, the writing here is noticeably warmer, the diction a little freer, as if registering a certain *détente* in the protocols of ordinary dialogue with those various collective subjects whose names end in 'studies' ('postcolonial', 'Irish' and 'feminist' and the rest). It may help, of course, that MacGowan is among the most literate song-writers of his

generation, but at any rate this is a welcome and convincing extension of the critical project beyond literature and drama. It is one of
the openings onto the material social world of cultural production
and circulation, inevitable in writing about popular music but, in
reality, no less necessary in the study of literature, where textual
reductionism remains the norm, even where a text called 'context'
has been brought into play. Among the many strengths of *Outrageous
Fortune* is that by its very tenacity in posing the broadest questions, it
forces literary studies to look and ideally go beyond familiar bounda-
ries. The elucidation of novelistic naturalism is one conspicuous
case, in effect creating the demand for an exploration of the wider
culture of Irish narrative, in which audio-visual media—typically in
this—have long been systemically dominant: cinema, yes, but more
importantly radio and television. How can you have a history of
narrative in modern Ireland without *The Riordans*? How, then, considering that remarkable institution and its offshoots, might we
characterize and specify the role of narrative forms in all media in
the construction and conduct of an Irish public sphere? And what
spheres of operation would be least inhospitable to counter-hegemonic
initiatives from the left? These are some initial questions; others will
have their own. They are the more easily put with the help of Joe
Cleary's indispensable book.

1990

Society as Nation as Culture

Any retrospect of Raymond Williams's *Culture and Society* should begin by acknowledging that the book comes to us through an already-long history of explicit retrospection.[1] It is a work much looked back upon. These acts of retrospection have occurred in every decade, and have differed in kind and relative salience, as of course in critical bearing. They form no consensus beyond the unchallenged assumption that the book was important and perhaps remains so. They do not substantiate a simple narrative of any kind, even if the inertial flow of textbook characterizations is noticeable—and probably inevitable, as derived acquaintance comes more and more to predominate over direct reading knowledge as the ground of Williams's currency and reputation.

The best-known retrospects are those of the 1970s: Terry Eagleton, not only the best known but also probably the most influential, and then the interviews that made up *Politics and Letters*.[2] With all qualifications made, it can be said that Eagleton and Williams's *New Left Review* interlocutors—I, at any rate—tended then to maximize the

---

1   This is the revised text of a lecture given to the Raymond Williams Society in London, November 2008, to mark the fiftieth anniversary of the publication of *Culture and Society* (London 1958. References are to the Pelican edition, London 1961).

2   Terry Eagleton, *Criticism and Ideology*, London 1976, ch. 1; Raymond Williams, *Politics and Letters: Interviews with New Left Review*, London 1979.

continuity between *Culture and Society* and the antecedent lineage of English cultural criticism and to minimize the continuity with a Marxism that Williams had first embraced, then seemingly abandoned, and was now rediscovering in new or unsuspected forms. The identifying term of this dialogic set was 'Left-Leavisism'.

The pattern of discussion in the 1980s was more complex. Williams's political engagements, in the domestic and international crises of the time, were now declaratively revolutionary, and Marxism was the terrain on which he forwarded the theoretical programme he sometimes called cultural materialism. At the same time, his work was now called into question on new grounds, as critical investigations of race and racism and the subordination of women claimed their places at the centre of cultural theory and politics.[3] Indeed, this might have been the decade that forgot *Culture and Society*, had it not been Williams's last—he died in 1988. Discourse on his work proliferated now, but in keeping with the protocols of the new situation. *Culture and Society* was widely recalled, of course: but this was retrospect as memorial.

Then, at the turn of the decade came the final crisis of the Eastern bloc and, in much of the West, the refiguring or dissolution of the Communist parties. At home, this coincided with the ascent of social-liberalism in an exhausted Labour Party and a long season of perverse apologia for commodity culture. In this hopeless conjuncture, *Culture and Society* showed its most radical face (as in truth did the contemporaneous work with which it was often mistakenly twinned, Hoggart's *Uses of Literacy*[4]). The core thesis of Williams's

---

3   See, for example, Paul Gilroy (*There Ain't No Black in the Union Jack: The Cultural Politics of Race and Nation*, London [1987], London 2002, pp. 50–51). Patrick Parrinder ('*Culture and Society* in the 1980s', in his *The Failure of Theory: Essays on Criticism and Contemporary Fiction*, Brighton 1987, p. 69) faulted Williams's 'common culture' as an idea foreclosed against 'the proliferation of cultures' characteristic of 'a multicultural society'. For critical reflections from feminist standpoints see Carolyn Steedman, *Landscape for a Good Woman: A Story of Two Lives*, London 1986; Jane Miller, *Seductions: Studies in Reading and Culture*, London 1990.

4   Richard Hoggart, *The Uses of Literacy*, London 1957.

conclusion—concerning the intrinsic historical creativity of social-
ized labour—had perhaps never seemed so coolly intransigent as it
came to seem in the nineties. Here now, beyond memorial, from an
earlier bad time, was 'a memory as it flashes up at a moment of
danger'.[5]

These evocations of the past forty-odd years are one way of saying,
by illustration, that *Culture and Society* is a classic—classic in the
sense that Frank Kermode proposed in his study of the category.[6] It
is, notably, diversely readable. Or, to put the matter in another way,
it is an elusive text, never quite where you suppose it to be, where,
perhaps, you would prefer it to be, whether wishfully or in a spirit of
resentment. And certainly the book has had a way of chastening
cocky hindsight with its own backward glance, as it goes on being
read and re-read, and always slightly differently.

1

What kind of work is it? Williams's translators bring their own judgements. In some languages, such as Catalan and Spanish, the title
retains its original form, 'culture and society'. In Italian, the historical
field and form of the book come to the fore: *Cultura e rivoluzione
industriale: Inghilterra 1780–1950*. The German edition abandons the
original title-form for something quite different: *Gesellschaftstheorie
als Begriffsgeschichte*, or 'social theory as history of ideas', with a subtitle continuing 'studies in the historical semantics of culture'. This is
an impressive miniature essay in critical specification, a contribution
in itself —and it may be that we owe it in part to the circumstance that
a literal translation had recently been pre-empted by another publication. *Kultur und Gesellschaft* was the title under which, in 1965,
Herbert Marcuse reissued his writings from the 1930s, including a
classic work of Frankfurt Critical Theory, 'On the Affirmative
Character of Culture'.[7] A few years later, there appeared a selective

---

5   Walter Benjamin, *Illuminations*, London 1970, p. 257.
6   Frank Kermode, *The Classic*, London 1975.
7   Herbert Marcuse, *Kultur und Gesellschaft*, 2 vols., Frankfurt 1965.

English version, called *Negations*, which Williams reviewed for his
university's house magazine, the *Cambridge Review*. In doing so, he
wrote the first, and probably the least influential, retrospect of his
own *Culture and Society*.

Williams's title, 'On Reading Marcuse', fairly indicated the
nature of his interest.[8] He was writing about Marcuse but also about
his reader, this reader, himself. In its opening phase, the review is
characteristically measured—respectful, emphatically mindful of
shared political commitments, yet intellectually distant. 'I think he
is more often wrong than right', Williams says, and the difficulties
extend beyond concepts and theses into matters of formation and
mentality: 'we see the world quite differently, at a level of primary
experience quite as much as in developed intellectual work.'[9] But
Williams reads on, and reports with 'interest and pleasure' a 'possible bridge' from Britain to this alien thought-world. It has been
common to classify such moments as instances of an island empiri-
cism saved from inanition by post-Hegelian theory. But the story
Williams goes on to dramatize here, with mounting intensity, is different. The particular interest of the essay on affirmative culture, he
says, is that 'its analysis corresponded so closely with a central
theme of *Culture and Society*, and that both were historical treatments, of very much the same problem', while being 'continents of
countries apart in method and in language'.[10] Williams describes 'a
marvellous moment of intellectual liberation' as he now reads across
'that gap'. He cites Marcuse's summary of affirmative culture and
declares: 'This is exactly my own conclusion' about 'the essential
origin and operation of the idea of culture, as it developed in
England after the Industrial Revolution, at a time when we were
very close, especially through Coleridge and Carlyle, to the German
thought to which Marcuse's arguments relate.' And in this, he says,

---

8   Raymond Williams, 'On Reading Marcuse', *Cambridge Review*, 90, 30
May 1969, pp. 366–8, reprinted in Eric Homberger, William Janeway and
Simon Schama, eds, *The Cambridge Mind: Ninety Years of the Cambridge
Review 1879–1969*, London 1970, pp. 162–6.

9   Homberger et al., *The Cambridge Mind*, p. 164.

10   Ibid., p. 164.

with an air of elation, there is 'a sense of meeting, after a long separation'.[11]

Great closeness, a long separation, but then the euphoria of meeting and recognition. The ill-assorted comrades turn out to be siblings, in a distinguished line. It is a moment of romance, in a writer in whom romance, perhaps surprisingly, exerts a steady pressure. And the central historical claim is none the less forceful on that account. For all the differences Williams registers, as hyperbolically as anyone could wish, there is a strict and consequential conceptual homology between his thought and Marcuse's at this point. Pressing forward through the free indirect mode that both writers favoured for the occasion—with debatable results—is a shared critique of what Williams called *the idea of culture* as a central discursive formation of bourgeois civilization.[12] Williams was more inclined to affirm the affirmative than Marcuse, who pursued his dialectic into a notorious formal equation of liberal and fascist culture. There is reason, then, to regret the loss of that phrase as the title of the book we know as *Culture and Society*, and the loss of the introduction, after its part publication in 1953, also as 'The Idea of Culture', for it did much to make clear, in its cool, distant framing, that the purpose of this work too was destruction.[13]

This objective parallelism of early Williams and the Frankfurt critique of culture is historically specific, not merely an echo from one developed capitalist society to another, and not as chronologically strained as it may seem to be. Marcuse's study of affirmative culture dates from 1937. Adorno's brilliant continuation piece, 'Cultural Criticism and Society', was drafted in the early 1940s and first published late in that decade.[14] Seeded in the same post-war years, between 1949 and 1952 the essential critical-conceptual work of

---

11   Ibid., p. 165.

12   Paul Jones advances a similar thesis in his *Raymond Williams's Sociology of Culture: A Critical Reconstruction* (London 2004, pp. 62–8), although in the context of a discussion of method—the practice of immanent critique.

13   Raymond Williams, 'The Idea of Culture', *Essays in Criticism* III, 1, 1953, pp. 239–66.

14   Theodor Adorno, *Prisms* [1955], London 1967, pp. 19–34.

Culture and Society had been done, as the essay 'The Idea of Culture' makes plain.[15] The Frankfurt School's debt to the early Lukács is well known. Here, then, it is worth emphasizing how, among the various thinkers that Williams invokes in his *Marxism and Literature*, the one whose work most strongly resonates with the core theme of the book is Lukács—and not the Lukács of novelistic realism but precisely the author of *History and Class Consciousness*, a shared precursor in a distinctive post-Romantic lineage of Marxist cultural thought.

2

What, then, can be said about the political significations of the project? The book's most telling associations, its formative associations, were with the Communist Party. This was something already fading from wider recognition by the middle 1950s, as Atlanticism consolidated its hold. With the adoption and re-narration of *Culture and Society* by the early New Left, it became hard to imagine. The cultural vision corresponding to the Communist Party's new political programme, *The British Road to Socialism*, was a concerted rally of the national culture. In the literary journal *Arena*, which had been founded for the purpose, this took two related forms: a polemical rejection of 'the American threat to British culture', and, in direct continuity with the inter-war Popular Fronts, a systematic effort to define a legitimating national past for communism. Thus, Jack Lindsay's Coleridge, the subject of the longest study in the record of the journal, was presented emphatically as both an English thinker and—with conspicuous reference to Hegel—a dialectician.[16] Edward Thompson looked back to William Morris for illumination of 'the moral issues today'.[17] Here was one of the intertexts of *Culture and*

---

15   See Dai Smith, *Raymond Williams: A Warrior's Tale*, Cardigan 2008, pp. 332–401, for the gestation of *Culture and Society*.

16   Jack Lindsay, 'Samuel Taylor Coleridge (I)', *Arena*, II, 6, February-March 1951, pp. 36–49; 'Coleridge (II)', II, 7, April-May 1951, pp. 29–43.

17   Edward Thompson, 'William Morris and the Moral Issues Today', *Arena*, II, 8, June-July 1951, pp. 25–30; also Edward Thompson, 'The Murder of William Morris', *Arena*, II, 7, pp. 9–27.

Society and, oddly enough, a warrant for everything in the book that supports the familiar continuist reading of it. It is odd indeed that the Englishness of *Culture and Society,* so often mistaken as the trace of Leavisian discourse, should turn out to be the sign of rather more substantial Communist affinities.

However, the relationship was not so simple. For the gist of Williams's critical argument, like Marcuse's before him, was radically at variance with the servicing assumptions of popular frontism. Marcuse's assertion of the deep twinship of liberal and fascist culture was an outrage against the humanist pieties of official and fellow-travelling discourse in the middle 1930s. Similarly, if in an altogether less dramatic way, the British Communist narrative of English culture was not well served by Williams's opening declaration of purpose, which he stated in damning terms that no communist could mistake: 'I wish to show the emergence of *culture* as an abstraction and an absolute.'[18] The theoretical judgement of the chapter 'Marxism and Culture' is equally unmistakable: the English Marxist debt to English Romanticism has been significant and significantly damaging.[19] *Culture and Society* is, then, complex in its orientation and address. Immersed in a certain stream of English social thought, but finally sharing less with English cultural liberalism than with the Communist cultural orientation of the time; communist but in an intransigent critical spirit that recalls the theoretical leftism of the 1930s—including, it should be said, the writings of Christopher Caudwell, who had suffered, post-mortem, the most withering of all Williams's particular judgements.[20]

Culture and Society appears to furnish all of us with some evidence for our discrepant, sometimes conflicting interpretations of what it has to say, and does so, I think, in consequence of its central polemical purpose, which was not to develop the idea of culture as a position or vantage-point but to disclose it as the site of struggle it had historically been. This entailed asserting continuities where

18   Williams, *Culture and Society,* p. 17.
19   Ibid., pp. 263f.
20   Ibid., pp. 268–9.

there was said to be rupture, and division, including self-division, where coherence was tacitly assumed. One example must suffice to illustrate this procedure and the ambiguities it nourished. Williams is discussing Morris's socialism, in an explicit contrast with Labour and Fabianism. He cites Morris's clairvoyant thoughts about the co-option of socialist measures for a modified order of capitalist rule, and, in doing so, claims them for what he calls 'the tradition'. Here, I would say, is Williams at his most tendentious, but that is not where my emphasis falls. What is most striking about this passage and others like it is the perfect ambiguity of its gesture to a reader. The gesture is one of inclusion, of association, but in what spirit? For one kind of reader at least, the spirit is affirmative, constructive—and in that interpretation lies a whole tradition of reading *Culture and Society*. But for another kind of reader—the kind who may have been more vividly present to Williams in the chill of the early 1950s—the spirit may have seemed provocative, the claim a discordant intrusion in a composed selection of values anointed as 'culture'. The gesture of sharing, if indeed it is that, is a calculated embarrassment, a politically directed check on the presumptuous fluency of the idea of culture as it circulated in post-war Britain.

3

That gesture is as necessary now as it was then, we can say to begin with, although the terms of engagement have undergone crucial alteration. It is not that Williams's terms—which were those of basic class relations—have become obsolete. For all that has changed, the capitalist ordering of social life has not changed. (Even the bright claims that all has changed utterly have a faded fifties look about them.) Yet in important respects *Culture and Society* is now distant from contemporary perceptions of cultural interest and possibility—as successive waves of contemporaries have been saying for several decades. I confine myself here to just one kind of case, which has become inescapable, and which, as it happened, actually announced itself all those years ago, but without consequentially entering the discursive space of the book.

There is a moment early on in *Culture and Society*, just a few pages into the first chapter, when Williams cites Edmund Burke on the true constitution of a nation. Here is Burke:

> A nation is not an idea only of local extent, and individual momen-
> tary aggregation; but it is an idea of continuity, which extends in
> time as well as in numbers and in space. And this is a choice not
> only of one day, or one set of people, not a tumultuary and giddy
> choice; it is a deliberate election of ages and of generations; it is a
> constitution made by what is ten thousand times better than
> choice, it is made by the peculiar circumstances, occasions,
> tempers, disposition, and moral, civil, and social habitudes of the
> people, which disclose themselves only in a long space of time.[21]

Williams then returns to his discussion, reporting that 'immediately after Burke, this complex . . . was to be called "the spirit of the nation" [and] by the end of the nineteenth century, it was to be called a national "culture"'. He adds: 'examination of the influence and development of these ideas belongs to my later chapters.'[22] It is a poignant moment. 'These ideas': Which ideas? Burke's head-word is *nation*, and Williams repeats it twice in the first sentence of his commentary. But it is clear from the context that his spontaneous conceptual translation of the term is 'society', specifically 'organic society'. He has good reason for doing so: that is a crucial aspect of Burke's usage. But society conceived of in this way is already more than a collective order or system, the merely social. It is, precisely, *national* society, or society as nation. Burke's 'people' are above all fathers and mothers and daughters and sons, generations in the shaping of an extended family. Their social being is inherently ethnic—and emphatically so, for Burke's ethico-political preference is set in stone. This organic constitution, he says, is 'made by what is ten thousand times better than choice'. Here is an idea of culture that Williams did not, in fact, pursue in his later chapters—or, for

21   Ibid., p. 30.
22   Ibid., pp. 30–1

that matter, in *The Long Revolution*, notwithstanding the theoretical status he accorded 'the system of generation and nurture' there.[23] In this idea of culture, the family is the stake, the symbol and the template of sociality. Its common collective mode is, as it was for Burke, the nation, in more or less marked association with ethnicity and race. In its most general character, it is the idea of culture as customary difference. This, rather than the meanings made familiar in literary criticism, sociology and cultural studies, is the politically charged sense of culture—its dominant—as it circulates in public controversy today, not least in Britain.

4

Culture is always culture, of course. That is its opaque charm. This time, what is at stake in the tautology is *customary difference*. Both parameters are essential: custom, or anything understood as custom, takes precedence over other modes of social validation, and its currency is difference. Thus, culture is what differentiates a collectivity in the mode of self-validating direct inheritance—whose value, in return, is precisely that it binds the collectivity in *difference*. The main substance of culture in this sense—its privilege or its fate—is ethnicity. This is often more obviously so in the case of racialized populations, but certainly not only then. The great contemporary exception is the supra-ethnic *Ummah*, Islam—which, nevertheless, is spontaneously ethnicized in countries such as Britain and France, whose Muslim populations were effectively founded by large-scale, regionally compact postcolonial migrations. Culture today consists above all else in customs we do not share with the others.

Culture as customary difference is not, in any final respect, a third variety, to be listed along with the high, minoritarian reserves

---

23   Others did, in different ways. Richard Wollheim, in his pamphlet *Socialism and Culture*, warned against the cultural centring of family, arguing that this would inevitably favour 'conservatism and conformism' (Fabian Tract 331, London 1961, pp. 12–13). Just a few years later, Juliet Mitchell placed the family at the strategic centre of feminist thinking in her pioneering essay 'Women: The Longest Revolution', *NLR* I/40, 1966.

defended by cultural criticism, and the popular forms and practices valorized by Cultural Studies. It exhibits essential features of both. It is a form of assertion of the cultural principle that is normative at least for the particular collective it identifies—how 'we' really, properly are—and in some cases makes universal claims, as in the spotlit case of purist Islam. At the same time, it is popular, more or less, in its human resources and appeal, understood as a necessary defence against the encroachments of the encircling, overweening other, which takes many forms: racism and bigotry, but also liberalism, modernity, Godlessness, materialism, selfishness, immorality, Americanization and so on. And if the discourse of culture as customary difference thus combines features of the two, this is not because it embodies a kind of dialectical resolution. On the contrary, it is because culture in this sense is the first form, the matrix from which the familiar varieties of cultural criticism (and, indirectly, cultural studies) emerged. Leavis's high humanism was energized by an eidetic imagery of native custom. In Thomas Mann, the continuity was still more pronounced. Culture—that is, a national sensibility—is what identifies us; the rest is civilization.

Culture in this sense found its first philosophical interpreter in Herder, in the late eighteenth century, and has had numberless learned advocates since. But no one quite authored it, in that reductive, bookish sense. Such cultures have been made and sustained with the active participation of many millions, and this way of putting the matter suggests something more than the inertial recurrence implied in the term *custom*. Herder spoke of *tradition*, meaning by that a process in which collectivities adapt their inheritance for changed conditions.[24] Tradition in this sense is inventive. However, the everyday meaning of the word tells its own story. Tradition is inventive, and much of what it invents is precisely 'tradition', a continuity symbolically assured by the observance of acknowledged custom. This, it has often been said, is a thoroughly modern

---

24   Johann Gottfried Herder, 'Ideas for a Philosophy of the History of Mankind' (Book IX), *J. G. Herder on Social and Political Culture*, trans. and ed. F. M. Barnard, Cambridge 1969, p. 313.

phenomenon. As Marx perceived, it is the spontaneous counter-discourse of capitalist modernity itself, just as old and with at least as many years of life to come.[25] What he could hardly have imagined, however, is that one hundred and fifty and more years later, after the surge and ebbing of socialist labour movements in every continent, the flowering and decay of secular nationalism throughout the old colonial territories, culture would be so widely honoured as the touchstone of social well-being.

5

It is a dialectical irony of the idea of culture that it should have made its way to the centre of public discourse in Britain thanks in good part to the workings of official policies whose purpose has been, in a sense, to contain it: the cluster of policies and precepts called multi-culturalism, which took shape from the 1970s onwards as part of a new strategy for managing race relations. The emphasis in what follows now about multiculturalism is critical, and, noting that, I start with two equally emphatic acknowledgements. First, multicul-turalist discourse—the more exact designation of my subject—has itself been a many-voiced phenomenon, and no set of generalizations such as these can hope to capture its many inflections. These remarks are an attempt to register and evaluate some key characteristics and tendencies of its dominant liberal variants. Second, the irreducible positive value of multiculturalism is that it has embodied, in British public life, an unprecedented attempt to acknowledge and embrace the historical fact of a multiracial society. It has been an important, if sometimes ambiguous, favouring condition of the struggle against racism. For now, we might say, some kind of multiculturalism is the horizon of all progressive thought and practice in its sphere. Nothing that needs to be said, from the left, in criticism of liberal multicultur-alism can simply overwrite that crucial development in policy and sentiment, the reach for a new civility that will be adequate to our

---

25   Karl Marx, *Grundrisse: Foundations of the Critique of Political Economy (Rough Draft)*, Harmondsworth 1973, p. 162.

real conditions of life in this respect.[26] But the criticisms have been made all along, and they bear recapitulation at a time when that discourse has entered a period of acute anxiety.

First, the idea of multiculturalism was always questionable as a line of solution to the crisis that prompted its adoption, that of racism and the struggles against it. Culture is an anodyne representation of race, which is a historically constituted relation of organized inequality, domination and subordination. To speak blandly of a plurality of cultures in coexistence is to obscure the historic dominance of one of them, that of Anglo-Britain, and an array of continuing social effects that are not mainly 'cultural'. Yet in the cultural multiplex as which liberal discourse pictures the UK's population, the leading theme has been 'diversity', as though that were a warrant of equality, and as though some kinds of diversity were not the effects of long-standing inequality. (Likewise, social exclusion is now deplored as an obvious evil, as though the goal of full inclusion in neo-liberal Britain were the outer limit of social aspiration for all of us, and as though 'exclusion' itself were not in truth a structural variety of its benign other, inclusion.) The promotion of culture as a defining social relation has tended to obscure the articulations of ethnic and class formation, which differ crucially from one part of the multicultural landscape to another. The resulting patterns of relative success or failure, adjustment or deadlock, inter-ethnic convergence or particularist assertion, may have at least as much to do with generic class situations or with historic changes in the division of labour as with the specificities of cultural inheritance.

Second, this shortcoming is in part that of liberalism generally: once capitalist social relations are excused fundamental questioning, progress can only take the form of improved life-chances for selected individuals. But in this context individuals are specified as members of communities, and here the idea of culture plays its own contradictory part in the working out of multiculturalism. The idea, as I began by saying, valorizes difference at the expense of intercultural

26   The phrase 'a new civility' is Tom Paulin's: see his *Ireland and the English Crisis*, Newcastle upon Tyne 1984, p. 22.

commonalities. Whatever the biographical reality (individual or collective) of our formation, what counts as culture is what distinguishes us from others with whom we may in reality share as much if not more. The kind of difference that counts is custom: confirmed, received difference. It is for this reason that the multiculturalist appeal to diversity has the paradoxical effect of promoting customary stereotypes even as it deplores their negative effects. For the commercial sector of the cultural multiplex there is an irresistible logic in this: niche markets in authenticities are potentially beyond counting, and without prejudice to the emerging market in hybridities, which has yet greater potential. The junk-word 'vibrant', without which no description of the metropolitan multiplex sounds quite right, belongs to the vocabulary of tourism and, even on the lips of the well-meaning, degrades the multiculturalist ideal of a shared home to a tainted image of exoticism for all.

Third, customary difference is most strongly confirmed in the plane of religion, whether as doctrine or as worship or as spiritual observance or as sanctioned behaviour. The culminating effect of this discursive logic, where the contingencies of inheritance and situation favour it, is to strengthen traditionalism, the systematic advocacy of customary relations and practices, and to confirm its beneficiaries as natural leaders of populations invariably called communities. The bonds of community are seldom merely confining, of course, even though they can tighten to the point of strangling. Unforced affections sustain them, as, in a contrasting way, do fears of an indifferent or hostile world beyond. But there is normally a price to be paid for this kind of cohesion, and those least likely to pay it are heterosexual males of a certain age and standing. The leading businessmen, the mouthy politicians, the clerics, all the father figures who come forward again and again as the authoritative voices of 'their' communities are heard at the expense of dissident, resisting voices off—those of feminists, very notably, and other independent community activists, and of others, not leaders or activists of any kind, who simply want to live and love unthreatened on something closer to their own preferred terms. This is the monocultural face of multiculturalism, of a politics through which, as Rahila Gupta puts it, 'the state more or less enters into an informal contract with the more powerful leaders in the minority community—disempowering women and trading women's autonomy for community autonomy'.[27] Proposals for a modified liberalism acknowledging group as well as individual rights would sanctify such bargaining at the level of political philosophy and constitutional precept.[28]

6

Such, today, in Britain and elsewhere, is the dynamic of the idea of culture. The *idea*, not the complex realities it presumes to interpret and regulate, in Britain's black and brown and white minority communities. There is no relevant minority I know of in which this idea of culture, however it is formulated, is pervasively and effectively dominant. (On the other hand, its restless, fluctuating existence in the collective psyche of the majority population—and in official liberal discourse—textures the experience of anyone living in Britain.)[29] It hardly captures the historical reality of multicultural, intercultural formation in Britain today—a reality for which, in truth, the idea of culture promotes a false description and a futile or

---

27 'Wake Up, Activists Are Pounding on the Doors of Ivory Towers', *Times Higher Education Supplement*, 28 May 2004, p. 21. See Rahila Gupta, ed., *From Homebreakers to Jailbreakers: Southall Black Sisters*, London 2003.

28 For an example, see Bhikhu Parekh, *Rethinking Multiculturalism: Cultural Diversity and Political Theory*, Basingstoke 2000.

29 It was Philip Goodhart, the editor of the monthly *Prospect* and a self-described 'sensitive member of the liberal elite', who reimagined the official dream as nightmare ('Discomfort of Strangers', *Guardian*, 24 February 2004, pp. 24–5, reprinted from *Prospect* for the same month), suggesting that social solidarity was being strained to snapping-point in the UK. In the ensuing controversy, against the background of a legislative ban on the wearing of religious tokens in state schools in France, suggestions that the proposed European constitution should formally honour the Christian heritage of its core region, civilizational resistance in high places—in France again, and elsewhere—to full EU membership for 'Muslim' Turkey, and all this in a sustaining conjuncture of US–British 'war on terror', the idea of culture became a political force (and counterforce).

damaging general prospectus. What I have been attempting to describe, with all due extremism, is the logic of a discourse whose public authority—credibility, at least—and impetus are far greater than its actual social reserves. And for an explanation in the most general terms of why this might be so, we may return to *Culture and Society*, and a famous passage from its Conclusion:

> The idea of culture is a general reaction to a general and major change in the condition of our common life. Its basic element is its effort at total qualitative assessment ... General change, when it has worked itself clear, drives us back on our general designs, which we have to learn to look at again, and as a whole ... The working-out of the idea of culture is a slow reach again for control.[30]

The main thing to note in this is that 'the idea of culture' recalled by Williams is in one basic respect different from the phenomenon outlined here. In the first, the effort of discovery is evident and sometimes dominant, but in the second it is the contrasting cultural mode—transmission—that prevails, commanding the rhetoric even where the practical realities are historically more complex. The reach for control is a reach for continuity, heritage, tradition, custom. But with that large and discouraging qualification made, we can see how Williams's distant generalities hold across the span of years from Burke to the present. What are the verities—religious, ethnic, national—sponsored under the idea of culture if not efforts at 'total qualitative assessment', with solutions to match? Williams was committed to the position that literature could have early access to emerging realities, in the forms appropriate to its own kinds. On this occasion, he came close to concluding something apparently similar, though less clearly affirmative, about the idea of culture. It is, he said, 'a general reaction to a general and major change in the conditions of our common life'. That is its great historical significance, but also its insufficiency. A 'reaction' is something less deliberate than a 'response', and not at all an apt classifying category for the learning

---

30   Williams, *Culture and Society*, p. 285.

process of which he speaks as a later stage of the change. The idea of
culture is a revelation in the way that a psychic symptom is revealing:
insistent in its registration of a real state of affairs yet not a simple,
sufficient account of it.[31] The idea of culture is not so much what
must be learnt as the warning that there is nevertheless something to
learn. That is the most general argument of Williams's classic, and
one that still claims us.

---

31   Elsewhere, in a notebook, he wrote: 'Theory of culture is a deep
response to a deep disturbance of the common life of exceptional complexity,
but this is its relevance.' (Cit. Smith, *Raymond Williams*, p. 443.) The choice of
but over *and* makes the crucial suggestion.

Britain after Nairn

In 1977, Tom Nairn published *The Break-up of Britain*. There would be no need for the question mark that some thought only prudent, he felt sure: that historical future was already upon us. Writing twenty-five years later, in a successor volume whose title likewise steals a march on the calendar, he doesn't even pause to say, 'I told you so.' The process of disintegration has begun 'and there is now almost no one who believes otherwise'. *After Britain* aims to show that New Labour has unwittingly pitched the old state into terminal crisis, to specify what must now be done in Scotland, and to make a first estimate of the challenge now facing the most enigmatic of Westminster's nationalities, the English.[1]

---

1 Tom Nairn, *After Britain: New Labour and the Return of Scotland*, London 2000. [Of course, Nairn is not the only one who must respond to the judgement of passing time: this essay was written in the millennium year 2000. My point in reprinting it now, with some adjustments for anachronism but no basic change in perspective, is that in important respects the lapse of twenty years has brought little alteration in the figure of the historical situation. It is not that drama has been wanting. North of the border, Labour lost heavily to the Scottish National Party, whose electoral prospects have in turn been dimmed by subsequent events within the party and on the parliamentary stages north and south. The Yes vote lost the 2014 referendum but the next year saw a stunning resurgence as the SNP all but swept the board in the Westminster elections, while the party itself multiplied in size (reportedly growing from 20,000 members in 2013 to some 119,000 in 2021). Two years later, the Scottish

The break-up is in the first place that of a territorial jurisdiction, Great Britain and Northern Ireland (plus the treaty possessions in the Irish Sea and the Channel). The historical condition of the break-up is the disarticulation of a certain 'sovereignty', which in Nairn's idiosyncratic usage denotes a basic constitutional formula, a master-discourse capable of stabilizing the positive and negative terms of what is politically thinkable. That formula took shape in the 1680s, when the English parliament frustrated the absolutist presumptions of the ('British') Stuart monarchy—not, however, to invalidate them as such, merely to realize them for itself, in the doctrine of 'parliamentary sovereignty'. The crucial territorial gain came two decades later, with the accession of the Scottish state to the Westminster constitution. This was the apparatus that oversaw the great expansion of British wealth and power over the next two hundred years, and which, after the Second World War, managed the diminuendo of Empire. Long stiffened in reaction to the American and French Revolutions, its basic formula weathered one hundred years of suffrage reforms, in the end seeing off the entire twentieth century. 'The purloined absolutism' of 1688 lived on, in a 'primitive-modern' apparatus of governance, the ultra-centralized, secretive, arbitrary, custom-ridden institution to which, in 1997, the electorate delivered Tony Blair.

New Labour, New Britain: there was no respite from the Blairist mission. Yet within three years, Nairn argued, Blair had demonstrated the futility of the project, bringing the old constitutional

---

electorate voted against leaving the European Union but saw its wishes swamped by the sheer weight of numbers in the South. Brexit has been an affront to democracy in Scotland, and the COVID-19 .pandemic, as well as offering rich opportunities for comparative performance assessment, furnished an unexampled daily reminder that Ukania is a multinational entity with four political capitals, not one. But for all that there has not yet been a clear and stable majority—something more compelling than a simple 50 per cent plus— for Scottish independence. The break-up of Britain, we might say, is something that goes on happening without ever being quite done. In this perspective, the contentions of twenty years ago remain live. The revisions I have made here bear chiefly on the explicit political context of the original, which was New Labour's first term in office, with its admixture of social-liberal policy inflections that were annulled with the onset of austerity inside ten years. 2023.]

formula to the point of rupture. Two large questions of state required early attention. One concerned the damage done to the Ukanian ruling bloc during the years of Thatcher's *garagiste* campaign against Tory paternalism in the party and the Whitehall apparatus—the same years that witnessed the Buñuelesque deconsecration of the House of Windsor. The other concerned a cluster of political commitments diverse in motivation and historic standing but convergent in final implication: the introduction of devolved government for Scotland and Wales, the restoration of a strategic authority for London, and an initiative capable of exploiting the new potential for a credible peace in Northern Ireland.

Only one coherent line of advance was available, according to Nairn and his co-thinker Anthony Barnett: a 'constitutional revolution' refounding Ukania as a democratic multinational state, with a recognizably 'modern' Basic Law and appropriately federalized representative structures. The opportunity was squandered. The Blair government reformed in the 'Celtic' peripheries, in each case according to the given circumstances, and thus incoherently. At the same time, it sought to renew the old prerogatives of the central state, diluting the long-standing promise of a Freedom of Information Act, temporizing over central electoral reform, and imposing an anti-democratic reform of the House of Lords—an infinite succession of appointed notables and celebrities to replace the old eternity of the bloodline. New Britain must first and last be 'Britain'. But it couldn't be. The discrepant constitutional changes on the periphery had undone the coherence of Old Sovereignty. As part of the Good Friday Agreement, Britain, like the Irish Republic, withdrew its claim of final jurisdiction over Northern Ireland; how 'the greater number' there would decide at length to exercise their power of self-determination was an open question. Scotland's union with Anglo-Britain rested on the original decisions of two parliaments, not that in London alone, and might be terminated with due notice; devolution, which Westminster unionists were prone to mistake for a concession or placebo, would vex the relationship to snapping-point. The Welsh Assembly, a more limited body in a more deeply incorporated country, would be alert to constitutional movement elsewhere.

Yet Blair perpetuated the arrogance of Westminster tradition, provoking popular electoral 'mutinies', as Nairn calls them, in Scotland and Wales (and also London, a less constitutionally fateful theatre, but an important anomaly, having the largest sub-state electorate in Britain). In the emerging conditions of a later union, that of Europe, new national and regional departures appeared less hazardous than they once were—or were plausibly argued to be. The alternatives to a unitary Britain were now tangible. But here again Blair stumbled, in the face of vocal Europhobic campaigning in the London parliament and press. Here were the multinational conditions and the late-British syndromes of a coming disintegration. The obvious third possibility—neither centralism nor disintegration but a federalized state—was a paper option, Nairn maintained. First, it had never had significant political support in London. Second, even a timely federalist initiative would have had to deal with the difficulty that led Scotland's treaty negotiators to settle for an 'incorporating' rather than a federal union in the first place: England's overwhelming demographic and economic weight in the island as a whole. This was one reason why the relations of inter-national equality essential to any acceptable federation seemed beyond reach. Another was that, as Nairn put it, there was nothing for Scotland-in-Britain 'to be equal to'. England, alone now among the countries in a state it had engineered and always dominated, was constitutionally inchoate and politically 'voiceless' and, by most appearances, not much concerned about the fact. The English would find their own way out of the Anglo-British imaginary only in the process of the break-up. Blair's incoherent 'modernizing' had confirmed English belatedness, at the same time as setting Scotland on an open road to 'de facto independence' and eventual formal separation. The end of that union would mean the end of 'Britain'.

1

Here, in rapid summary, are the principal theses of *After Britain*. But anyone familiar with Tom Nairn's writing over the years will know that simple précis does not properly capture his rhetoric, which is a study in the arts of engagement. Satire comes readily to him, and seldom more readily than on this occasion. His language deserves a little attention, in something of its own high-troping spirit. Imagine that a twister makes its way across Nairn's textual landscape, sucking up everything in its path. Then, quite quickly, the storm abates and releases its cargo, which makes a single, very strange heap. It includes a house, a computer and a wooden spoon; the *Titanic*, with iceberg; a leopard (Sicilian) and an elephant; a rotting fish, a polyhedron, and assorted insects, including a butterfly that officers a ship; and on top of all this, a tub of Pot Noodle.[2] No, not Kansas: Britain. And the chief oddity in this figural jumble is that it suggests diversity in an analysis that is, in contrast, essentially simple. This archaeology-cum-zoology of Ukanian modernity somehow compensates for the fact that Nairn's literal sweep of the landscape discovers only one significant life-form and one technology: the post-1688 ruling bloc and its prosthesis, the Westminster state. The reality of this state is itself Gothic: it has survived all hazard to become the binding final purpose of the political action it licenses. Nairn just once describes it as 'capitalist'—and then, as it happens, with reference to something in itself metaphorical: the 1997 Labour government's self-projection as BlairCorp, a 'modern' enterprise complete with annual reports, brand managers, focus groups and the rest.[3] Britain's business is being 'Britain'.

Scotland's tropology is different: sparser, and quite coherent in feeling and sense. In this landscape, Nairn sees a nomad, a moor-lander, a mountain preacher and a 'Gaberlunzie man'; there is a river (of doubt or loss), and a 'little white rose'.[4] Scotland, as imaged here, is recognizably a country with human forms. (The walking stereo-types of the civic bureaucracies appear too, as creatures evolved for the cramped ecology of the Union.) The ambient language of pain and healing in which these figures move confirms the thought that

---

2 Tom Nairn, *After Britain*, London 2000, pp. 22, 155, 39, 32, 34, 161, 116, 158, 50, 138, 59–60, 69.

3 Ibid., p. 77.

4 Ibid., pp. 99, 120, 287, 96, 286.

here we have a lyric specialization of vision exactly complementary to the surrealist extravagance that predominates in the long discussion of Blairism. If Britain is essentially a monstrous state, part hippogriff and part cyborg, Scotland is essentially anthropomorphic, a collective person.

Metaphors sometimes belie the intent of the thesis they seem merely to embellish; here they have the opposite effect, confirming that the literal historical and political judgements must be taken at their word, and not merely read into reasonable 'balance' with other more or less valid considerations. Nairn grants full historical personality only to states (including their symbiotic elites) and people-as-nations. Other manifestations of solidarity and antagonism—say, class relations— have a secondary, intermittent existence, often as little more than modes of appearance of the two great agencies. 'Blessing and curse together,' he writes, 'nationality is simply the fate of modernity.'[5] It may be so. But the ambiguity conceded in that opening phrase does not make up for the indeterminacy that the main proposition 'simply' denies. There are older, far more stubborn human fates—eros and death—but not many suppose them to account for the pattern of human history. The logic of capital accumulation, with its associated patterns of class struggle, has some claim to be counted as the possible fate of the epoch, but here it registers only in the bland forms of 'modernization' and 'development'. 'The fateful eternity' of the Cold War—which some, even now, may perceive as an international capitalist struggle to contain and reverse the advances of historical Communism—has turned out to be 'one dismal chapter in a longer and far more interesting story'.[6] A story too long and much too interesting to summarize, apparently, though it is a fair guess that its title includes the word 'nation'.

Left-wing critics of the great monodrama come in two varieties. The first comprises those who, like the younger Daedalus, aspire to fly, with the same results. These are the 'departure-lounge internationalists' (in other parts of the North Atlantic archipelago known

---

5 Ibid., p. 199.
6 Ibid., p. 103.

as 'metropolitan Marxists') who think to expunge the stain of nationality with the aid of 'Socialism, Liberalism and other formulae of the moment'.[7] If they do not come to see more clearly, they are prone to fall into complicity with the great-nation chauvinists who, less highmindedly but with greater actual force, deny the aspirations of nationality. The local illustration is of course 'British Socialism', which is Nairn's taxidermic rendering of 'Labourism'—itself a term which, in his own departure-lounge days, he imported from Italian Communist discourse for his contributions to NLR's theses on Britain. This plebeian-unionist version of manifest destiny is now 'a Heritage site', frequented mainly by the lost souls of Labour's left. In its post-socialist form it is 'British', pure and simple: the Blairist drive to rejuvenate Ukania's old regime—to which the real-world alternative is nationalism. In fact, Nairn maintains, the historic priority of class identifications in British politics has been a distinctive local effect of state-formation in the island: 'Britain', he writes, in one of many brilliant observations, 'was a multi-national class before it was a multi-national state; and the latter remains in essence a manifestation of the former.'[8] But lest we infer from this that the break-up of Britain might then count as a properly socialist (not only nationalist) objective, he points to the Catholic working class of the West of Scotland, who have made their way beyond such understanding. Of their first-ever recorded majority vote for independence he writes: '"Class" was being transmuted into "Nation" before our eyes.'[9] Home at last.

2

Nairn is an unusual nationalist, in good part because of his systematic practice of comparative historical discrimination (for which the Marxism of the departure lounge is due some credit) and because of his unabated sympathetic interest in other national worlds. His

---

7   Ibid., p. 128.
8   Ibid., p. 176.
9   Ibid., p. 196.

theoretical-political vision of the nation in modernity is secular in commitment and global in range. There is no taint of ethnic essentialism in his scheme, though he also seeks to avoid the shortcomings of the familiar constructionist alternative which, in both its cynical (Gellnerian) and naive (post-structuralist) forms, has difficulty in theorizing the real *longues durées* from which ethnic romanticism spins its mythologies. The 'Scotland' for which he urges independence is the territory of the state that went out of existence in 1707, and its current population. If a Scottish national identity has survived the three centuries of the Union, it is because British state policy required only 'subsumption', not assimilation, and because key civic institutions accordingly survived as an autonomous sub-state system: spirits and genes have had no part in the matter. The new, democratic-republican Scotland would be an equal partner in a post-Ukanian Council of the Isles and a developing European Union. But about the possible social order of the new state, Nairn has nothing to say, not even to his fellow-Scots, who are the named or implied addressees of much of his book.

Nairn's settled polemical habit is to dismiss appeals to social questions as the spoiling tactics of Labour unionists, or the doxologies of departure-lounge internationalists who still will not understand that nationality is the fate of modernity. Undoubtedly it has often been so. However, the left is not so easily stereotyped, even in these times, and the logic of Nairn's axiom is not what he takes it to be. It is possible to endorse his demand for Scottish independence and general vision of a post-British archipelago of states, and still to insist on the limitations of his theoretical and political nationalism. The proposition that nationality is fate settles very little, without the further proposition that the social character of nationality is itself fatal. Only if both are true can it be inferred that nationalism is the necessary politics of the epoch. But Nairn expressly—and convincingly—rebuts the second proposition, for Scotland and, by implication, for all cases. Nationality is a politico-cultural condensation of historical social relations of all kinds and, in so far as these are contestable and changeable, so too is it. The people of the Irish Republic were 'Irish' in 1950 and they are 'Irish' today, yet, over that seventy-year period, the national imaginary has been recomposed—not through the collective self-elaboration of national character, but through a complex, sometimes traumatic sequence of social struggles for and against the prerogatives of capital, clericalism, and patriarchy. Modernity may dictate that our social existence is always understood to be, among other things, a 'national' condition, but, by the same token, any appeal to nationality is always a coded declaration for, or against, a substantive social state of affairs. In that sense, even where the issue of territorial sovereignty is in play, the privileging of nationality-as-such is either insufficient or evasive. Nairn's axiom conceals a paradox: the peculiarity of nationality as a fate is that it is itself fatally contingent.

The effort to contain this paradox within a discourse that franchises only states and people-nations as historical agents shapes a distinctive order of emphasis in political interpretation and judgement. The chapter on 'The Unmaking of Scotland'—a phrase that looks to the future, not the past—illustrates Nairn's insistently historical perspective on nationality. His central concern, in this admirable intervention in cultural politics, is identity, which he is inclined to image as personality. Another chapter, 'The Last Day', shows a rare sensitivity to the inner disturbances that attend upon moments of transition, the fluctuations of gravity, the almost bodily sense of anachronism that comes when, suddenly, as it must seem, the crucial decision has already been taken. Of course, 'identity' no more exhausts the reality of a society than 'personality' sums up the reality of a human being. But there, in those terms and their metaphorical pairing, the emphasis of Nairn's discussion lies. The third, directly political, term in this set of equivalents is 'constitution', which, for Nairn, is a *passe-partout* in the analysis of late-British politics and the struggle towards Scottish independence.

3

Some things are too obvious to be clearly visible. Constitutional questions are so obviously crucial in any discussion of the British state that we may mistake their truly fundamental place in Nairn's thinking, as the final reality of politics in general. His account of

British local government reform since the 1960s is notable both for its ingenuity and for its symptomatic quality. This long, continuing sequence of new beginnings, as he reads it, is a record of displacement activity, in which the unspeakable question of reform at the centre has been rephrased as the admissible—but unanswerable—conundrum of efficient municipal governance. The infamous Poll Tax—a flat-rate imposition on all adults, regardless of income and household status— was not merely a crazy episode in the story of Thatcherism: it was a particularly acute passage in the case-history of a chronic disorder— that of the state itself. The Poll Tax crisis concentrates all the elements of Nairn's political vision: a reckless centralist measure, still more recklessly piloted in Scotland, and answered there and, later, in the south by popular 'mutinies'—mass non-compliance beyond the limits of the law, and a climactic riot in the capital.

The difficulty is that Nairn can only interpret it as he does by erasing the political record of the preceding fifteen years. Two issues dominated British politics in the 1970s: labour militancy and public spending. There were others—an upsurge in racist agitation and terror, devolution itself—but these were the issues that made or broke the governments of the decade. Edward Heath's Conservative admin- istration set out to control the trade unions, and was destroyed by them. Four years later, another great strike wave settled the electoral destiny of its Labour successor. One critical difference between these two phases of militancy was that, by 1978, the issue of social spend- ing had become central in political life. The protagonists of the second wave were public-sector workers rather than miners and engineers; not only wages but welfare services themselves, as they had been known for a generation, were at stake in 'the winter of dis- content'. Thatcher came to office determined to re-run the conflicts of the past decade, this time resolving them to the definitive advan- tage of capital and its social hinterland, the right-thinking petty bourgeoisie in which she had grown up. The intensified centralism of her government had little to do with constitutional displacement activity, everything to do with the desire to avenge the two great social affronts of her lifetime: the victory of welfarism in 1945, and the fall of Heath in 1974. The war on labour culminated in the

miners' strike of 1984–85. The Poll Tax was the matching climax on
the second front: a drastic redistribution of the local tax burden from
rich to poor.

The Poll Tax episode is as significant as Nairn believes it to have
been, but for reasons that he quite systematically depreciates. It was,
after all, a crisis of fiscal policy, the kind of business that he regularly
counterposes, prejudicially, to the serious high-political practice of
'constitutionalism'. He is disdainful of those whose criticism of
New Labour dwells on such matters. 'Economics' (his own impatient
phrase) is another feature of the British *misère*. The alternative,
which Blairism botched and Scotland must now pursue, is the formulation of a new constitutional order. The general objection to this
is that, temperamental preferences set aside, budgets and constitu-
tions cannot so easily be opposed: each, in its own register and
time-scale, is a political synopsis of a social order and its priorities.
There may be a price to pay for high-minded indifference to 'economics' and such things.

4

Independence may be no more than ten years away, Nairn reckons.
The critical task for the Holyrood Parliament is to assume the functions of a constituent assembly, deciding upon 'its own constitution,
principles and modes of operation'. This curious summary betrays
the insufficiency of constitutionalism as a line of political march. It is
in part tautological, and in greater part reductive, suggesting the
work of a Standing Orders Committee rather than the momentous
struggle to determine the *Grundgesetz*, the Basic Law, of a whole
society. In this, the national-territorial question would be quickly
settled. Far harder questions would remain. Would the new constitution place general conditions on the right to property? Would it
entrench a right to strike, thus overriding the corpus of anti-labour
statutes handed down by Westminster? In what guaranteed sense
would the new society be 'secular'—if at all? How widely and deeply
would 'equality' be understood? Would the standard right to freedom
of expression be buttressed by a right of access to means of

dissemination—and corresponding restrictions on private ownership of media? The list goes on, prompting a more down-to-earth question: where, at present, is the politics that might draw popular energies into the making of a constitution? Nairn is quick to sense philistinism in those who query the call to constitutional revolution. But philistines are always other people—other people who, in the main, will be attracted to the work of a constituent assembly, as they have been to devolution and even independence, in so far as it comes to appear as a possible solution to the abiding problems of their social existence.

There have been grounds for believing that this critical dynamic might quickly take hold in Scotland. Two-thirds of the electorate, a stunning majority of all devolutionists, supported tax-varying powers for the devolved parliament—a vote which, in the post-Thatcher ideological world of New Labour, signalled an unthinkable willingness to increase the rate of income tax for social purposes. The Scottish National Party leadership steered a social-democratic course to Labour's left, with electoral success. But as it moderates its line, turning to compete for 'middle Scotland' on the familiar centrist terms, the case for early independence, and the associated constitutional upheavals, appears just so much weaker, more abstract, the possible benefits outweighed by the likely risks. If the emerging choice for Scotland is Blairism or Blairism, why not stay put? After a decade and more of ruthless austerity under successive Tory leaders, the alternatives no longer seem so nearly blank. Nevertheless, it remains that Nairn's strategy is a conclusion in search of its own sufficient condition, which is an array of popular demands converging in the perception that independence is a practical necessity. The likelier political basis for convergence will be unruly experimentation, a complex process that tests the concrete possibilities and limitations of devolution, on the social terrain defined by Westminster's management of capitalism in Britain. The struggle to foster a popular left alternative is the low road to the constitutional sublime—but perhaps it is the only one currently open.

Short of an electoral crisis at that level, 'de facto independence', or devo max, may prove a habitable state for the Scottish majority. Nairn

knows far too much about Ukanian political culture to underestimate the level of inertia in the system. Besides, not even Scottish
independence would put an end to Old Sovereignty. The day after,
there would still be 'Britain', the Union of England, Wales and
Northern Ireland. It is too early to be confident that Wales will follow
Scotland into independence—even if current indications seem to
favour that wager. The direction and tempo of Northern Irish developments can only be guessed at. It is as good a conjecture as any that
the break-up of Britain will turn out to be a characteristically 'British'
process—something, like metric measures, that encroaches on the
official imagination without ever quite becoming banal reality.

5

Then there is England, about which Nairn writes with arresting,
sombre insight. The English ruling class dominated the state, giving
the world, including England, its essential imagery of 'Britain'. The
price the English have paid, he argues, is a kind of collective estrangement from political self-representation—which has been the always
already accomplished work of 'their' larger-than-life state. The most
obscure of Britain's national questions has been that of England—
which, as Westminster's old monopoly disintegrates, must at last be
posed and dealt with. The 'question' may in fact be plural, Nairn
believes: the nation may discover in itself another composite, and the
prospect of a cluster of small states. That vision is less charming than
it may seem, given that regional disparities of wealth in England are
among the starkest in Europe. However, a more tangible danger lies
in the more likely course of development, which is the emergence of
'England' as a distinct site of political elaboration. Nairn is well aware
that this is the preferred terrain of the right. But his better nature
checks the flow of his speculation, whose ulterior logic appears to be
this. If Britain has been above all the historic vehicle of an English-
cum-Scottish ruling bloc, and if that state has been, for the English as
a whole, a surrogate locus of collective identity, then it follows that
the national-popular resources for an emancipating post-British politics in England will be meagre. Like Orwell before him, Nairn is

inclined to imagine a deep nation, 'England's England', essentially untouched by the 'British-imperial class' that has occupied its imaginative common lands for so long. But he has already excluded that possibility as a matter of theoretical principle. Historical England, the only available 'national' material for a new polity in formation, has been Anglo-Britain. There was nothing else it could be, on Nairn's own account. Moreover, the new polity would be hard put to become anything else, for a practical reason that Nairn overlooks. It makes sense to think of Scotland, Wales, and Northern Ireland as quitting Britain; sovereign powers, once exercised from London, would be assumed by governments in Edinburgh, Cardiff, and Belfast-or-Dublin. But England could not quit the old state in the same way: after all, there is nowhere to 'go'. In effect, England would inherit Ukania, armed forces, laws, monarchy and all, becoming at best a residuary body, at worst the afterlife of the old regime. There is no existing Englishness that might redeem the population of England from this. The spontaneous tendency of a new English nationalism— already manifest in the Conservative Party—would be to recharge the presumptions and resentments of late-British political culture, to tend the flame of British pre-eminence in an embattled loyal heartland: England as Sherwood Forest.[10]

This ugly Robin Hood nationalism has been quite comprehensively reactionary—and simply dangerous for the black- and brown-skinned sons and daughters of the country, who as yet cannot uncontroversially claim 'British' identity, let alone call themselves 'English' (hyphenated or not), should that be their intuitive preference. Nairn

---

10 [Granted, it didn't always seem so. By 2010, as the Conservatives under David Cameron returned to government in coalition with the Liberal Democrats, it was even credible to trace the outline of a political regroupment on the Europeanist centre-right. But the evidence of the following decade went all one way: Brexit and the ascent of Boris Johnson, the recurring panics over immigration, the shambles of Westminster's response to coronavirus— indecisive, incoherent, owing as much to the dynamics of Conservative factional rivalry in parliament as to any other consideration—and, an epitome if one were needed, the *Windrush* affair, a post-imperial scandal taking its name from a gentle river in the Cotswolds. 2023.]

and others have been tempted to see in the events surrounding the death of Diana, Princess of Wales, the intimation of a progressive counter-Englishness. The thought is fanciful. Diana Spencer's personal project for the monarchy was nothing other than a novelettish companion piece to Blairism itself: a photogenic makeover of the official lifestyle. Her cult, familiar in many ways from centuries of royalist folklore, was and is regressive, personally as well as politically. Nairn's image of a capital 'barricaded with flowers' seems designed to evoke the memory of revolutionary Lisbon. Others may think back to a village some way north of it, by the name of Fatima.

Nairn has heard other dark predictions for England from Scottish unionists, and dismisses them as so much scaremongering. But this prediction is actually his own, in that it emerges, without prejudice to Scottish independence, from the logic of his own theses on Britain. A southern-dwelling socialist may ask whether Nairn's concern to defend the English against manipulative caricature—an honourable reflex in itself—has not been exaggerated in the interest of his prior theoretical commitment, which is to nationality, as the only sustainable agency of human betterment in modern history. Here, as in the case of Scotland, he takes pains to rebut charges of ethnicism, and to insist on the real and superior alternative of 'civic' nationalism. He is right, of course, to reject claims that nationalism always ends in ethnic cleansing. But that smallish mercy is not enough. The set-piece contrast between civic and ethnic nationalism is politically convenient, in so far as it distracts critical attention from the first to the second, allowing the former easy polemical advantage without risk of comparable scrutiny. Civic nationalism may not be ethnicist, but it is a variety of nationalism none the less. As such, it is inherently under-determined in social composition and trajectory. The United States of America has been the most purely civic of nations, historically; its constitution is held sacred as an act of creation; democracy and equality are watchwords of the official culture. Viewed thus, it is exemplary. Yet that civic order has fostered the most purely capitalist society on earth, and assumed an international role without comparison in its destructive egoism. Nairn can hardly want that for the republics of the North Atlantic archipelago, but he denies himself the political language in which he might say so, preferring the canonical vocabulary of republican constitutionalism. This reluctance to venture into the actual and possible social reality of nations is not only politically limiting; it condemns his case to inconsistency. A civic nationalism that does not specify and defend an order of social priorities—a version of national civility, in other words—falls short of its own definition.

The political lessons to be learned from *After Britain* are not unionist, but they are not simply Nairnist either. There are two, and in both cases the more advanced Scottish situation illuminates the more daunting English prospect. First, and specifically, the process of break-up will probably be more complicated, irregular—and perhaps inconclusive—than Nairn allows. There is unlikely to be an effective, popular majority for independence in Scotland until Westminster's counter-strategies have been tested to their perceived limits, and that will entail substantive, not purely constitutional, challenges to the existing order of social interests. That process, necessary for Scotland, will be a rich political learning resource for the left in England, where constitutional questions are widely shunned as precious, tedious, or dangerous, and the 'nation' is an estate of the right. Scottish outcomes have fundamental significance for all of us. Second, and generally, Scotland already suggests what a glimpse of a possible Anglo-English future confirms. If nationality is a modern fate—which is to say, a central politico-cultural structure of capitalist societies—then it follows, for socialists, that it is far too grave a matter to be left in the care of nationalism. The left these days has too few answers, too many of them too simple. But at least they speak to the national 'question' in its only unmystified form, which is neither nationalist nor nihilist: not *Whither our nation?* but *What kind of social order do 'we' want for it?*

2000

Conradian Histories

It is an old commonplace that modernist art is reflexive, drawn more or less strongly to explore the material element of its existence—pigment, say, or language. With the so-called linguistic turn in the human sciences, and specifically the literary criticism of the late twentieth century, the commonplace has rejuvenated itself, and pressed its interpretive claims with corresponding energy and confidence across an ever-wider field of literary history. So it is that Joseph Conrad too has come to be read as yet another exemplary modern, as questioning of his medium, with its Delphic promises of sincerity and truth, as of human motives. There is a lot to explore here, but also an attendant danger, which is that the interpretive appeal to 'language', conceived just so abstractly, settles little. The more often and more widely it is reiterated, the less it explains. There is always a better account: better because more closely specified, more historical, that is, and materialist. The undoubted crisis in Conrad's work is in one sense inevitably linguistic—after all, it is writing, which is done in language—but its dynamic and characteristic textual figures emerge from a quite specific cultural and institutional context of literary practice. Conrad was not merely 'a worker in prose' or a maker of 'art', as he was prone to say.[1] He was not, indeed, a teller of

---

1 Joseph Conrad, preface, *The Nigger of the 'Narcissus'* (1897), edited and introduced by Cedric Watts, London 1988, pp. xlviii–xlix.

'tales', however insistently his subtitles lodge that claim on his behalf. The longer and shorter printed narratives that constitute his literary achievement belong, inescapably, to the world of the *novel*. That is the locus of Conrad's crisis as a writer, which worked itself out in a distinctive and paradoxical literary practice. The characteristic forms and strategies of his narratives (including the shorter fictions, which in this perspective are not different in kind) are shaped by an impulse to abolish the novelistic, or at least outwit it.

For the younger Thomas Mann, the novel, or 'literature', was the cultural epitome of modernity, as distinct from poetry and music, which sheltered the superior values of tradition.[2] Walter Benjamin, in a classic essay, likewise emphasized the essential modernity of the novel, defining it by contrast with the anterior narrative form of the oral 'tale'. The storyteller, he writes,

> takes what he tells from experience—his own or that reported by others. And he in turn makes it the experience of those who are listening to his tale. The novelist has isolated himself. The birth-place of the novel is the solitary individual, who is no longer able to express himself by giving examples of his most important concerns, is himself uncounselled, and cannot counsel others. To write a novel means to carry the incommensurable to extremes in the representation of human life.[3]

This is manifestly relevant to Conrad, but, paradoxically, perhaps too close, for critical purposes, to his own constant theme of isolation: he might almost have written these sentences himself, or put them in the mouth of his best-known fictional storyteller, Charley Marlow. It will be more helpful to develop Benjamin's insight in other, less psychologistic terms. Two general historical conditions detach the novel

---

2 Thomas Mann, *Reflections of a Nonpolitical Man* (1918), trans. Walter D. Morris, New York 1983.

3 Walter Benjamin, 'The Storyteller: Reflections on the Works of Nikolai Leskov', in his *Illuminations*, ed. and introd. Hannah Arendt, trans. Harry Zohn, London 1979, p. 87.

irrevocably from the world of the tale. The first is institutional, involving a change in the *social relations* of narration. Storytelling as a form presupposes a basic community of values binding teller and audience: shared intuitions of what is interesting, intelligible, pleasing or repugnant, fitting or not. Indeed, being oral, it depends on the actual co-presence of the two: the moral affinity is confirmed in time and space. Novelistic narrative, in contrast, is mediated as printed text for the market. Both the physical and the cultural supports of the tale fall away. Writing is temporally prior to reading, which, like writing, is now privatized, and practically variable in a way that listening is not. The audience is not only privatized; unknowable to the writer at work, it is also, in principle, unknown in its cultural disposition. Thus, the social relationship that grounds and is fertilized by the tale is cancelled; in linguistic terms, novelistic communication lacks the long-familiar 'phatic' guarantee.[4]

The second condition is strictly cultural. The shared values that stabilize the tale as institution may or may not be officially sanctioned, but they are in any case *customary*, matters of inherited common sense and virtue, whose continuing authority is itself a positive value. This is the world of 'wisdom', from which the novel takes its leave, irreverently even if not in revolt. The tonal dominant in novelistic culture, which has always been predominantly realist, is contrastingly *critical* and *secular*. As Mann understood, the novel is the prose of 'civilization' and the Enlightenment. Its cosmology is godless even where its ethics remain scriptural, more or less. Ordinary believers may recoil from lewd representations, but far from entertaining miracles and evidence of inspiration in their fictional reading, they feel cheated by the intrusion of even purely mundane improbability. Dispositions that find easy articulation in poetry are inhibited in the culture of the novel, for which the

---

4 The phatic function of communication, in Roman Jakobson's classic definition, consists in monitoring and confirming the integrity of the communicative medium—as when, in a telephone conversation, a speaker says 'Yes, . . . yes . . .', meaning not 'I agree' or 'It is so' but 'I can hear you'. In the expanded sense invoked in this essay, the phatic function bears also on the *social* conditions of the communicative act.

currency and prestige of the human sciences are a historical given, welcome or not. Pragmatically at least, what finally counts as valid is some idea of rational knowledge.

These twin features of the novelistic were the discursive conditions of Conrad's literary practice. But, as any of his readers will know, they figure in the works themselves, as negative terms in his characteristic thematics. Isolation, as Conrad imagines it over and over again, is a destructive condition whose outcomes are disgrace, corruption, madness, and death. Its avatars are Jim (*Lord Jim*), the Capataz and Decoud (*Nostromo*), Stevie, Verloc, and Winnie (*The Secret Agent*) and of course Kurtz (*Heart of Darkness*). None survives. Modern knowledges, and their associated norms of inquiry, have a recurring part in these human disasters, appearing at the same time trivial and mischievous, and in no case equal to the moral realities they affect to explain. There is already an appearance of paradox in this, and it is not dispelled by the recollection of the historical materials on which he set his themes to work. 'Exotic' or not, his fictional worlds are figures of the defining sites and crises of historical modernity: colonialism and the global thrust of capitalism, class struggle, the swelling of the metropolis, the revolutionary threat to Europe's old regimes. For this alone, Conrad would merit a prominent place in the canon of the modern novel. But there the paradox returns, and it is not merely that this novelist of modernity was a conservative disaffected from the new moral ecology he explored—there was nothing remarkable in that. It is that he was profoundly at odds with the conditions of his own writing practice, the novelistic itself. Conrad's 'task', as he struggles 'to make you *see*', is to resolve that paradox—or rather, to manage it, for resolution proper is hardly attainable. The labour of containment is the central process of his writing, the effective substance of his rhetoric.

Two related propensities, so strong they might even be termed compulsions, shape and texture Conrad's narratives. The first, here called *hyperphasia*, seeks in the first place to restore the communicative guarantee that the novelistic is constitutionally unable to underwrite. Its further function is to regulate the flow of modern knowledges and the historical pressure that drives them. In this respect, hyperphatic anxiety serves the interest of the second compulsion, that splitting of knowledge and belief that Freud explored as *disavowal*.[5]

i. Telling Tales, or Hyperphasia

In 1897, with three novels and a number of stories to his credit, Conrad returned to work on the novel that was to round off a 'Malayan trilogy': *Almayer's Folly, An Outcast of the Islands* and, now, *The Rescuer* or *Rescue*. He did so under pressure. His attempts to escape from what he himself already called 'Conradese' had not been successful; *The Sisters* was left as a fragment, and no magazine could be found to take a shorter work, *The Return*. Depending on writing for his income, Conrad could not afford to be disdainful of popular taste; his simple purpose was to make the novel 'good enough for a magazine—readable in a word'.[6] Yet this entailed his engaging with romantic-sexual material that had already proved intractable in *The Return*. ('There are things I *must* leave alone.'[7]) And he also resented his vulnerability to the literary market, describing the book as 'an infamous pot-boiler'. *The Rescue*, and Conrad with it, passed into crisis. He became aware 'how mysteriously independent of myself is my power of expression', and was soon severely blocked:

> I sit down religiously every morning, I sit down for eight hours every day—and the sitting down is all. In the course of that working day of 8 hours I write 3 sentences which I erase before leaving the table in despair.[8]

---

5   See Sigmund Freud, 'Fetishism' (1927), *On Sexuality*, The Pelican Freud Library Vol. 7, London 1977, pp. 351–7. For a discussion of disavowal as a process in culture generally, see Octave Mannoni, 'Si, lo so, ma comunque . . .', in his *La funzione dell' immaginario*, Bari 1972, pp. 5–29.

6   Letter to Edward Garnett, cit. Ian Watt, *Conrad in the Nineteenth Century*, London 1980, p. 128.

7   Ibid., p. 128.

8   Ibid., pp. 128, 130.

The path to redemption was at once institutional and rhetorical. Over the same period of months, Conrad had formed a strong relationship with *Blackwood's Edinburgh Magazine*, a prestigious and rather conservative monthly, which now began to publish the stories he was writing as a relief from the torments of *The Rescue*. The first of these, *Youth*, saw the adoption of a new formal device: narration at one remove, or secondary narration, through the instance of a character, Marlow. The new association with *Blackwood's* was providential: the magazine paid well and valued continuing relationships with authors. Conrad expressed his 'unspeakable relief' at writing 'for *Maga* instead of for "the market"'. More than this, he could now sense an audience, a community of understanding:

> One was in decent company there and had a good sort of public. There isn't a single club and messroom and man-of-war in the British Seas and Dominions which hasn't its copy of Maga.[9]

The invention of Marlow secured this imagined community and gave it objective cultural currency. To dwell on the obvious element of nostalgia in this would be to underestimate the force and generality of the desire it accommodates. There is more than one thing to say about the strategic value of secondary narration in Conrad. To begin with, it is crucial to recognize that Marlow is not a personified primary narrator like Nick Carraway in *The Great Gatsby*. He is himself narrated, held in an englobing primary discourse whose point of enunciation is itself normally personified, however minimally. (Even in *Lord Jim*, where the primary narration is not attributed to a character, the occasional use of frequentative verbs carries an anthropomorphic suggestion: the narrating instance 'knows' Marlow of old.) These narrating characters and their fellows—sailors, lawyers, accountants, well-travelled men of affairs—are the respectful, infinitely patient audience for Marlow's stories, the audience Conrad believed he had found in *Blackwood's*. In their first publishing context, then, the Marlow narratives invent a community talking to

---

9 Ibid., p. 131.

itself. The sense of their second and definitive context—that of book publishing—is still more striking. The random, anonymous readers of the novels and shorter fictions are drawn into narratives of a man telling stories, in the controlling perspective of an audience whose objective cultural-institutional coordinates are quite different from their own. The novel-reading public is refashioned by the thing in its hands as the listening community of the tale.

1

The meaning of this paradoxical narrative rhetoric emerges more distinctly in comparison with the work of another turn-of-the-century writer of fiction, Sholom Rabinowitz. Born, like Conrad, in Ukraine and only two years younger than him, Rabinowitz turned to writing a little earlier, in the 1880s under a pseudonym that is in itself a miniaturized version of his writing—Sholom Aleichem. The heartland of this fiction is the *shtetl*, the village world of East European Jewry, in a period when its deeply traditionalist culture was straining under the antithetical pressures of official persecution and enlightenment. The big city is Odessa, and the wider world is itself a local affair:

> I doubt if the Dreyfus case made such a stir anywhere as it did in Kasrilevke.
>
> Paris, they say, seethed like a boiling vat. The papers carried streamers, generals shot themselves, and small boys ran like mad in the streets, threw their caps in the air, and shouted wildly, 'Long live Dreyfus!' or 'Long live Esterhazy!' Meanwhile the Jews were insulted and beaten, as always. But the anguish and the pain that Kasrilevke underwent, Paris will not experience till Judgement Day.[10]

Inevitably, since the events come to the villagers second- or third-hand, in the oral reports of Zeidel, the only newspaper-reader among them, and acquire their force in the excited talk that follows. Talk is

---

10   Sholom Aleichem, 'Dreyfus in Kasrilevke', from *The Best of Sholom Aleichem*, eds Irving Howe and Ruth R. Wisse, New York 1980.

the model as well as the main diegetic substance of Sholom
Aleichem's texts, as the opening of 'Dreyfus in Kasrilevke' already
suggests. They begin suddenly, often importunately, and nearly
always in, or as, a speech situation. 'The Pot' is a monologue, one of
many such records of a one-sided conversation:

> Rabbi! A question's what I want to ask you. I don't know if you know
> me or if you don't know me. Yente's who I am, Yente the dairy-vendor.[11]

In the stories proper, the main narrator is usually personified, or at
least assumes the grammatical signs of personality and the rhetorical
licence of informal conversation.

These texts are devoted to an ambiguous art of the fragment. Read in
a cluster, they appear as so many random samples from the continuous
conversation of Kasrilevke and the many places like it. In this, Sholom
Aleichem is bardic, the remembrancer of a common world. But his
humour is often that of the gallows, and fragments can also testify to
disintegration. The Tevye sequence narrates the breakdown of *shtetl*
culture. Or rather, Tevye narrates it, in successive encounters with a
character whose 'vocation' is writing books, one Sholom Aleichem. All
these encounters end with explicit partings, routine at first but, by the
end, historic. They last meet after a pogrom ('Get Thee Out'), on a train,
and Tevye does not know where next year will find him. His parting
words always include reference to books, about which he is ambivalent.
He is not sure that he wants to be recorded in print, and on one occasion, when he has told the story of his daughters' marriages, positively
forbids it. 'Write me often', he says, in the closing lines of 'Chava';
letters, like the shared writing of the scriptures, are sustaining. But

> don't forget what I asked you. Be silent as the grave concerning this.
> Don't put what I told you into a book. And if you should write,
> write about someone else, not about me. Forget about me. As it is
> written: *'And he was forgotten—'* No more Tevye the Dairyman![12]

---

11   Ibid., p. 71.
12   Ibid., p. 178.

The irony of these words, and of the entire sequence, illuminates and undermines Sholom Aleichem's practice as a writer, including the wishful fiction of his pseudonym. His texts resemble Conrad's in their effort to capture speech and its typical genres as the moral substance of social relationships. Here too, the inscribed position of reading is that of an initiated listener. The writer's signature itself certifies the communal bond: *sholem aleichem* is purely phatic, a customary greeting inviting the specular response *aleichem sholem*. However, Tevye's story of his family troubles, and his injunction against repeating it in print, throw this symbolic settlement into disorder and self-contradiction. Chava has forgotten her faith and must now be forgotten. Sholom Aleichem must likewise forget her story, if he is to keep faith with Tevye. But to do so would be to thwart the basic commitment of his writing, which is to saving the speech-world of the *shtetl* for literate posterity. Either way, fidelity entails a breach of faith. The bond cannot endure. 'Greetings to you, Mr Sholom Aleichem', says Tevye, opening the last story of the sequence, 'heartiest greetings'. There is reason for concern: 'I've been expecting you for a long time and wondering why I didn't see you any more.'[13] Sholom Aleichem has been travelling 'all over the world'; Tevye and his family, having been driven from their villages, are travelling too, to a destination still unknown to them. As in all the stories, Tevye's last word to the writer called Greetings is 'goodbye'.

Two circumstances, one collective and the other individual, might be said to moderate the phatic crisis in Sholom Aleichem's case. The first is that he wrote in Yiddish, which, to a greater extent than any of its neighbouring European vernaculars, could claim to be the medium of a common culture. (Isaac Deutscher, a Polish Jew from a later generation, wrote compellingly about this.)[14] For as long as there were Yiddish readers, the speech-world of Kasrilevke would not quite perish. Second, he accepted the historical probability of that loss; his nostalgia and occasional sentimentality were, in a way, a measure of his realism. Conrad was differently placed, in both respects. He clung to English with fierce, obscure commitment. It had adopted him, he

---

13   Ibid., p. 179.
14   Isaac Deutscher, *The Non-Jewish Jew and Other Essays*, London 1968.

wrote in *A Personal Record*: 'If I had not written in English I would not have written at all.'[15] But it was hardly clear, at this point in the history of an already multinational language, to what moral family, what community of sentiment, he thus belonged. Like Spanish or Portuguese, English was the common birthright of widely scattered, mutually alien speech-communities. Second, his fictions, unlike those of Sholom Aleichem, did not record and reflect upon the life of an inherited world. They imagined an adoptive culture in the perspective of a grateful, devoted outsider compulsively drawn to the great transforming agencies at work in it. There is little nostalgia in Conrad. He was fascinated by the defining historical forces of his time. But that is not to say that he could quite believe in them, in either sense of that term. These were the uncertainties that shaped his narrative hyperphasia.

2

One characteristic effect of hyperphasia is quantitative: envisaged as a short story, *Lord Jim* grew into a long novel.[16] The elaboration is everything. Jim's history is quickly related. A young English seaman joins the *Patna*, which has been chartered to carry two hundred Muslim pilgrims on their way to Mecca. The craft is unseaworthy, and after an accident, seems in danger of foundering. The captain and his cronies decide to abandon ship, and Jim follows. The *Patna* is saved by a French naval vessel. An official inquiry is ordered, and Jim, facing the proceedings alone, is stripped of his mariner's licence. In disgrace, above all in his own eyes, he takes refuge in one job after another, moving on when word of the *Patna* episode catches up with him. Eventually, he finds a kind of redemption in the remote upriver district of Patusan, becoming the guarantor of peace and security for the local population,

---

15   Cit. Edward Said, *The World, the Text and the Critic*, Cambridge, MA 1980, pp. 98, 99.

16   Joseph Conrad, *Lord Jim* (1900), London 1957. For this and other novels later discussed, references are given in the text, a roman and an arabic numeral for the chapter and page respectively, thus: (II, 3).

who acknowledge him as *Tuan* (Lord) Jim. But Nemesis arrives in the form of a boatload of outlaw raiders. A phase of armed confrontation ends in confusion and violent death. The locals' suspicions fall, mistakenly, on Jim, who finally, in effect, gives himself up for execution. The story of *Lord Jim* is simpler still. A ship's captain named Marlow attends the Inquiry. He is gripped by the *Patna* events but above all by Jim, whom he befriends. He takes pains, over a lengthy period, to gather a complete account of the episode, and in later years seizes any opportunity to disclose all that he has seen and heard and tried to make out about Jim. What the novel narrates, for nine-tenths of its length and all but four of its forty-five chapters, is Marlow's discourse on Jim, spoken for the greater part in an after-dinner gathering, and concluded in personal correspondence with one of that party.

What Marlow narrates is a sequence of spoken encounters: the testimony given at the Inquiry, then a lengthy interview with Jim; conversations with Captain Brierly, who is badly disturbed by the scandal, and then with his chief officer, who gives his account of the hours before Brierly's suicide; with a French naval colleague who reports the latter stage of the *Patna*'s voyage, and then with Gentleman Brown, the 'ruffian' who triggers the final catastrophe and survives to give his own version of it. Another conversation, with the seagoing entrepreneur Chester, yields the story of a partner, Robinson, as this emerges from the untraceable conversations of others—what 'they say' about him. *Lord Jim* is not, strictly speaking, what Conrad claimed in his subtitle, 'A Tale'. It is a novel about a tale about other tales (about others still). Although Jim has been the protagonist of an intensely dramatic action, the primary narrator of *Lord Jim* catches sight of him only in the least romantic phase of his career, as a water-clerk soliciting custom for a ship's chandler. That is appropriate, in a novel where nearly all that actually happens is talk.

3

Talk, for Conrad, is the linguistic site of solidarity, but here the talk is of a failure of solidarity, and of normative identity—of 'character'. In its most abstract formulation, the moral drama is that of heroism

pursued, forfeited and at last regained. The heroic code supports
Jim's account of himself, as both Marlow and the anonymous narrator agree. His seagoing 'vocation' was animated by 'a course of light
holiday literature' (I, 11), as was his life's finale:

> And that's the end [Marlow says]. He passes away under a cloud,
> forgotten, unforgiven and excessively romantic. Not in the wildest
> days of his boyish visions could he have seen the alluring shape of
> such an extraordinary success! For it may very well be that in the
> short moment of his last proud and unflinching glance, he had
> beheld the face of that opportunity, which, like an Eastern bride,
> had come veiled to him. (XLV, 313)

For one moment, Marlow himself seems to honour Jim's code, or at
least to acknowledge its attractions:

> I was aggrieved at him, as though he had cheated me—me!—of a splen-
> did opportunity to keep up the illusion of my beginning, as though he
> had robbed our common life of the last spark of its glamour. (XI, 103)

However, the burden of his obsessive questioning lies closer to home.
Jim was 'one of us': Marlow reiterates this proposition over and again
as concession or as affirmation, compassionately or in disbelief.

> There he stood, clean-limbed, clean-faced, firm on his feet, as
> promising a boy as the sun ever shone on; and looking at him,
> knowing all he knew and a little more too, I was as angry as
> though I had detected him trying to get something out of me by
> false pretences. He had no business to look so sound. I thought to
> myself—well, if this sort can go wrong like that . . . (V, 36)

Worse, Marlow confesses, for all his experience, he would have mis-
judged Jim himself:

> I liked his appearance: I knew his appearance: he came from the
> right place; he was one of us . . . I would have trusted the deck to

that youngster on the strength of a single glance, and gone to sleep
with both eyes—and, by Jove! it wouldn't have been safe. There are
depths of horror in that thought (V, 36, 38).

The horror is internal and communal. What Jim has put in question
is 'us'.

'We' are, in the first place, the practitioners of 'the craft', the merchant marine, and the keepers of its 'honour' (V, 40). Brierly, the
'complacent', 'self-satisfied' paragon of the Blue Star Line leads the
Inquiry, and is destroyed by what it discloses—though not so much
to him as to others. The horror, for him, is not what happened on the
Patna, but the 'shame' of the official investigation. 'Why eat all that
dirt?' he protests; and why make 'us', therefore, do the same? (VI, 54).
The disaster lies in the scandal, 'this infernal publicity': 'there he sits
while all these confounded natives, serangs, lascars, quartermasters,
are giving evidence that's enough to burn a man to ashes with shame'
(VI, 56). Brierly, frustrated in his wish that Jim should simply disappear, dispatches himself. The news of his death, conveyed to his
'people'—who are acquainted with Jim's—goes unacknowledged.

Brierly's particular fear of scandal, and the terms in which he evokes
the Inquiry, suggest that 'we' are not, or not finally, the community of
'the craft'—which also includes some of those with whom he disgust-
edly refuses affinity. 'We', as a later, contrastive reference to 'one of us'
reveals, are the category of 'white men'. But only a category, not a community, for which far more intimate conditions of affiliation must be
satisfied. Marlow is unfailingly sensitive to national and racial difference. Much of the time, this is the dominant in his characterology, a
sufficient sign of personality and a leading clue to conduct. The master
of the *Patna*, obese and with 'a bullet head', is a German-turned-
'Flensborg or Stettin Australian' whose defiant threat to the authorities
is 'I vill an American citizen begome' (V, 37). Personal nationality is
marked, in the case of the French lieutenant, with an insistence beyond
its apparent relevance. The only nationality for which special terms
apply is the English. Of course, there is no room to doubt that Jim,
Brierly, Marlow and the rest are English. But what is the more notable
then is how their nationality is indexed. 'Home'—a recurring term—for

Brierly and Jim is 'Essex' or, as Marlow once says, facetiously, 'the land uprising above the white cliffs of Dover' (XXI, 70). 'The British Isles', 'Great Britain' and the national specification 'Scot' each appear once, as symbols in the sentimental history of another German, Stein. The 'English' language is named on a half-dozen occasions. But Marlow never applies that adjective to himself or his compatriots, or names the country they come from. We might settle for interpreting this as a case of the ideological gesture that Roland Barthes called 'exnomination'— the dominant term in a system, *qua* dominant, is unmarked—were it not that normative Englishness is elsewhere ironized.[17] 'Englishmen' and 'the English' are identified as such only twice in the novel, the first time by the Flensborg or Stettin Australian who is chiefly responsible for Jim's disgrace—'You Englishmen are all rogues' (V, 37)—and the second time by the outlaw Gentleman Brown and the treacherous Cornelius, the renegades who will bring about their compatriot's death:

> 'What is he? Where does he come from?' inquired Brown. 'What sort of man is he? Is he an Englishman?'
>   'Yes, yes, he's an Englishman. I am an Englishman too. From Malacca.' (XXXIX, 277)

Brown's first three questions are also Marlow's; the fourth is the question he avoids, even suppressing the noun from his vocabulary. Cornelius's answers dramatize the aporia that Marlow can scarcely outwit, for all his show of subtlety. Indeed, he utters the thought metaphorically when he reflects that Jim 'looked as genuine as a new sovereign, but there was some infernal alloy in him' (V, 40)—some mixing of metals that weakens the mettle and debases the currency of England and Empire. This, in a discourse so finely attuned to the blood-lines of nation and race, suggests the unspeakable dilemma: Jim is an Englishman—but, having acted as he did, how can he be? Marlow likes to imagine that Jim at last succeeded in Patusan where he had failed on the *Patna*, creating a virtual Pax Britannica for the 'native-ruled' district, and that his death was a moment of heroic

---

17   Roland Barthes, *Mythologies*, trans. Annette Lavers, London 1972, p. 138.

fulfilment. 'He is one of us . . . Was I so very wrong after all?' (XLV, 311).
The locals, including his lover, would agree. So far as they can see, Jim
has betrayed them, as they feared he would. 'They never could understand' the 'exact relation' between Gentleman Brown and 'their own
white man' (XLV, 311)—the split figure of the Imperial Englishman.
Marlow too cannot, or will not, understand. 'It seemed to me', he
says, as he recalls his first evening with Jim, that 'I was being made to
comprehend the Inconceivable—and I know of nothing to compare
with the discomfort of such a sensation' (VIIII, 75). Here is a scene of
trauma. It is coercive, and its sense is non-sense: rational disclosure of
something that lies beyond imagining. Marlow's defence is his rhetoric. 'Why these vapourings?' he asks in an irritable moment, referring
to Jim. This question applies to his own monologue, and the answer is
that the alternative would be an intolerable acknowledgement.
Marlow's narrative strategy is in large part one of protraction, an
exhausting proliferation of the telling in relation to the putative action
of the tale. His rationale, which exploits the ambiguous semantics of
his proprietary term 'Inconceivable', is philosophical. Threatened by
the encroachment of rational inquiry on a reality that he finds morally
unimaginable, he affects a higher curiosity whose paradoxical termi-
nus is the validation of mystery. He and his kind profess a 'faith
invulnerable to the strength of facts' or 'the solicitation of ideas' (V,
38). Marlow's prolix monologue is a filibuster, a process designed to
delay conclusion. His narrative quest for Jim's reality has the appearance of curiosity but is antithetical in motivation: compelled by the
suggestions of an image that no logos can be permitted to translate, it
exemplifies the opaque, pseudo-cognitive syndrome of fascination.

4

The same compulsions drive Conrad's next Marlow narrative, *Heart
of Darkness*, registering more graphically in a shorter work of
simpler formal design.[18] The scene of narration, which is said to

---

18   Joseph Conrad, *Heart of Darkness* (1902), ed and introd. by Paul O'Prey,
London 1983.

confirm a 'bond', is a fully realized social occasion—a sailing-party—and wholly englobes the sailor's narrative, thus leaving the unnamed primary narrator to close the novel. Marlow's story of his journey, via Brussels, to West Africa and so up the Congo River to its farthest navigable point, itself yields elements of a third narrative, the assorted reports, comments and fragments of overheard conversation that are the legend of Kurtz—whom eventually he meets, thereafter joining the ranks of his own legend-bearing characters. Now, he wishes to account for his response to what he has seen, and 'the kind of light'—'no, not very clear'—that it 'seemed to throw on everything about me' (I, 32).

This is a more anxious Marlow, and a more anxious audience. All three narrative planes show a greater or lesser weakening of phatic guarantees. The motives sustaining the talk of Kurtz are at every point questionable—envious, spiteful, self-deceiving or naive. Marlow's own contributions to the legend, on his return to Brussels, are, in calculated effect, lies. The literary remains of Kurtz's career are either defective or misleading as acts of communication. The letters from the Intended, which Marlow returns in a sealed packet, record the intimate history of an illusion; the text of Kurtz's 'vast plan', once shorn of its murderous postscript, is their public counterpart. Whereas his main informants in *Lord Jim* are, for all their moral inequalities, men of his own 'craft', seamen, here they are so many once-met acquaintances on a journey from a company bureau in Brussels to a remote colonial outpost in Africa—to which he has been drawn by recollection of a boyish whim. Even the 'bond' so confidently affirmed in the opening paragraphs of the novel is not perfectly secure. Marlow, the first narrator observes, is not free from 'the weakness of many tellers of tales who seem so often unaware of what their audience would best like to hear' (I, 32). Some time later, in mid-narration, Marlow invokes the cognitive value of the 'bond': 'Of course, in this you fellers see more than I could then. You see me, whom you know . . .'

The circumstantial reality is less reassuring. According to the narrator,

It had become so pitch dark that we listeners could hardly see one
another. For a long time already, [Marlow], sitting apart, had been
no more to us than a voice. There was not a word from anybody.
The others might have been asleep.

With this phatic fading comes interpretive anxiety:

> The others might have been asleep, but I was awake. I listened, on
> the watch for the sentence, for the word, that would give me the
> clue to the faint uneasiness inspired by this narrative that seemed
> to shape itself without human lips in the heavy night-air of the
> river (I, 58).

He might be reading a novel.

The intensified hyperphasia that distinguishes *Heart of Darkness*
from *Lord Jim* coincides with a shift in the terms of representation,
from the earlier novel to the later. We can say that Marlow's obsessive meditation on the person of Jim is a displacement of attention
from the system of social relations—imperialism—that shaped his
projects and their outcomes. But we must then accept the corollary,
which is that this is indeed so; the displacement has occurred; *Lord
Jim* is centrally a novel of character. *Heart of Darkness* is not wholly
different in this respect. Kurtz, the visionary 'extremist' is Jim composed in another key; the 'sordid buccaneers' of the Eldorado
Exploring Expedition are functional equivalents of Gentleman
Brown and his crew. Marlow is, as usual, much concerned with
'character'. Yet now, unmistakably, Conrad extends his field of
vision to encompass the impersonal relations of 'the new forces at
work' in European and African history (I, 43), to probe the logic of
the 'fantastic invasion'.

That European activity in the Congo amounts to an invasion is
established beyond doubt. The pages in which Marlow narrates the
cumulative discovery of his journey from Brussels to the Central
Station, never less than sardonic, rise steadily towards a pitch of
unrestrained, generalized denunciation. The summary judgement on
the 'explorers' illustrates the manner: 'To tear treasure out of the

bowels of the land was their desire, with no more moral purpose at
the back of it than there is in burglars breaking into a safe' (I, 61). Yet
the same passage, with its ambiguous second clause, reminds us that,
for all his straining after universal truths, Marlow's indictment may
not be strictly general. The burglars of West and Central Africa are
named—they are France and Belgium—and Marlow has already distinguished them and other colonial powers from one that is not quite
named. Looking around the waiting-room at the Company's prem-
ises, he pauses at a map of Africa. 'There was a vast amount of red',
he notes, 'good to see at any time, because one knows that some real
work is done in there', as well as 'a deuce of a lot of blue, a little green,
smears of orange, and, on the East Coast, a purple patch, to show
where the jolly pioneers of progress drink the jolly lager-beer' (I, 36).
The punctual turn to the idiom of the smoking-room ('a deuce of a
lot') and its associated cultural standards ('the jolly lager-beer' signifying German-ness) confirms the identification of Britain as a
special case.

It would be easy to make too much of this claim to exceptionality.
Marlow does not return to it. Perhaps the fate of Kurtz, who as an
imperialist with a 'redeeming idea' embodies an unstated will to
emulate the British, must be taken as definitive in implication. The
principal narrator's last words may suggest as much:

> The tranquil waterway [the Thames] leading to the uttermost ends
> of the earth flowed sombre under an overcast sky—seemed to lead
> into the heart of an immense darkness (III, 12).

But only *seemed*: the hesitation is characteristic, and scarcely avoid-
able, given the main purpose of Marlow's tale, which is to reflect 'a
kind of light'—in some sense, to explain. 'The conquest of the
earth, which mostly means the taking it away from those who have
a different complexion or slightly flatter noses than ourselves is not
a pretty thing', Marlow declares—'when you look into it too much'.
And then: 'What redeems it is the idea only' (9I, 32). Forced by circumstance to 'look into it', or at least *at* it, Marlow becomes
captivated by 'the idea'. He wonders first whether Kurtz will

succeed, and, later, why he has failed, but this pair of questions is already a substitute for curiosity. In *Heart of Darkness* as in *Lord Jim*, Marlow's fascination is a means of keeping knowledge at a distance. He knows the basic reason for Kurtz's presence at the Inner Station: the Company is 'run for profit' (9I, 39). But as he narrates the journey upriver, the terms of his discourse shift, cynicism and indignation making way for an anxious meditation on the forest and its peoples, in their symbiotic relations. This world is 'incomprehensible', 'mysterious'; it overwhelms mind and yet, in an animistic turn, comes to seem the controlling mind in the situation. The 'stillness' is that of 'an implacable force brooding over an inscrutable intention' (II, 66). This is the force that 'found [Kurtz] out early and had taken on him a terrible vengeance for the fantastic invasion' (III, 97). Indeed, it is still more fantastic, for it finally takes over the attributes of the invaders: it is 'the heart of a *conquering* darkness' (III, 116, emphasis added). History mutates into nature and then into spirit, which envelops the invaders in its darkness—which at last overcomes the 'flicker' of civilization on the Thames itself. Marlow has undertaken 'amongst other things not to disclose any trade secrets' (I, 36) and he does not do so. 'The conquest of the earth, . . . when you look into it'—*really* look into it, in his preferred manner—is not what it seems, either to its complacent advocates or to its anti-imperialist critics.

Indeed, it may not be happening at all. The thought is certainly hyperbolic, but it is not, in textual fact, perverse. Secondary narration has a dual function in Conrad's narratives. It serves his compulsive hyperphasia, reconstituting, in the imaginary space of the novel, the contrasting conditions of enunciation of an older, unalienated narrative institution, the tale. In doing so, it symbolically restores the moral bond on which successful communication depends. In its other function, its role is apparently the contrary, qualifying narrative knowledge-claims and, at the limit of implication, querying the reality of the situations they putatively disclose. Formally speaking, the ultimate arbiter of fictional reality is the primary narrator: whatever it is, personified or not, that says *fiat*: let the world be and be thus. Only this instance can discriminate among the conflicting claims and evaluations of characters. In so far as this authority is weakened, problems of interpretation deepen, and reading becomes less secure. Conrad's primary narrators are ill-placed to arbitrate, because they know little or nothing of what they now report at one remove. Secondary narrators may in their turn depend heavily on the reports of others—and they on others still. Marlow has rather little direct authority for what he reports of Kurtz's actions, and discloses little, in fact, of what he has heard from the man in person. The narrative organization is recursive ('I say that he said that he said . . .') and, in fictional effect, tantalizing; there is no formal guarantee that these things have happened, or happened quite in this way. The more important point, for Marlow, is that they defy comprehension: much of his utterance is not narrative at all, but an elaboration of this theme. In the novels themselves, empirical uncertainty and interpretive bafflement are the twin modalities of the unshakeable conviction that these stories, and the larger history they instantiate, are *unbelievable*. Conrad, as a novelist, has been brought to know something, but cannot accept what he knows or that he knows it. His novels find their form in the struggle to contain an unbearable acknowledgement. Secondary narration is a strategy for accommodating this compulsive splitting of knowledge and belief. The brilliant, opaque protagonists of *Lord Jim* and *Heart of Darkness* who so fascinate Marlow are fetishes in the psychoanalytic sense, prized images of Empire that allow him to look, indeed to gaze, without seeing. Here at work in the plane of collective rather than personal history, is the process of disavowal.

ii. Figures of Disavowal

If the first paradox in Conrad is that his distinctive formal contribu-tion to modern narrative originated in an impulse to undo the typical conditions of the novelistic as such, the second is that Anglophone culture in the twentieth century owed its first, still compelling, visions of contemporary history to a writer so alienated that his novels cannot credit its reality. In the first decade of the new century, he wrote about colonialism (*Lord Jim* and *Heart of Darkness*), the politics of capitalist development in the Americas (*Nostromo*), revolutionary conspirators and their official adversaries in Eastern Europe (*Under Western Eyes*) and the West (*The Secret Agent*). His work registered the impact of working-class militancy (*The Nigger of the 'Narcissus'*), the sexual panic that flared in the persecution of Oscar Wilde (*Typhoon*), the new, scientific claimants to authority in human affairs. And all this he confronted not merely with distaste— which was manifest, and often violent—but in disbelief. Contemporary history, as the teacher of languages judges in the case of Russia (*Under Western Eyes*), is 'inconceivable'.

The labour of disavowal, which thus becomes a condition of possibility of fictioning the present, is borne by the device of secondary narration. *Nostromo* illustrates the practice on its grandest scale, with more than a dozen narrators offering their disparate answers to the implicit conundrum of the novel: Who or what makes history? Overhanging these narrative conjectures, as the mountains physically overhang the life of Sulaco, is the popular legend of the treasure of the Punta Mala, 'the evil point', and an implied answer that puts the question in its place: history is made by not-history, by brute nature. *Under Western Eyes* illustrates another rhetorical stratagem. Opening the first chapter of the novel, the reader is immediately addressed by an unattributed first-person pronoun, which therefore may be read as marking an authorial guarantee. A few sentences pass before the *I* is occupied by its character, the English teacher of languages who narrates the text. Such irony supplements the work of secondary narration and sometimes overtakes it as Conrad's leading device, assisting darker, more extreme instances of disavowal.

1

'Irony', today, circulates too widely and too fluently in cultural commentary to specify any of the diverse textual processes it names. There is point, once again, in approaching Conrad's practice indirectly, by way of a contrastive detour through the writing of another

master-ironist of the early twentieth century, James Joyce. Here are
the opening lines of *A Portrait of the Artist as a Young Man*:

> Once upon a time and a very good time it was there was a moo-
> cow coming down along the road and this moocow that was
> coming down along the road met a nicens little boy named baby
> tuckoo . . . (I, 7)[19]

In a common reading that sees this novel as dramatizing the growth
of a personality, critical emphasis falls on the diction of the passage—
the baby-talk of *moocow*, the ill-formed *nicens*—and its naive syntax.
In this way, free indirect style renders early childhood. Yet the
opening words set these features in a different light. The novel begins
with, or as, the beginning of a story, conventional in form and ambiguous in provenance: the language of the telling may mark Stephen's
childish effort at reiteration, or equally Simon's sentimental view of
how a father speaks in a nursery. It is impossible to resolve this or any
more interesting uncertainty in the novel, because there is no narrative exterior, no textually given authority to which the issue might
be referred. *A Portrait* is already another of its own kind, a 'Once
upon a time . . .' thing. In the beginning was the word, Joyce leaves us
to consider, but not the first word. In the beginning there was the
already-uttered, or genre. The course of Stephen's inner life is a
journey in discourse of various kinds and degrees, from schoolboy
argot and saloon-bar gentility to the formal heights of philosophy. He
is drawn to the obscure recesses of this symbolic universe—what, he
wonders, is *smugging*?—but finds no alternative sense there. When
he sins, he does so in the terms of the hell-fire sermon. 'Another life',
as he first grasps it, commits him to obsessive ritual observance and
initiates him, word-perfect, into the commonplaces of Irish devo-
tionalism. Even the release into art is deceptive. The discursive order
he now inhabits is that of artistic autonomy, which the narrative
reduces to a self-contradictory posture. Evocation turns mechanical;

---

19   James Joyce, *A Portrait of the Artist as a Young Man* (1916), London
1968.

associative processes are foreknown; idle glances and even smiles are already scripted. The dispositions thought proper to the artistic calling emerge as a version of the everyday paralysis. Spontaneity of mind is just the higher commonplace. *A Portrait* holds Stephen at a distance from himself to the end. His mother is preparing his 'new secondhand clothes', he records in his penultimate journal entry, anticipating in this small semantic disturbance the graver ambiguity to come:

> Welcome, O life! I go to encounter for the millionth time the reality of experience and to forge in the smithy of my soul the uncreated conscience of my race (V, 252).

Stephen's intended sense of 'forge' is *shape*, as his heroizing metaphor makes plain, but he cannot suppress—or even see—its other meaning, to *counterfeit*, or utter false coin.

If Joyce's irony is evidently directed at Stephen, its final implication concerns the relationship between the novel and its readers. *A Portrait* develops the Flaubertian critique of the bourgeois commonplace to the point of questioning the bohemian artist who thinks to expose and reject it; in doing so, it suspends the familiar contract between novelist and reader. This irony is not local or temporary in its incidence; it is pervasive and sustained, disqualifying given angles of vision and norms of judgement without ever validating more secure alternatives. It is art that reveals, not the artist-figure (who, as Joyce's title suggests, is just another subject for genre painting), and what it reveals is open to more than one evaluation. The notorious 'detachment' of the artist detaches the reader, with opposite subjective effects.

2

Conrad's irony functions differently. One strategic goal of his novels and stories, on the contrary, is to strengthen the bond between text and reader, to reinvent conditions of utterance for which, indeed, 'commonplace' would be an exact and positive description. Of course, his secondary narration has paradoxical implications, symbolically binding audiences but at the same time complicating the knowledge-value of the stories they hear. At a certain extreme, the paradox reverses its terms, now generating extended irony. That extreme is reached in *Heart of Darkness*, as Marlow, back in Brussels, makes his visit to the Intended. At this point, his narration modulates from report, which has dominated throughout, to scenic presentation, and a relatively spare exchange of direct speech. A short excerpt gives the sense of this rhetorical shift:

> 'And of all this,' she went on, mournfully, 'of all his promise, and all of his greatness, of his generous mind, of his noble heart, nothing remains—nothing but a memory.'
>
> 'We shall always remember him,' I said, hastily.
>
> 'No!' she cried. 'It is impossible that such a life should be sacrificed to leave nothing—but sorrow. You know what vast plans he had. I knew of them too—I could not perhaps understand—but others knew of them. Something must remain. His words, at least, have not died.'
>
> 'His words will remain,' I said.
>
> 'And his example,' she whispered to herself. 'Men looked up to him—his goodness shone in every act. His example—'
>
> 'True,' I said; 'his example, too. Yes, his example. I forgot that.'
> (III, 119–20, 121)

The irony of this scene has no bearing on issues of knowledge and evaluation in the plane of the text-reader relationship; it is strictly objective, inhering in the given reality of the situation. Marlow knows what the Intended does not, and also what she believes to have been the case. She, confident in what she believes, cannot imagine that Marlow might have grounds to believe otherwise. He conveys his truthful evaluation in words he knows she will translate into her illusion, which will then persist as the authorized version. His tale, on this occasion, is a masterpiece of non-communication. Dramatic irony is thus a necessary supplement to secondary narration in Conrad: it is the form assumed by his narrative hyperphasia in those moments where he imagines the final loss of shared belief, the snapping of the bond.

In *Heart of Darkness* that moment is an episode in a narrative whose scene of enunciation, by contrast, seems to promise phatic security. But ambiguity enters immediately, in the person of Marlow's host: 'On the whole river there was nothing that looked half so nautical. He resembled a pilot, which to the seaman is trustworthiness personified' (I, 27). He *looked*, he *resembled*; it was 'difficult to realize' the fact. He is 'the Director of Companies', and 'his work' lies not seawards 'but behind him, within the brooding gloom' of London. These uncertainties, like the following evocations of the city's reversible history—first as colonial outpost, then as colonizing centre—qualify the easy contrast Marlow will shortly assert, between Britain's Empire and the others. Even so, however, the marking of the city seems emphatic, as if registering the pressure of a further meaning. London may or may not be Brussels, but it is indisputably 'the biggest, and the greatest town on earth' (I, 27). Its constant index is 'gloom': 'a mournful gloom', 'the gloom to the west'.

> The sun sank low, and from glowing white changed to a dull red without rays and without heat, as if about to go out suddenly, stricken to death by the touch of that gloom brooding over a crowd of men (I, 28).
>
> The place of the monstrous town was still marked ominously on the sky, a brooding gloom in sunshine, a lurid glare under the stars (I, 29).

London, the type of the modern metropolis, is a site of cosmic disorder.

This is the universe of *The Secret Agent*, a place of unnumbered metamorphoses, where the law of non-contradiction has fallen into abeyance.[20] Even its best-adapted creatures may become disoriented at times: late in the action, Ossipon, the lecherous *anarchisant* student of moral pathology, '[feels] himself losing his footing in this treacherous affair' (XII, 225)—and for once, most readers will

---

20   Joseph Conrad, *The Secret Agent* (1907), London 1963.

sympathize. This London is not merely the prototypical modern city; it is, with Paris, a cradle of the novel. Indeed, with its atomized social relations, secularized mores, and disenchanted knowledges, it actually *is* the novelistic. Hence the desperate rhetoric of *The Secret Agent*: whereas the Marlow narratives simulate the moral conditions of the tale on the objective ground of the novel, this 'simple tale' pursues the immanent logic of modernity, dramatizing the moral extremities of a novelized world.

There is no Marlow-figure to tell the story of how the pornographer and anarchist Verloc, under pressure from the foreign embassy for which he spies, induces his autistic brother-in-law to bomb the Greenwich Observatory; how Stevie stumbles and blows himself to pieces; how the police investigations go forward dubiously motivated and at cross-purposes; how Verloc's wife, Winnie, discovering that her husband has destroyed the brother-son who has been everything to her, murders him; and how at last, betrayed a second time—by Ossipon—she takes her own life. Secondary narratives play a familiar but now subordinate part in the organization of the text, which is given as an impersonal narration addressed, so to speak, to no one in particular. Two kinds of scene predominate.

The first is the solitary walk through the streets. None of these journeys is socially transparent, or benign in motivation or outcome. Verloc has been summoned to the embassy, and is anxious lest any of his political associates should happen upon him. Chief Inspector Heat, of the Special Crimes branch, patrols here and there, monitoring the anarchist demi-monde. The Assistant Commissioner, with his private interest in the outcome of the Greenwich investigation, descends into cosmopolitan Soho, dressed for the part and eluding his own uniformed officers as if a criminal himself. For the Professor, the supreme technician of terror, walking the streets is a political activity, an occasion for resentful fantasies and a show of defiance: the police are aware (he says) that he is a walking bomb. The few companionate journeys in the narrative are only apparently exceptional. Watching Verloc and Stevie leave home together, Winnie wishfully imagines them as father and son; in fact, they are on the first leg of their deceptive route to Greenwich. Deep family loyalty prompts Winnie and Stevie to accompany their mother to South London; but the occasion of the journey is her voluntary self-exile from the Verloc household, and the conversations that occur in the course of the trip will, on one available reading of events, lead to their deaths.

Conversations, normally duologues indoors, make up a second scenic group. Heat and his superior assess the Greenwich case with mutual resentment, in a conversation that taps little of the inner speech on either side. Heat's main concern is his occasional informant Verloc, whom he proposes to safeguard by framing a vulnerable parolee, Michaelis—who, it happens, is the counterpart object of the Assistant Commissioner's concern, being the protégé of his wife's valued acquaintance, a great society hostess. It irritates the Assistant Commissioner that he must 'take so much on trust' in his isolated position of command. His own superior, Sir Ethelred, in contrast, is too distracted by his plan to nationalize the fisheries to pay close attention to the fish who inhabit the 'slimy aquarium' of Soho. Ossipon and the Professor, in a matching discussion, fail to penetrate the enigma of the day's news, even though Ossipon immediately suspects a provocation and the Professor has supplied Verloc with the bomb. Knowing little of him or his household, in reality, they cannot correctly infer his role in the event, much less that the luckless bomber was someone else—and something else again. The household itself, supposedly a focus of intimate feeling and political solidarity, conforms to the rule of alienation. Conversation is sparse, unless the usual anarchists—grotesques all—turn up to talk at or past one another, while Verloc inhabits his double identity, Winnie gets on with things, and Stevie sits on the far side of an open door, lost in his drawing. What Stevie draws is in one aspect an expressive figure, in another a diagram:

> circles, circles; innumerable circles, concentric, eccentric; a coruscating whirl of circles that by their tangled multitude of repeated curves, uniformity of form, and confusion of intersecting lines suggested a rendering of cosmic chaos, the symbolism of a mad art attempting the inconceivable (III, 45–46).

Here, in stylized form, is the non-communicating world of *The Secret Agent*, which will eventually mean the death of Winnie and, through this, the loss of the last social bond.

'The inconceivable' in this case is the identity—perhaps even the fact—of 'the secret agent'. The distinction implied in the singular form of the noun is not self-evident, in a world where everyone acts clandestinely, whether for love (Winnie and her mother) or gain (Verloc) or *raison d'état* (Vladimir) or social advantage (the Assistant Commissioner) or professional convenience (Heat) or self-styled revolutionary ends (the Professor). All are secret agents in a way, and even a 'realistic' shortlist leaves three obvious candidates, Vladimir, Verloc and the Professor, and a fourth who cannot be discounted, namely Stevie. And if the identity of the secret agent remains ambiguous, it is because the narrative remains undecided about 'his' motivation. *Who?* depends on *why?* or *how?*—questions to which the novel entertains two answers which, although compatible as accounts of an uncontroversial record of events, are antithetical in final historical implication.

The more strongly emphasized of the two explanations is, so to speak, 'externalist' in kind, and begins with Vladimir, who seeks to further the domestic priorities of his own state in the contrasting political environment of Britain, using a local agent to organize an unlawful event that takes two innocent lives. Here Conrad reiterates the great theme of English conservatism, elaborated from Edmund Burke's *Reflections on the Revolution in France*. The states of continental Europe are characteristically rigid, intrusive apparatuses of rule that shape a correspondingly doctrinaire and extremist reflex in their political opponents; their defining types are secret police and terrorists. In Britain in contrast, where civil society enjoys greater autonomy, political rule is less formal, more flexible, an evolved liberal constitution grounding more reasonable terms of political engagement. This is shared wisdom in *The Secret Agent*. Vladimir finds England 'absurd' in 'its sentimental regard for individual liberty' (II, 33). The Professor, who like all Verloc's revolutionary associates is 'European', thinks the country 'dangerous, with her idealistic conception of legality', and adds: 'The social spirit of this people is wrapped up in scrupulous prejudices, and that is fatal to our work' (IV, 67). Winnie embodies that spirit. On first hearing of the explosion, she comments: 'I call it silly... We ain't downtrodden slaves here' (IX, 168)—and specifically, as she has protested on another occasion, 'not German slaves... thank God' (III, 57). Revolutionary activity is 'not our business', she maintains; and the Assistant Commissioner, concluding his investigation and satisfying official interest in the events, agrees that it has been a foreign affair. What matters now 'is the clearing out of this country of all the foreign political spies, police, and that sort of—of—dogs' (X, 185). Every anarchist can be accounted for; it remains only 'to do away with the *agent provocateur* to make everything safe' (X, 186).

However, neither judgement can be taken as dependable. Winnie is not an exhibit for the Professor's gallery of English 'prejudices'; fully aware, as she repeatedly says, that 'things do not stand being looked into', she is a self-conscious pragmatist, in politics as in her marriage. The Assistant Commissioner, whose curiosity is his temperamental vice, not a professional principle, cannot hear the ambiguity in his confident report of his findings: 'We could have gone further; only we stopped at the limits of our territory' (X, 186). He means that he has observed diplomatic protocol, not intruding into sovereign space of the embassy. But what is there to read in his words is the suggestion that he has not even entered 'our' territory—that he has not looked inwards, into England, and seen there the evidence for an alternative 'internalist' explanation of events. Yet the narrative leaves no doubt of this, or that Stevie, instrument and victim of the Greenwich plot, may be the incendiary reality misrecognized as 'the secret agent'. Like the anarchists whose non-conversation he overhears, Stevie is an isolate. It is precisely this that defines his condition: what he lacks is not so much ordinary intelligence or feeling as his sister's pragmatism, the 'common sense' that might moderate the reach of his curiosity and his compassion, which is extraordinary. Like the Professor, he 'lacks the great social virtue of resignation' (IV, 69). Moreover, he has already shown himself ready to take violent measures against perceived wrongdoing—as when he launches a firework attack on his employer, outraged by stories of the oppression of others (I, 18). That episode of terroristic virtue suggests the inference

to be drawn from a later episode, which in fact provides the only
direct evidence of his disposition in the approach to the bombing
attempt. Arrived at his mother's place of exile, Stevie is drawn into
conversation with the cab-driver, who details the drudgery of his
working life and the poverty of his family. 'Bad! Bad!', he exclaims, as
'convulsive sympathy' surges in him. 'Poor! Poor!' Then, a little later,
as he and Winnie set out for home: 'Bad world for poor people' (VIII,
143). It occurs to him that the police might help. 'The police aren't for
that,' is Winnie's half-distracted reply. Stevie is suddenly angry. 'What
are they for then, Winn? What are they for? Tell me.' Then Winnie
breaches the rule by which she lives:

> 'Don't you know what the police are for, Stevie? They are there so
> that them as have nothing shouldn't take anything away from
> them who have.'

With that, the explosive formula is complete. Compassion, inciting
curiosity, leads to terror. The cab-man and Winnie have primed
Verloc's instrument. In due course, the bomb will arrive, and not
from Soho but from a 'little country station' in Kent (V, 89), the so-
styled Garden of England. Foreigners have little to do with it.

This doubling of interpretive possibilities marks the crisis of political perception on which disavowal must do its work, somehow
recuperating an unbearable anxiety within the terms of the accepted
narrative. This radical ambiguation of the event is itself rendered
suspect, resting as it does on an opposition of national types that may
after all be groundless. England's political culture stands in favourable contrast to that of continental Europe, but who may confidently
distinguish their corresponding human types? Vladimir, whose
spontaneous 'guttural' intonation is 'startling even to Mr Verloc's
experience of cosmopolitan slums', can produce 'an amazingly
genuine English accent' (II, 29, 38). His adversary, the Assistant
Commissioner, is English, but has been shaped by his time in a tropical colony, and has a taste for 'foreign' disguise, and for Soho, that
'denationalizing' milieu whose restaurants, with their 'fraudulent
cookery', deprive patrons of 'all their national and private

characteristics' (VII, 125). Verloc is English-born, but his father was French. Even Winnie is indeterminate: if her mother's boast is to be credited, she too is partly French. Of course, these complications resolve nothing: their point is the further ambiguity they generate. Like Marlow's prolixity, they serve to fend off the threat of disenchantment.

Only the Professor is exempt from this drama of nationality: he has no proper name to place him, and his origins are unmarked. In fact, he largely escapes the semantic organization of the text as a whole, by virtue of his sheer abstraction. His pure hatred of the existing order entails no corresponding solidarity with either the masses, who are 'an odious multitude', or the revolutionaries, whom he despises. Whereas Stevie embodies unmoderated compassion, he affects pure cerebration; and unlike his political associates, he is formidably skilled, and incorruptible. His politics are socially meaningless, consisting in the pursuit of an ideal detonator; he is an aesthete of the revolution. If there is something fetishistic in the Professor's technical obsession, there is something the same in his place in the novel, which is disproportionate to his limited narrative function—making the bomb. Under-employed and abstract, he appears at once marginal and central, a figure whose purpose is simply to be present. The novel's closing vision is of him, not anyone who has acted with real consequence or suffered commensurate harm. The Professor is, in effect, a rhetorically simpler version of Jim or Kurtz, in a story with no equivalent protagonist. Like them, he is an object of fascination, a character in whom Conrad can at once register and obscure his perception of historical danger.

The Professor, like Jim and Kurtz, is centrally defined by his relationship with a local population. They are visible, self-consciously paternalist functionaries in their respective colonial systems; he, in contrast, is secretive, malevolent, an anonymous member of the crowd—'unsuspected and deadly, like a pest in the street full of men' (XIII, 249). Yet he is hardly the alien aggressor the simile implies. No one in this world is transparent, or secure in their social being; and the street and its men are already in the grip of a protean disorder. The morning sun works its alchemy in reverse in the streets of the

West End, 'old gold' turning to 'copper' and then 'rust'. The number-
ing of the houses has fallen inexplicably out of series. The friezes in
the Silenus Restaurant depict a medieval outdoor scene, but the
music comes from a mechanical piano. The bomb plot destroys a
family, which in much conservative thought is the very model of
social order. But that family has had reality only in Winnie's
dreams—Verloc habitually takes his meals 'as if in a public place'.
Stevie's lethal compassion is fired by the social misery of another
family and his own history embodies a record of familial decline:
bullied in his early years by a violent father, he has grown up in his
mother's boarding-house, an interior no longer quite a home, if not
yet its opposite, a hotel. Verloc looks from his bedroom window at
'that enormity of cold, black, wet, muddy, inhospitable accumulation of
bricks, slates, and stones, things in themselves unlovely and unfriendly
to man' (III, 54). The South London night, as Winnie's mother leaves
for a solitary life as the tenant of a charitable foundation, is 'sinister,
noisy, hopeless and rowdy' (VIII, 133). The cumulative force of these
indications is irresistible. The modern city, acme of gregariousness, is
the vanishing-point of solidarity. If Conrad's 'perfect terrorist' is a
figure for the 'inconceivable' social revolutionary, his London figures
the inconceivability of lasting social order. The secret agent, now,
is not a person at all, but the history that has created 'the street full
of men'.

3

An American coda . . . In the symbolic geography of *The Secret
Agent*, poised as it is on the Greenwich meridian, danger comes from
the East. The events of the decade following its appearance lent substance to Conrad's imaginings. By the end of 1918, the old regimes of
the Romanovs, the Hapsburgs and the Hohenzollerns lay in ruins,
crippled by four years of warfare, then felled by revolutionary
attacks—the work of insurgent crowds, be it said, not the feckless
caricatures who inhabit Verloc's parlour. These transformations reso-
nated throughout Europe, as inspiration or menace, not exempting
England, the heartland of liberalism and 'resignation'. The subtler

dangers of territories farther east (and south), the colonial settings of
Lord Jim and *Heart of Darkness*, were a threat of another, politically
less tangible kind. At the same time, however, Conrad's narratives
discern the portents taking shape in the opposite quarter, in a
country now salient in 'the West'. The New World is no more reassuring than what survives of the Old. The German-Australian who
has abandoned the *Patna* sees it as a place where not even English
justice can pursue him: in his own damning words, he 'vill an
Amerigan citizen begome'. The Professor commends the United
States as 'fertile ground for us': 'They have more character over there,
and their character is essentially anarchistic . . . The great Republic
has the root of the destructive matter in her . . . Excellent' (IV, 67).
And the 'root' is being transplanted abroad: the financial power
behind the silver mines in *Nostromo* is the US banker Holroyd. Here
again, historical experience gave body to Conrad's apprehensions.
The Great War brought a first involvement in European politics for
the country that now boasted the world's largest economy; henceforward, the tendencies of developed capitalism would often be
construed simply as 'Americanization'. However, while Conrad and
European writers of younger generations could not but try to evaluate the cultural promise or threat of American capitalism, there were
others, across the Atlantic, to whom that mighty reality appeared in
the form of an intimate historical enigma—as if the very idea of capitalism in America were finally unimaginable. F. Scott Fitzgerald was
one such, producing in *The Great Gatsby* a truly Conradian *envoi* for
'the American century'.

  The story begins with the ambitions of a Middle Western farmer's
son, Jimmy Gatz; continues with his transformation, through the
fortunes of patronage and war, then bootlegging and fraud, into the
rich, flamboyant Jay Gatsby of West Egg, Long Island, the host of any
parasite's dreams. The motive for his great displays of hospitality is in
truth unsociably private. He hopes to recapture his lost love, Daisy,
who has come to live directly across the bay, in the more prestigious
East Egg, with her husband, Tom. The parties themselves accomplish
little, but with the help of his neighbour, Nick Carraway, who is
Daisy's cousin, he succeeds, or nearly. His romance intersects

disastrously with Tom's current sexual intrigue; misidentified as the driver in a hit-and-run accident in which Tom's lover, Myrtle, dies, he too dies, shot by her distraught husband. Gatsby's funeral is a dismal, ill-attended affair; Tom and Daisy, the real authors of Myrtle's destruction, slip away from the area; Nick returns to the Middle West to muse on the significance of his summer in the East, at length delivering the monologue that is the exclusive textual substance of *The Great Gatsby*.

There is so much of *Lord Jim* in the novel, both as imagined action and as narration—so much, too, of *Heart of Darkness* and, in another way, *The Secret Agent*—that it is worth emphasizing the respect in which Nick's situation differs from Marlow's. He does not speak: his medium, as he immediately declares, is writing for print—'this book' (I, 8).[21] The implied audience, likewise, is largely unmarked, taking discernible form just once, in the educated facetiousness of 'that delayed Teutonic migration known as the Great War' (I, 9). His Ivy League background and its later social echoes seem no more than circumstantial. He frequents the Yale Club, but only to dine and use the library. The 'investments and securities' that he finds there are the matter of the books he reads; the fellowship of the club—an enabling value for Marlow—appears only negatively, in the shape of the usual 'few rioters' (III, 57). None of this suggests the hyperphasia that motivates the resort to secondary narration in Conrad. *Gatsby* is a novel at peace with its institutional conditions of existence. And yet, for all that, its crowning stylistic achievement is to fashion itself in a medium to which it has no access, that of speech. The Carraway figure is a simulated voice—something to return to, in a narrative whose supreme object of desire, Daisy, is normally represented as that and little more.

It is of course a normative, WASP voice—only the Jewish gambler, Wolfshiem, and assorted plebeian characters, including Gatsby's father, have their words marked down by the old device of pseudophonetic transcription (as in 'Oggsford' for Oxford). And one

---

21   F. Scott Fitzgerald, *The Great Gatsby* (1925), intro Tony Tanner, London 1990.

locution identifies it more closely. Nick is writing from his home-
town, '*this* Middle Western city' (I, 8)—a context-dependent form of
words that invokes a preferred audience, and aligns it in the symbolic
space of the narrative, whose poles are East and West. This axis is a
biographical constant for the main characters. Like Nick and Gatsby,
Tom, Daisy and her friend Jordan all come from points west; ambition of various kinds has drawn them, as if naturally, eastwards, to
New York. For Nick, as he looks back from the Middle West, this
geography is a moral emblem. The journey east is one into danger,
the 'valley of ashes' that lies between the Eggs and the City, sur-
mounted by a *deus absconditus* in the form of a huge, unseeing pair
of spectacles advertising the optometrist Dr Eckleburg. There is
nothing in the narrative to motivate this unreal landscape; in this
sense it is not even symbolic, rather a simple allegorical figure of
spiritual exhaustion. 'I see now', Nick concludes,

> that this has been a story of the West, after all—Tom and Gatsby,
> Daisy and Jordan and I, were all Westerners, and perhaps we
> possessed some deficiency in common which made us subtly
> unadaptable to Eastern life (IX, 167).

But what has he 'seen'? Why is the East like this, and in what does the
West differ? Nick is convinced that he has learnt something; his
story, like Marlow's, is rich in philosophical generalization. He has
had 'privileged glimpses into the human heart' (I, 8), and specifically
into the hearts of Americans; these are the substance of his avowed
learning. What he has actually seen is something quite different.

Compared with ordinary life in New York as it presents itself to
Nick, the valley of ashes is a mere curiosity. The visible world as a
whole is phantasmagoric. Natural objects seem artificial: a dog's fur
is 'a weather-proof coat' (II, 30), and in West Egg the leaves prolif-
erate 'just as things grow in fast movies' (I, 9). Artefacts are liable to
the reverse transformation, Daisy's living room appearing as a windy
seascape. In this world, objects come to animate life—'a hundred
pairs of golden and silver slippers shuffled the shining dust' (VIII,
144)—and are even spoken to:

'No thanks', said [Jordan] to the four cocktails just in from the
pantry. 'I'm absolutely in training.' (I, 16)

Gatsby's parties, where drinks 'float . . . through the twilight' and
even the moon rises 'out of a caterer's basket' (I, 44), intensify such
phenomena, and confirm a morally ominous but also mysterious
connection with wealth and theatre. Turkeys, emblematic for the
nation, are 'bewitched to a dark gold' (III, 41). Representations multiply and distract, as an actress is 'erroneous[ly]' identified as 'Gilda
Gray's understudy from the Follies' (III, 42). Such logics of substitutability extend to personal relations, one guest arriving 'always with
four girls . . . never quite the same ones in physical person, but . . . so
identical one with another that it inevitably seemed they had been
there before' (IV, 62). Deceiving and disordering in its effects, the
phantasmagoria is nevertheless regular in its forms, whose underlying process is unveiled just once, in a single paragraph:

> Every Friday five crates of oranges and lemons arrived from a
> fruiterer in New York—every Monday these same oranges and
> lemons left [Gatsby's] back door in a pyramid of pulpless halves.
> There was a machine in the kitchen which could extract the juice
> of two hundred oranges in half an hour if a little button was
> pressed two hundred times by a butler's thumb (III, 41).

The careful sequencing of this passage, and its regular mismatching
of grammatical and real agencies, divulge the secret of the floating
cocktails. The phenomenal world of West Egg now appears in relation to an objective system of goods, markets and (occluded) labour.
The Great Gatsby offers a brilliant visualization of what Marx
explained as 'the fetishism of commodities':

> It is absolutely clear that, by his labour, man changes the forms of the
> material of nature in such a way as to make them useful to him . . .
> The mysterious character of the commodity-form [or the use-value
> produced for exchange] consists . . . simply in the fact that the com-
> modity reflects the social characteristics of men's own labour as

objective characteristics of the products of labour themselves, as the social-natural properties of these things . . . It is nothing but the definite social relation between men themselves which assumes here, for them, the fantastic form of a relation between things.[22]

However, the commodified object-world of the novel is not commensurable with its relatively few indications of labour. Domestics, small farmers, mechanics and fisherfolk cannot account for its characteristic accessories—the opulent food and drink, the telephones, the automobiles and the vast wealth. When Nick describes Daisy as being 'appalled by West Egg, this unprecedented "place" that Broadway had begotten upon a Long Island fishing village', he is in effect joining her in disavowal of American economic reality. Yet he cannot do otherwise, for to acknowledge it would be to accept that there is no final, anthropological difference between East and West, that one is the product and necessary function of the other. American capitalism is a systemic unity, and its human token, in the novel, is none other than the young man from the hinge of the agricultural and industrial economies—a Middle Western hardware business—who has come East to learn about finance. But Nick cannot accept the material reality of his home region. His preferred image of it might be a Hollywood set. 'That's my Middle West', he says, thinking back to his college days:

—not the wheat or the prairies or the lost Swede towns, but the thrilling returning trains of my youth, and the street lamps and sleigh bells in the frosty dark and the shadows of holly wreaths thrown by lighted windows on the snow (IX, 167).

The alternative to radical disenchantment is his story of 'the great Gatsby'.

Curiosity about the secrets of money is overtaken by fascination with the enigmatic figure who lives next door. Gatsby, like Kurtz, is

---

22 Karl Marx, *Capital Volume 1*, trans. Ben Fowkes, Harmondsworth 1976, pp. 163–5.

before all else a rumour. 'They say he's a nephew or a cousin of Kaiser Wilhelm's', Myrtle's sister reports: 'That's where all his money comes from' (II, 35). According to another source, 'Somebody told me they thought he killed a man once' (III, 45). A third informant can confirm that he had spied for the enemy during the war—'I heard that from a man who knew all about him, grew up with him in Germany.' Gatsby has more than one version of himself, and seems to acknowledge the essentially rumorous quality of his existence when he mistakenly assumes, on his first encounter with Nick, that his neighbour already knows who he is. The truth, as he later discloses it to Nick, in fact confirms the validity of the rags-to-riches story it seems to travesty, renewing mystification where another success story—that of the Carraways—might dispel it. Gatsby has received his social training from a multimillionaire whose fortune had grown from silver and other metals speculation; his shady professional skills he owes to Wolfshiem, the man who fixed the World Series. In other words, wealth comes from the earth and proliferates in the hands of speculators and tricksters: the secret of money is safe. Nick distils Gatsby into a psychological essence: uniquely, in a human landscape where anticlimax appears to be an inexorable general law, Gatsby has 'an extraordinary gift for hope, a romantic readiness such as I have never found in any other person and which it is not likely I shall ever find again' (I, 8). His story, it may be, epitomizes a peculiarly American striving for a future that is always already past. In the ultimate reduction, Nick's Gatsby becomes a self-fashioned work of art: 'If personality is an unbroken series of successful gestures, then there was something gorgeous about him, some heightened sensitivity to the promises of life' (I, 8).

Like Kurtz, he has been driven by 'his Platonic conception of himself'; like Jim, 'he turned out all right at the end' (I, 8). Like both, he embodies opacity as revelation; his role is to fascinate. The decisive function of Fitzgerald's personification, as of Conrad's, is disavowal of an intolerable apprehension—here, that of capitalism itself. And thus Freud converges with Marx in the space of a shared metaphor. Nick's Gatsby is his fetishistic defence against the reality of a fetishized society. Only the image of Gatsby the illimitable enables him to recompose his relations with the West he must not know, 'that vast obscurity beyond the city, where the dark fields of the republic [roll] on under the night' (IX, 171). And likewise only by this means, perhaps, could Fitzgerald imagine Nick's account of himself, this monodrama of bourgeois conscience, and embody it in a speaking voice that, for all the evidence to the contrary, is not, like cousin Daisy's, 'full of money'.

iii. Fascinations

Fascination has been the constant point of return in these readings: fascination, that is, in the sense of a pseudo-cognitive disposition having everything in common with curiosity, which it resembles and often mimics, except the essential, namely the will to find out.[23] Curiosity is transitive, driven by the desire to pass from knowledge state *a* to knowledge state *b*. Fascination is intransitive, fulfilled in the presence of an object that is compelling but opaque. Jim (in *Lord Jim*) and Kurtz (in *Heart of Darkness*) are objects of fascination in this sense. These brilliant, opaque inventions, seen at one remove via Marlow's stories, are the means by which Conrad can narrate his contemporary world while saying, as it were, 'don't believe a word of it'.

The theoretical undergirding of this analysis is Freud's metapsychological concept of disavowal, which denotes a mental process in which a given reality is simultaneously acknowledged and denied, avowed but at the same time disavowed thanks to the formation of a fetish or something like it that preserves an anterior, less disturbing belief.[24] Fascination, as I understand it, is the mode of apprehension

---

23   In its original form, as 'Critical Considerations on the Fetishism of Commodities', this was given as the Hinkley Lecture in the Department of English at Johns Hopkins University in October 2006. The script appeared more or less verbatim in *ELH*, 24.2, Summer 2007.

24   Freud's case was sexual fetishism in male heterosexuals, which he interpreted as a defence against the knowledge that women have no penis. See his 'Fetishism' (1927), in *On Sexuality*, vol. 7 of Penguin Freud Library, ed. Angela Richards, Harmondsworth 1977, pp. 351–7; and 'Editor's Note', pp. 347–9. See

proper to such fetishistic investments. Fitzgerald's Gatsby is another invention of the Conradian kind; and since what Nick has to report is among other things a phantasmagoric experience of commodities, it seems necessary also to refer to the relevant part of Marx's *Capital*. And so, as it is put in the preceding section, two strong general theories converge in a shared metaphor. But the phrasing is a giveaway: too comfortable in its suggestion to be altogether credible. What can be said in a more critical vein about this tropic encounter?

Slavoj Žižek has been the boldest exponent of an articulated practice of historical-materialist and psychoanalytic reason in the past fifty years, and his summary account of commodity fetishism is telling:

> The fetishist illusion resides in our real social life, not in our perception of it—a bourgeois subject knows very well that there is nothing magic about money, that money is just an object which stands for a set of social relations, but he nevertheless acts in real life as if he believed that money is a magical thing.[25]

Faced with this formulation, which simply rewrites Marxian fetishism as a case of Freudian disavowal, it seems superfluous to speak of a relationship at all; and 'convergence'—my word—is a timid description of such a fusion. Regardless of the independent theoretical merits of his construction, which we need not prejudge, Žižek's fusion simply overrides the discrepant logics of the concepts it brings together. Two related discrepancies call for particular notice.

First, although commodity fetishism and disavowal both involve a disturbance of the knowledge function, they do so in contrasting ways. In cases of disavowal, the acknowledgement is uppermost. Žižek is right about this.[26] Were this not so, there would be no need

also Freud, 'Splitting of the Ego in the Process of Defence' (1938–1940), in *On Metapsychology: The Theory of Psychoanalysis*, vol. 11 of the Penguin Freud Library, Harmondsworth 1984, pp. 461–4.

25   Slavoj Žižek, *The Universal Exception: Selected Writings, Volume Two*, eds Rex Butler and Scott Stephens, London 2006, pp. 254–5.

26   Compare Mannoni: the fetishist '*knows very well*', yet cannot add 'but all the same' (pp. 11, 12, my translation). That is the work of the fetish. Compare

for the counter-function of denial, or for the opaque form it assumes. But commodity fetishism, in contrast, plunges the subject into a primary condition of unknowing, from which neither theoretical elucidation nor social point of vantage can redeem it. Unlike Freud, who could discern a range of variation in the relative forces of acknowledgement and denial in disavowal, Marx was categorical in his judgement of the experience of commodity exchange. Mystery rules, in a process that inverts that of disavowal.

The second discrepancy arises from a fatal distribution of logical properties. Disavowal is implicitly anthropological in range; it is a human universal. But within that specification, it is contingent, a potential always present but not necessarily active. Commodity fetishism, by contrast, is strictly bounded in its historical incidence. It is a feature of capitalism—or, at least, of regularized commodity production. But within that specification, there is no contingency to speak of. Fetishism is a necessity. In the one case, then, we have a universal contingency, in the other a historically specific necessity. Viewed so, the 'convergence' between Marx and Freud is better imaged as an intersection, where paths meet only in order to part again. In logical terms, it is a crux. It happens too—and quite apart from any consideration deriving from Freud—that this crux marks the site of another one, a crux internal to Marx's own reasoning. It is time to look again at *Capital*.

1

In the thesis of commodity fetishism, Marx put forward a strong general claim about the condition of subjectivity in capitalist societies: 'The commodity reflects the social [that is, interdependent] characteristics of men's own labour as objective characteristics of the

also Roland Barthes, who, in a different context, makes the closest association between fascination and ignorance: 'Cette ignorance est le propre de la fascination' ('Roland Barthes par Roland Barthes', in his *Oeuvres complètes*, ed. Eric Marty, 3 vols., Paris 1995, 3:85). He is talking about family snapshots from his childhood.

products of labour themselves.'[27] Clearly it matters a great deal in cultural theory and analysis whether this claim is valid or not, and, if yes, how far. It matters today, when commodifying processes continue to extend their social reach, when it is necessary to speak not only of the range and degrees of commodification but of intensities of commodification, when capitalism stands ready, at last, to take possession of the entire planet. A theory that cannot account for the culture of commodities is hardly a cultural theory at all.

Now, commodity fetishism has not been a neglected topic over the years. The volume of writing it has inspired is large—and also repetitious in key respects, even amidst the important differences. The continuing interest is understandable and necessary, then, but it is also disturbing. This thought prompts an observation which, though hardly fine-tuned, is fair enough, I believe, and disquieting. The theory of commodity fetishism has been generally honoured in Marxist tradition—and latterly in circles where Marx is honoured for not much else—but treated in practice as a convenience to be cited or overlooked according to circumstance. This is not merely a sub-critical state of affairs; it is a lapse of logic. After all, there is nothing corresponding to this intermittence in the theory. However, it may be that there is a grain of insight here too. The theory of commodity fetishism, as Marx's posterity has known it and significantly modified it, is too strong.

Jean Baudrillard launched his critique of the political economy of the sign with the claim that a full account of commodity fetishism must incorporate use-value as well as exchange-value, must grasp needs themselves as a system, not just the natural or acquired wants of persons in the mass.[28] Guy Debord's *Society of the Spectacle*, another French initiative from the same years, the late 1960s, was clearly indebted to the Marxian analysis of commodity fetishism, but the concept-trope of the spectacle represented a drastic upping of the

---

27   Karl Marx, *Capital: Volume 1*, introd. Ernest Mandel, trans. Ben Fowkes, Harmondsworth, 1976, pp. 164–5. This translation follows the old convention, long discredited, whereby the masculine 'man' can stand for 'men and women' or 'human beings'. Here and elsewhere I have left this as it is.

28   See, for example, Jean Baudrillard, 'The Political Economy of the Sign', in *Selected Writings*, ed and introd. by Mark Poster, Cambridge, UK 1988, p. 63.

critical stakes, in effect denoting any aspect of contemporary social relations—capitalist or not, indeed—that works to induce passivity in the subject population: 'The spectacle in its generality is a concrete inversion of life, and, as such, the autonomous movement of non-life.'[29] Both Baudrillard and Debord made explicit acknowledgement of Georg Lukács's *History and Class Consciousness*, which is without a doubt the most influential account of commodity fetishism ever written, and the source from which the idea of reification surged into twentieth-century Marxist cultural theory.[30] Another, more telling way of stating this relationship is that the theory of commodity fetishism furnished Lukács with the occasion for implanting the exogenous concept of reification at the centre of the critique of capitalism, thereby subsuming a determinate theory of commodity culture into a general vision of the fallen life-world of capitalist modernity—a world in which processes and relationships appear as things, and quality is reduced to quantity, obeying a universal rule of rationalization and measurability. 'Reification requires that a society should learn to satisfy all its needs in terms of commodity exchange.'[31]

Baudrillard and Debord had a shared purpose, the entirely laudable one of trying to develop a theory of contemporary capitalism and its subjects; and they appear to have shared with their early mentor the purpose of developing the critique of commodity fetishism by extending its range of reference and intensifying its basic thesis. However, it may be that in inflating the claims of the theory of commodity fetishism—as they did—such thinkers merely compounded a mistaken move in Marx's own account; that the thesis he classically propounds in the closing section of his chapter on commodities is itself already a logical leap beyond what his general arguments allow. There are other problems here, but this one holds quite general critical interest for cultural theory.

---

29   Guy Debord, *The Society of the Spectacle*, trans. Donald Nicholson-Smith, New York 1994, p. 12.

30   See Georg Lukács, *History and Class Consciousness* (1923), trans. Rodney Livingstone, London 1971.

31   Ibid., p. 92.

2

About the pages that Marx devoted to the fetishism of commodities
we can be relatively brief. In his own words:

> A commodity appears at first sight an extremely obvious, trivial
> thing. But its analysis brings out that it is a very strange thing,
> abounding in metaphysical subtleties and theological niceties . . .
> The mysterious character of the commodity-form consists simply
> in the fact that the commodity reflects the social characteristics
> of men's own labour as objective characteristics of the products of
> labour themselves, as the socio-natural properties of these things.
> [The commodity-form] is nothing but the definite social relation
> between men themselves which assumes here, for them, the fantastic
> form of a relation between things . . . I call this the fetishism which
> attaches itself to the products of labour as soon as they are produced
> as commodities.[32]

'As soon as . . .': the phrasing is simple and final. The production of
commodities—that is, private production for exchange—is in and
of itself the production of fetishes—of irreducible false appearances.
    This was not among Marx's first thoughts about commodity pro-
duction. In the first draft for *Capital*, the *Grundrisse*, he entertained
the possibility that this illusion was socially variable in its occurrence.
For wage-earners, he was ready to speculate, money was perhaps
no more than 'coin', what he termed a 'self-suspending' mediation
between labour-power and subsistence goods, a token facilitating the
barter of work for food and shelter.[33] But by the time he came to write
the first chapter of *Capital*, a late addition which therefore ranks as
one of the last parts of the work he cleared for publication, his position had hardened. Fetishism is universal and necessary in conditions
of commodity production. In fact we can go further and say that

---

32   Marx, *Capital: Volume 1*, pp. 163–5.
33   Karl Marx, *Grundrisse*, Harmondsworth 1973, pp. 284, 254.

Conradian Histories   113

there is no precedent for this claim in the language or logic of *Capital* itself. Considering this, I want to turn now not to the discussion of fetishism itself but to an earlier part of the chapter on commodities, in which the notion of fetishism has no part, that devoted to the analysis of 'the value-form, or exchange-value'.[34] My question will be, how and how far does the analysis permit us to speak of a fetishism of commodities?

At this point in his exposition, Marx has established the twofold character of the commodity.[35] It is a use-value, fulfilling a determinate human need, and an exchange-value, something worth such-and-such a ratio of another something in the market. Commodities have value because of the amount of work they entail—or, to speak precisely, their value, their exchange-value, is determined by the amount of socially necessary labour-power expended in their production. Now, he will move from this general account of the commodity to reconstruct the process through which commodity exchange eventuates in the special commodity we know as money. The temporality implied in the three principal stages of this analysis is more logical than real, even where it intersects with documented historical processes. It turns on a distinction between two forms or aspects of value, the relative and the equivalent.[36]

First, a simple exchange occurs, use-value A for use-value B, and in the process there is an agreed determination of value, exchange-value. A is worth two of B. In this instance, B appears in the aspect of the equivalent form of value, as the measure by which the relative value of A is determined. In a simple reversal, we may say that B is worth half of A, and now B emerges in its relative form to be measured by the equivalent now manifest in A. Each in turn illustrates the role of a particular equivalent.[37]

In the next stage of this theoretical narrative, the commodities and their possible exchanges multiply. Here is a market in which A =

---

34   Marx, *Capital: Volume 1*, p. 138.
35   That is, by the end of *Capital: Volume 1*, part one, chapter 1.2, pp. 131–7.
36   See Marx, *Capital: Volume 1*, chapter 1.3 (a), pp. 139–54.
37   Ibid., pp. 152–4.

2B = 3C = .5D and so on. Now, Marx writes, the choice of the particular equivalent is 'a matter of indifference'—at least in the sense that any particular commodity can assume the role of the equivalent, at any appropriate time.[38]

The third stage is distinguished by the emergence of a reserved commodity that serves as a general equivalent, a single measure for all exchanges. Initially, this will have a significant use-value in its own right. Linen is Marx's example; in special market conditions, such as those of prisons, tobacco may come to serve as the reserved commodity. In its final form, however, this general equivalent has little or no use-value other than that of being itself, or money. Thus, Marx writes, 'the simple commodity-form is . . . the germ of the money-form', and with that he passes directly to the matter of fetishism.[39]

He might equally have written 'the germ of the fetish'. In the simple exchange, a particular use-value—corn or oil or potatoes—manifests itself as the equivalent form of value, as the immanent presence of worth itself, and there, as something inherent in the structure of exchange, is the potential for fetishism.[40] However, it is only as the embodied equivalent that the commodity may turn fetish, and we should not forget that every exchange requires two commodities, and that the other one cannot also, at the same time, take that role.

The limiting implications of this thought become clearer when we pass to the second stage, that of expanded exchange. Fetishism remains a structurally given potential, and, as commodities enter endlessly varied chains of exchange, the potential becomes mobile throughout the network. At this point we can imagine episodes or hotspots of fetishism but still not the saturated totality that Marx projected.

With the emergence of money, the equivalent form of value finds a fixed and specialized means of representation. Marx writes: 'The money-form is . . . the reflection thrown upon a single commodity

38   Ibid., p. 155.
39   Ibid., p. 163.
40   See Ibid., p. 149.

by the relations between all other commodities.[41] And it is in this mode that capital attains what he calls 'its finished form', interest-bearing capital: 'its pure form, self-valorizing value, money breeding money' or in other words its 'most superficial', that is most nearly opaque, 'and fetishized form'.[42] Here Marx's analysis points away from the notion of fetishistic saturation towards an alternative account in which the system of commodities is fetishized, not as a mass of exchangeable products but in the special, synecdochic form of money.[43] That is plausible, though even then the fetish may not be stable for all exchanges: all of us have known occasions when money has seemed worthless if it could not secure that special thing and none other, when value seemed to withdraw into a singular opaque object of fascination and desire.

Marx's discussion of the fetishism of the commodity sits a little oddly in the first volume of *Capital*. There is no mention of fetishism, either before or after it, in the published work. Had it been excised in advance of publication, as other material was, we may doubt whether the loss would have been noticed. It is something of an excursus, or perhaps a cadenza for a work—the analysis of the commodity—already substantially complete. What I have tried to show is that in at least one crucial respect it is also ill-founded in the general logic of the book. Yes, fetishism is a disposition inhering in the structure of commodity exchange; yes, the potential for it is everywhere in the ensemble of exchanges; and it may be that the system as a whole

---

41   Ibid., p. 184.

42   Marx, *Capital: Volume 3*, London 1981, pp. 515, 516, 515.

43   We might pursue the thought that the fetishistic trope of the system as a whole may appear still more magical than the consideration of 'money breeding money' alone suggests. Marx notes, in a short passing sentence, 'a second peculiarity' of the equivalent form: 'In it, concrete labour becomes the form of manifestation of its opposite, abstract human labour'. (*Capital: Volume 1*, 150) If money is the acme of the commodity, then surely the acme of labour, its highest pitch of skill, is art-making. No compounding of abstract labour can satisfy the intuition and the demand inherent in the notion of genius. The bourgeois art market is in this sense the jewel of jewels in the crown of capital, the site where money and genius merge in undead labour, the mode in which artistic mastery goes on creating value beyond the grave.

promotes the fetishism of money. But none of these propositions is sufficient for the argument that commodity fetishism is general and necessary in conditions of regular commodity production.

That was the argument I had in view in suggesting that the theory of commodity fetishism in its classic form is too strong, and considering how it might be modified in a way that makes it at least self-consistent—and also more interesting. The great convenience of the classic theory has been that for those situations for which it seemed intuitively apt, it furnished a ready-made explanation: it must apply in this case because it applies in all cases. And yet for many and perhaps most cases it could be left in abeyance, in flat defiance of its own logic. The revised version proposed here excludes that kind of intellectual procedure in advance. If commodity fetishism is not a generic necessity of capitalism, then for any apparent instance of it we have to attempt to say how and why it is so. The terms of interpretation and explanation need not be unique case by case—that would be another kind of magic—but they should certainly be specific. A more modest theory would claim less but have the virtue of being able to unearth new problems, with the attendant possibility of actually discovering something from time to time. It would then be better able to play its part in elucidating the culture of capital.

3

Marx had his cadenza; here, now, is another. It is time to return to Conrad and *Nostromo*, a novel of particular interest in connection with fetishism. The idea of the fetish is already part of the novel's field of reflection,[44] used to characterize the kind of significance the San Tomé silver mine has acquired for its administrator, Charles Gould, and his workers. (The presence of this term is the more notable given its absence from the narrative where you might expect to find it, *Heart of Darkness*.) The fetish is the mine, but we should not draw hasty conclusions from this. The miners are said to have attributed autonomous (and benign) spiritual powers to their own everyday

---

44   As are such terms as *fascination* and *curiosity* and kindred items.

creation and in doing so to have made it a fetish.[45] In the case of Charles Gould, however, who has raised this old family enterprise from a state of ruin, 'fetish' denotes the object of an obsession driven by filial guilt (N, 190). Here and elsewhere, the lure of precious metal is associated with evil spirits and a curse. Conrad's materialism manages to be cynical and mystical all at once. Rather like his characters in *Nostromo*, when he thinks of capitalism he is thinking of something else—or perhaps thinking of it in a different way. Judged as textual tissue rather than fictional reality, the silver of the mine counts for rather little compared with the silver that adorns and identifies the named protagonist of the novel. Here if anywhere in the novel are the signs of fetishism. Perhaps we should take the book at its word—its title—and attend more closely to the figure of Nostromo.

What is he, this brilliant, daring, resourceful dock-workers' foreman? What does the narrative have to say about him? First of all, that he is wonderfully useful, 'a sort of universal factotum', his employer says, as he proudly 'lends' him for one task or another to the Europeans in the harbour town of Sulaco (N, 48). 'A perfect handyman', he is *nostro uomo*, 'our man' Nostromo, and this is only one of his many names (N, 267). The trope of antonomasia, or variant naming, is conspicuous in the novel, where it serves as an instrument of Conrad's ironic perspectivism, but Nostromo is addressed or referenced by as many as seventeen names. In this way substitutability is indexed in his character, as it is in his conception of familial identity. Family relations are conventionally thought of as irreducible, but Nostromo's capacity for filiality by arrangement is particularly striking, involving him in son-like relationships with at least three father figures at different times. Sonship comes as part of the service.

In both respects he is a figure of exchanges, and his mode of appearance is silver: silver cords and tassels, silver buttons, silver trappings for his horse, and the animal itself is silver-grey. In a text that is full of metallic gleaming, silver is Nostromo's property before it is Gould's. This commitment to self-display is a sign of Nostromo's

---

45 See Joseph Conrad, *Nostromo*, Harmondsworth 1963, 329. Hereafter abbreviated *N* and cited parenthetically by page number.

narcissism. It is a modality of his commitment to investing in himself and the accumulation of personal prestige. This is not lost on some observers in Sulaco, who can see that 'his prestige is his fortune', and Nostromo himself holds that 'a good name is a treasure' (N, 268, 216). In due time the metaphor will turn literal, as his prestige turns into a real fortune in silver bullion.

A universal factotum, exchangeable, silver, and capable of self-augmentation—or as Marx put it, 'self-valorizing value'—Nostromo is money. And he is more than that. According to Martin Decoud, he is an agent of progress, who has brought to the harbour the secret of estimating labour-time. He comes from Genoa, one of the great trading ports of medieval and early modern Europe and a centre of gold minting since the thirteenth century. His original first name is Giovanni Battista, John the Baptist, the precursor of a new dispensation . . . No wonder then that, as Decoud remarks to his sister, Nostromo has this knack of being 'on the spot' just when he's needed (N, 192). Like Diggory Venn in Hardy's *Return of the Native*, he is not altogether a realist creation. If Diggory can move around Egdon Heath seemingly untrammelled by ordinary space and time, it is because he is in some sense a part of the heath, or its sprite. Nostromo too is a sprite, we might say, the sprite of capital.

Nostromo is one of Conrad's figures of fascination, fetishes of a kind that attract the gaze while obstructing the vision. In him, Conrad figures the emerging order of capital in the terms of an anti-thetical and obsolescent style of storytelling, figures expanding capitalism as a romantic, seafaring adventurer. In the list of his attributes, Nostromo iterates those of commodities and money. *Who or what makes history?* is the question this novel insistently presses. Nostromo, says Captain Mitchell, the self-appointed bard of Sulacan independence, and Mitchell, we have known all along, is stupid. But that is not to say he is mistaken.

A final observation has to do with what the novel itself suggests to us about fetishism—not in how it deploys the term but in the story it tells. Look again at Nostromo the character and contrast his appear-ance and bearing before and after the consignment of silver falls into his hands. He now has a secret and must lead a partly clandestine life, but that is not all there is to note. Nostromo before the fact is brilliant, theatrical, daring, a genius of sorts. After the fact he is Captain Fidanza, a coastal trader, no longer 'picturesque' in 'the new conditions', as the novel puts it (N, 432). That invocation of 'new conditions' has more than one plausible reference. One of them is captured in the information that 'the vigour and symmetry of his powerful limbs [were] lost in the vulgarity of a brown tweed suit, made by Jews in the slums of London, and sold by the clothing department of the Compañía Anzani in Sulaco' (N, 431). These phrases owe something of their contemptuous charge to everyday anti-Semitism, but that is not their main point. What they evoke is an established international trade network in which Fidanza has found his banal place. He is no longer seeking his fortune, just 'growing rich very slowly' (N, 428).

Clandestinity does not quite account for the disenchantment of the magnificent *capataz*, Nostromo. The novel prompts consideration of another possibility the opposite of Lukács's ascriptive reality. We might call this Conrad's Conjecture. What if fetishism is not, as has normally been assumed, a distinguishing characteristic of fully formed capitalism? What if, on the contrary, it is a feature of its brilliant, bold, baffling emergence? Where and as capital becomes dominant and stable as a system, the phenomenon subsides or becomes intermittent, no longer to be explained as a natural constant in regularized commodity exchange. The literary eulogies to money that Marx invoked— Shakespeare's Timon and Goethe's Mephistopheles—are, after all, incunabula of the transition to capitalism, not documents from a mature setting.[46] There may be something worthwhile in this thought, there may not. But the question it poses is at any rate historical, open to adjudication on the evidence, and that itself is not nothing.

2002–2007

---

46 See Marx, *Capital: Volume 1*, pp. 229–30; and Marx, 'Economic and Philosophical Manuscripts', in *Early Writings*, ed. Quintin Hoare, trans. Rodney Livingstone and Gregor Benton, New York 1975, pp. 375–9. Compare Marx's comment on the historical immaturity betokened by the 'fetish of metal money' in the 'Manuscripts', p. 364.

Intellectual Identities

A cartoon from Turkey in the 1980s depicts a man hacking at the wooden projection he is sitting on.[1] It is a commonplace image of self-defeating activity, though in this case the man is clearly a bourgeois and the branch-equivalent, drawn to a far larger scale, is a pencil. Another cartoon from the same political context shows an imprisoned pen—but the enclosure is a birdcage, only the nib is confined, the body, again massively drawn, lying outside the open door, like a giant unaware of its own strength. In a third image, a man sits reading. His spectacles, absorbed air and slightness of build leave no room to mistake his social type: he is a man of the pencil and pen—an *aydin* or 'enlightened one'. In this scenario too, conditions are bad, but in a different sense: the pages before him can scarcely be readable: the print is obscured by something like a large blot, which, however, is not the ink-as-blood that features in other drawings of this genre, but the shadow cast by the object that blocks the electric light above him—his own head.

Such images rehearse—the more strikingly for the extremity of their political situation—a persistent crux in post-Enlightenment culture, that is, in the modal culture of 'intellectuals'. The conviction has motivated a whole tradition of intellectual self-declaration, from Zola to

---

1 Initiativ Solidarität mit den Intellektuellen derTürkei, Hrsg., *Diktakatur*, Duisberg 1985.

Chomsky, from Arnold to Said. The counterpart suspicion found some
of its most notable sponsors among the Marxists of the Bolshevik
generation, for whom professions of intellectual honour typically signified illusion, nuisance, even danger. Apparently binary opposites, the
conviction and the suspicion are perhaps better seen as inseparable
elements of a general discursive ambivalence. After all, the leitmotiv of
the affirmative tradition has been not honour but betrayal—in the
phrase that Julien Benda added to the common parlance of the educated West, *la trahison des clercs*. The brusque moral sociology of
Bolshevik polemical tradition, itself rather 'intellectual', was to be
developed in Gramsci's thought to accord critical strategic value to a
politics of intellectual life. The energy and variousness of intellectuals'
discourse on their own kind are the deceptive appearances of inertia.

i. Teachers, Writers, Celebrities

The special interest of Régis Debray's *Teachers, Writers, Celebrities* is
that it attempts to move beyond the received terms of understanding.[2] His purpose is to situate *les clercs* in their constitutive material
relations, but without dissolving the category into a generic logic of
classes, instead analysing the specificities of intellectual life as a
determinate social practice. These notes attempt first to situate the
book in the history of French writing about intellectuals and in relation to other relevant traditions; then to examine the historical
specificity of the French intelligentsia and suggest some pertinent
comparisons and contrasts with Britain and the United States—and
in doing so to trace the outlines of a contingent historical formation
that might aptly be called intellectual corporatism.[3]

---

2   Régis Debray, *Le Pouvoir intellectuel en France* (Paris 1979), translated
as *Teachers, Writers, Celebrities*, London 1981.
3   'Intellectual corporatism', as I understand the phenomenon, arises when
an ideology of collective unity and independence takes hold in a given intelligentsia or segment of it. 'Corporatism' as intended here differs from
conventional Gramscian usage in that it does not imply the 'hegemonic' posture
as its opposite—that would be, if anything, its ideal moral completion.

1

'Le clerc ne trahit jamais.' Debray's studied declaration at once evokes and challenges a whole tradition of intellectual self-reflection. The homeland of this tradition is France, and its inception, in its modern form at least, may be dated from the appearance of Julien Benda's *La Trahison des clercs* in 1927. The cultural matrix of Benda's book was liberal humanism, its politics, amidst the crisis of post-war Europe, an unworldly rejection of all national particularism or social partisanship in the name of the disinterested service of humanity as a whole. *La Trahison des clercs* is internationally significant as a statement of this outlook; its added significance in France is that it laid down the protocols of a distinctive cultural *occasion* that was to recur in subsequent crises and under the auspices of radically contrasting positions.

Benda's symbolic counterpart between the wars was Paul Nizan, whose *Les Chiens de garde* (1932) was one Communist intellectual's 'great-minded harangue' (Debray) against the political quietism of academic philosophy. Some fifteen years later, after the Liberation, Nizan's friend Sartre launched *Les Temps Modernes* with a declaration of intellectual commitment, and wrote *Qu'est-ce que la littérature?* to demonstrate that the writer was, *qua* writer, necessarily on the left. The antitype, in the Cold War fifties, was Raymond Aron's *L'Opium des intellectuels*. May 1968 and its aftermath saw a great proliferation of such documents, of which Sartre's 1970 interview 'l'Ami du peuple' and the Godard-Gorin film *Tout va bien* were among the better-known instances. The confusions and disappointments, the reversals and the desertions of the later seventies proved no less conducive to this traditional activity than the antithetical conditions of ten years before. The bad objects of the Parisian high intelligentsia might vary (approximately, from Power to the Gulag to the Devil—and back) but an unassimilable 'plebeian' stance was widely advocated as appropriate to the age. And here, now, in Debray's book, was another—oppositely intended—challenge.

This tradition, then, is not confined to any particular political or intellectual position; it has been a prominent and constant theme in the national culture of twentieth-century France. This consideration is decisive for any attempt to understand the phenomenon. For the moment, however, it is more pertinent to note a related, intrinsic feature of the tradition: in spite of the wide variety of its tributaries, it has retained a marked discursive coherence. It has characteristically been an *ethics* (or, in the twin classical sense, a politics) of intellectual life. Benda's text was patently and proudly a work of moral prescription founded on an ontology of the intellectual as social being. Nizan's was structurally similar, even if the imperatives were now political and the ground of being was history as class struggle. The socialist politics of *Qu'est-ce que la littérature?* were premissed on the existentialist ethics of Sartre's technical philosophy, the intermediary being an aesthetic conception of the novel as a 'pact of freedoms'.[4] Rationalist, phenomenological or dialectical-materialist, liberal or socialist, these and kindred writings sustained a common discourse whose basic character was always (not only or even principally in the pejorative sense) *moralist.*

Teachers, Writers, Celebrities lies uneasily among its predecessors, for the main novelty of the book is precisely its practical challenge to moralism and the analytic options and occlusions characteristic of it. It represents, in fact, a major break in the tradition. Ethics is displaced here by politics, ontology by history and sociology. Benda invoked the changeless truth of a calling and prescribed its functions accordingly; Debray seeks to analyse the formation and re-formation of a determinate occupational bloc. Sartre's investigation of the relations between intellectuals and their audience concluded that writing was constitutionally leftist, that the vocation of writer was a political fatality; Debray's object, by contrast, is to discover the structured tendencies of intellectual behaviour in successive cultural production-systems and to show how these dictate the posture of the intelligentsia in given political situations. The 'mediological' discourse so initiated is markedly more historical, markedly more materialist than anything in its parent tradition.

---

4   See Ronald Aronson, *Jean-Paul Sartre—Philosophy in the World*, London 1980, pp. 122–42.

Indeed, the novelty of the book remains clear in international comparison. In complaining that France was the 'political paradise' of the
intelligentsia but the 'purgatory' of its analysts, Debray was under-
estimating the extent to which the selfsame or similar, essentially
philosophico-literary discourse on 'the clerisy' permeated the cultures
of the advanced capitalist world, not excepting the younger, scientific
disciplines that claimed to have superseded it. Such notions are active
in the work of Parsons, for example, and just as clearly in that of
Gramsci—whose nearly complete isolation, as a Marxist, in this field of
theory and research tells its own tale.[5] Whether Debray himself has
entirely settled accounts with this 'erstwhile philosophical consciousness' is a consideration that will be taken up. But the main emphasis
should fall on the originality of his book. Precedents may be cited
for its various themes and analytic strategies—its combination of
theoretical argument and concrete analysis, the historical sketch of the
French intelligentsia that forms the centre of the book, the insistence
on the specific economics of culture and, related to this, the systematic
integration of statistical with more conventional ('qualitative') kinds
of evidence. What is novel here is the combination, and the purpose
that it is designed to serve. No one, Marxist or other, has made so
concerted an attempt to analyse what might be called, in Marx's
terms, the 'social being' of 'social consciousness', the intelligentsia as
a social category at work, in one of its major modern incarnations. By
this alone, Debray's book sets a standard for future research.

2

That is one context in which to read *Teachers, Writers, Celebrities*.
But certain others, two in particular, will probably hold greater
significance for an English-language audience. The first of these is

---

5   See Parsons's contribution to Philip Rieff, ed., *On Intellectuals*, New
York 1969; and Gramsci's discussion of 'traditional intellectuals', which effec-
tively adopts the self-image of intellectual corporatism (Antonio Gramsci,
'The Formation of the Intellectuals', *Selections from the Prison Notebooks*, eds
Quintin Hoare and Geoffrey Nowell Smith, London 1971, pp. 5–14).

Frankfurt Marxism. Debray's history of the French intelligentsia is conceived in the form of a study of the development of the national cultural apparatuses—the schools and universities, publishing, the press, radio and television. It is an exercise in 'mediology', and much of its argumentation pertains not so much to intellectuals as to the laws of motion of the institutions in and by which they are deployed. Two processes are given analytic priority. The first, economic process is that of the absorption of cultural production into general commodity production, in an era when the capitalist economy is said itself to be undergoing an inner transformation, the relative determining powers of production and distribution being switched to the advantage of the latter. The second, technical process involves the development of the forces of cultural production and the institutional rearrangements induced by it. The analytic object so constituted is akin to what the Frankfurt tradition called 'the culture industry'; and the substance of the analysis is no less redolent of Critical Theory, above all in its historical pessimism.[6] Debray may not altogether suppress the distinction between the technical resources of the media and the social relations within which they are utilized, but he denies emphatically that it underwrites the possibility of cultural emancipation. The electronic media are bringing forth a culture in keeping with their own unalterable nature, he argues. The modern culture industry falls under one historical law and one only: the law of increasing symbolic immiseration, in obedience to which the criterion of intrinsic worth is displaced by that of 'mediatic surface', the complexity of the message is sacrificed to the volume of its reception, cultural labour is deskilled and its products quality-controlled to ensure the optimal incidence of sensation. A society whose 'high intellectuals' reserve their main energies for appearances on Friday-night television, Debray maintains, is in truth a 'mediocracy'. 'The darkest spot in modern society is a small luminous screen.'

These echoes of the Frankfurt School are notable enough in a writer of Althusserian and Leninist background. But such arguments

---

6   See, for example, Theodor Adorno and Max Horkheimer, *Dialectic of Enlightenment*, London 1979.

stir stronger, more familiar and far more improbable associations.
For many of the topics and themes of his book, and even, in places,
its tones and cultural accents, were anticipated fifty years before in
the early writings of F. R. and Q. D. Leavis. The former's *Mass
Civilization and Minority Culture* and the latter's *Fiction and the
Reading Public* showed the same preoccupation with the contemporary economic reorganization of culture that now motivates Debray
(though he naturally thinks of the economy as capitalist, a specification that the Leavises thought secondary in the essentially
monolithic conditions of 'industrialism').[7] 'Standardization and levelling down' was their conventional shorthand for the same
tendencies that Debray now describes as inherent in mediocratic
culture. His acid accounts of intellectual life in the Latin Quarter and
Montparnasse recall the Leavises' attacks on the 'coteries' of metropolitan London. His analysis of the circuits of influence and
advantage, in reviewing and promotion, is parallel to theirs. For
Bernard-Henri Lévy, actor-manager of the vaunted New Crusaders
and their *Nouvelle philosophie,* read (say) Michael Roberts, the strate-
gist of the *New Signatures* and *New Country* anthologies in the early
thirties. For Pivot, the telejournalist with the power of life and death
over the season's new titles, read Arnold Bennett, the star reviewer of
the London *Evening Standard*. In temper too there is a striking simi-
larity. Cool and concentrated, but then suddenly mocking, indignant
or openly angry, both the Leavises and Debray here display a tense
combination of fatalism and defiance. Debray might well cite, as he
has done in the past, Gramsci's famous borrowing, 'pessimism of
the intelligence, optimism of the will',[8] for this motto registers the
stress at the heart of his book, the same stress that was defined in
the perhaps more lucid Leavisian phrase, 'desperate optimism': the
stress of a cultural voluntarism armed only with its conscience and
always already defeated, if its own strategic estimates are to be
believed.

---

7   Cambridge 1932 and London 1932 respectively.
8   Régis Debray, 'Schema for a Study of Gramsci', *Prison Writings*,
Harmondsworth 1975, pp. 161–6.

This is not to say that Debray's mediology is 'really' a belated, stray variant of *Kulturkritik*. The theoretical constitution of the book will prompt many questions, but these are best posed in the light of prior and more widely applicable historical questions. How should we regard this improbable confluence of English cultural criticism and French Marxism, and what does it suggest about Debray's relationship with the national history that he discusses? But first, is there anything further to be said about the specificity of the French case, or by way of pertinent contrast, about the differing cases of England and the United States?

3

Debray distinguishes three 'cycles' in the past century of French intellectual history: the academic, which he dates from 1880 to 1930; that of publishing (1920–1960); and the mediatic, initiated in 1968 and still in its ascendant phase. These chronological periods delimit not lifespans but hegemonies. Just as the university displaced the Church in the last years of the nineteenth century, so in the inter-war years publishing and its culture displaced the university milieu, reorganizing the latter in a subaltern position. Then, in the 1960s, the press and broadcasting apparatuses restructured both, creating a pyramidal culture in which a mediatic elite became paramount over a subordinate publishing sector and an abject educational system. There was a symbolic succession from Alain to Gide to Glucksmann.

This was not, it need hardly be said, the common destiny of the West. But, to the extent that it was rather a distinctive French experience, general theses concerning the development of capitalist commerce and of communications technology cannot fully explain it: by definition blind to national variation, they are at once too much and too little. Other elements besides these were involved in shaping this distinctive historical passage.

The so-called second industrial revolution came very late in France, and when it did arrive was correspondingly intensified in its rhythms and effects. The trustification and technical rationalization of industry, the introduction of scientific 'research and development', the production of machines by means of machines and the opening up of the mass market had begun in the United States at the end of the 1890s, and by the end of the First World War had already largely transformed the American urban economy—the baptism of Ford's assembly line in 1915 symbolized the start of the new era. Over the same period, the multiple conjunctions of commercial pressure and opportunity with technological innovation were responsible for a whole complex of culturally decisive changes: the transformation in the status of advertising and the financial reorganization of the press, the growth of publishing of all kinds, the ascent of Hollywood and the consolidation of a nationwide broadcasting network. By 1930 the cultural format of 'mass', 'consumer' capitalism had been designed and patented. In Britain, it was the war itself and the ensuing depression that triggered the process already known as 'Americanization'. The results, in an economy weakened by technical senescence and over-reliant on the stored fat of Empire, were naturally unequal. Yet within twenty years the economy had been considerably remodelled (most evidently in the sphere of distribution) and the national culture had been transformed—by the promotional revolution, the huge expansion of publishing and the cinema, and the creation of the British Broadcasting Corporation.

The American motif was prominent among the attractions of Weimar Berlin for young English writers at that time; Paris, in contrast, was the gathering-place of American intellectuals drawn to an older Bohemian style. It was not surprising, for no comparable transformation was experienced in inter-war France. The component processes of the second industrial revolution unfolded slowly and piecemeal, each in its own space and according to its own tempo, in a society that remained archaic overall. A further twenty years and a full constitutional cycle passed before le défi américain finally forced a quickened and coordinated pace of modernization on Gaullist France, the breakneck pace that led to the social collision of 1968.

Higher education forms a second plane of comparison. All three countries laid the foundations of their modern university systems around the same time: roughly, in the last quarter of the nineteenth century and first ten years of the twentieth. The great university reforms of the Third Republic date mainly from the 1880s. In England, where the foundation of London University had already weakened the hegemony of Oxford and Cambridge, the next decade saw the first 'redbrick' institutions of learning chartered as independent universities. Across the Atlantic, in the same years, the first public universities emerged from the old system of land grant colleges. However, the French case stood apart from the British and the American in two decisive respects. The emergent systems in the latter cases were based on recent foundations—Liverpool or Sheffield, Wisconsin or California. The old institutions—Oxford and Cambridge in England, and in the United States the Ivy League colleges—were by-passed, so to speak, in an ambiguous gesture that signified both supersession and untouchability. But the French reforms concerned precisely the old foundations, the Sorbonne and the *grandes écoles* of the Latin Quarter. Beneath this contrast lay a fundamental difference. The late nineteenth-century innovations in England and the United States belonged to waves of educational expansion that were themselves part of broader processes of economic and cultural change. The innovations of the Third Republic were in this sense socially blank, as the next half-century revealed. By 1930, the national academic corps had grown by under a quarter to 1,405, less than half that of slightly less populous Britain. At the same date, the United States, little more than three times the size of either country, possessed more *institutions* of higher education than France did academic *personnel*, and could claim a university and college student population ten times that of France's secondary schools.[9] In sum, the reforms of the 1880s had not been expansionist or even, in any sense that Britain or the United States might have echoed, modernist. The French 'multiversity' lay far ahead still—as far ahead as the second industrial revolution. The *grandes écoles* remained the exclusive, hierarchical institutions they had long been. Yet, as Debray explains, they had indeed been reformed: not so much in what they were or

---

9   See Debray's figures, and for the US see Donald R. McCoy, *Coming of Age*, Harmondsworth 1973, pp. 116–44.

how they functioned as in what they represented.[10] The consequences
for French culture were decisive.

4

The purpose of the reforms was directly, expressly political: it was to
win the university to the role of a secular, democratic successor to the
Church, to create in it the loyal and effective ideological custodian of
the new, third Republic. The teaching community, with the Sorbonne
and the École Normale at its head, was to be invested as a republican
clergy—in the words of the Charter of the Union for Moral Action—
as 'a militant lay order based on private and public duty'. The initiation
of the new order in the struggle over Dreyfus—the moment when the
noun *intellectuel* was added to the language—is powerfully recounted
here, but its lasting significance is insufficiently stressed. 'The primal
scene of politics', Debray observes elsewhere in the book, is the prince
with his scribes. If that is so, then the screening memory, in the collective psyche of the French intelligentsia, is of Conscience in the
company of the Republic.

The entente between the University and the Third Republic was
the formative experience of the intellectuals, the mould of a dual
posture that could seem at times the defining attribute of intellectuality as such. In its 'negative' moment, the posture was factional,
one of permanent readiness in the defence of threatened allegiances;
but there was also the inseparable 'positive' moment that claimed
generality, in cultural terms (transcendent values) and often also
politically (popular-democratic typicality). *La Trahison des clercs* at
once exemplified and depended upon the paradigmatic authority of
this dual posture, the posture of a 'republican clergy'. When the old
Dreyfusard attacked the 'organizers of political passions', he cited
only opponents of the Republic, on the extreme left (Sorel) or right
(Maurras). Durkheim, conceivably the most effective intellectual-
politician of the pre-war era, was nowhere mentioned. The Third

---

10 See Debray, *Teachers, Writers, Celebrities*, chapter 2, especially
pp. 58–63.

Republic was more than a political allegiance; it was the *république des professeurs*, the constitutional ground of Reason itself.

This was not a doctrine or a programme; it was rather an objectively constituted repertoire of postures and occasions, a part of the cultural inheritance of generations of French intellectuals and of the audiences to and 'for' whom they spoke. As such it persisted into the publishing and mediatic cycles of the middle and later decades of this century, as a necessary support of the milieux and the practices that Debray describes. True enough, a phenomenon like the New Philosophy presupposed late-capitalist distribution and promotion and the electronic media; and the French apparatuses, being of relatively recent date, are advanced of their kind. It also presupposed the unique degree of centralization that makes Paris the political, academic and lay cultural capital of the country (a fusion of roles elsewhere distributed among, say, Washington, Boston and New York, or London and Oxbridge). But it was quite unimaginable in the absence of the cultural syndrome that ensured that the road to Damascus would be lined with editors and paved with contracts, outside a culture in which the Pauline style was known, expected and prized.

Underlying Debray's tricyclical history there is a continuous tradition whose forcing-house was the reconstitution of the republican state after 1871. Its epitome is the career of Jean-Paul Sartre—brilliant *normalien*, privileged stipendiary of the house of Gallimard, regular focus of controversy in the media and, in the end, petitioner at the Elysée Palace. Merleau-Ponty once charged that Sartre's dramatic style of socialist 'commitment' was dictated by his unreconstructed philosophical individualism, by 'a conception of freedom that allows only for sudden interventions into the world, for camera shots and flashbulbs'.[11] But if Sartrean 'commitment' was a distinctively existentialist creation, the press cameras that sensationalized its public moments plainly were not. Sartre inherited not only a philosophical tradition that went back to Descartes, but the established morality, the spontaneous ideology of a corporation. His great

11   Cit. Aronson, *Jean-Paul Sartre*, p. 226.

personal distinction was that he accepted the role of 'intellectual' with the utmost self-consciousness and passion, and reached its limits in the rarest and most creditable of ways—by pressing its possibilities to the point of exhaustion.

5

The stock contrast that is the British intelligentsia was shaped by a radically different political history. No one could take the Third Republic for granted: the opposite of a historical fatality, it was a project to further or to thwart, a point of controversy in its own right. But in Britain a remarkably continuous state history had the effect of largely withholding basic constitutional questions from political debate; the great issues of nation and state remained, in local parlance, 'above party politics'. The inevitable beneficiary of this history has been the Conservative Party, since the First World War the 'natural party of government' in Britain. The real hegemonic strength of Conservatism may be judged not by its celebrated pragmatism but by the fact that it alone of the parliamentary parties in the past century has had a proven capacity for disruptive confrontations from the 1920s to the present day. That the power of political initiative is monopolized by the oldest and most continuist of the parties is both cause and consequence of the exceptional constitutional quietism of the polity.

The culture and the intelligentsia formed in this matrix were correspondingly distinctive. The institutional sequence university-publishing-media was repeated, but within a shorter time span and accordingly to a different principle of combination. Here, the older would characteristically *license* the newer, ceding this specialized function or permitting the extension or duplication of that, or it would encroach upon the newer, after an initial recoil perhaps, to secure its own advantage in the new territory. In neither case was there a decisive transfer of hegemony. The university expansion around the turn of the century was part of a far-reaching process of cultural change, but it scarcely dimmed the radiation of Oxford and Cambridge: if by the mid-1920s these institutions taught only one in every three university students,[12] their traditions weighed just as heavily on the other two—whose Oxbridge counterpart, now the elite of an elite, in fact enjoyed the old prestige to the second power. At the beginning of the twenties, relations between the university and the lay culture based on publishing were close only among the most archaic and reactionary circles of both, the scholar-gentlemen and the bellelettrists (the Bloomsbury Group was an exceptional case). For the rest, the contemporary reciprocal hostility of specialized teachers and writers made glib by commissions and deadlines was already quasi-institutional. Yet within twenty-five years the old guards had been dislodged, each by new generations below them, and a new relationship was instituted in which the power of the university was manifest. The end of the forties saw the closure of England's last successful literary magazine of extra-academic provenance, *Horizon*. Throughout the fifties, the eclipse of 'creation' by 'criticism' and of the freelance writer by the academic was widely but unavailingly complained of. By the end of the decade, the major reviewing spaces in the weekly journals and supplements and the prime ideological occasions—'the new Naipaul' or whatever—were largely reserved by a corps of professor-journalists, many, perhaps a majority of them from Oxford and Cambridge. The experience of the electronic media has been in important respects similar. The BBC, as befitted a national broadcasting service, was apparently born venerable. What it lacked in years was made up in the funereal propriety that Reith prescribed as its institutional style. Yet a long time passed before radio, and far longer before television, won the assent of British intellectuals and their established institutions. The politico-cultural innovations of the wartime service, the inception of the Third Programme and, ultimately, the creation of the Open University (complete with vice-chancellor 'and all the trimmings', lest any misunderstand[13]) were among the crucial steps in the acceptance-colonization of broadcasting.

---

12   C. L. Mowat, *Britain Between the Wars*, 1918–1940, London 1968.
13   Thus Jennie Lee, the Labour minister responsible (see Raymond Williams, *Politics and Letters*, London 1979, p. 371).

It would be perverse to argue that the electronic media are the least powerful of cultural institutions. But it would be equally perverse to insist that when the doyen of Oxford history appears on prime-time television to discuss, say, the Second World War, truth's last citadel has fallen to mediatic barbarism. British continuism has the effect of rejuvenating the older institutions at the expense of the newer. But the rejuvenation of the old, seen from the other side, is the legitimation and regulation of the new, and this is the real strategic value of cultural continuism. The university in effect acts as a licensing authority for other cultural institutions, recognizing and/ or regulating the extent and demarcation of their various claims to knowledge and endowing them with something of its own accumulated prestige. The resulting institutional configuration is perhaps unique in its conservative adaptability.

The people whose work was in these institutions were not accustomed to think of themselves as 'intellectuals'. No form of corporate consciousness either drew them together or defined a social role for them as individuals. If the French intelligentsia formed a 'republican clergy', their English counterparts were decidedly Anglican in temper: aware of higher things but careful not to become tedious on that account, and not really in much doubt of the basic good sense of the nation and those who governed it. It is not, of course, that they constituted a kind of collective 'happy consciousness' willingly allied with the dominant classes. But two contrasting political histories produced two distinct types of intellectual formation. 'Independence' here signified not a self-defining corporate invigilation of a transcendent general interest but the freedom to pursue one's particular (usually occupational) interest without ideological distraction or politico-juridical interference, in conditions where 'the Constitution' was not a redoubt to be defended or stormed, not even an arena of free civic activity, but a half-noticed, hardly changing country landscape.

The sectoral distribution of political allegiances also differed from one country to the other. In France, according to Debray, academics and teachers have traditionally inclined to the left, writers to the right. This was so during the Dreyfus affair, in the political crisis of

Intellectual Identities 135

the mid-1930s, and is the case again today. But in Britain, it is probably true to say, the intellectual radicalization of the thirties was more
marked in the lay culture dominated by writers than in the universities. The new phase of political division that opened in the mid-1970s
has taken yet another form. In keeping with the apparent international pattern of the misnamed 'crisis of Marxism',[14] the rupture has
occurred within the nationally dominant politico-cultural formation of the workers movement: not, as in France, Marxism of any
kind but *Fabianism*. The old centre-left consensus has been largely
dispersed, leaving the intelligentsia polarized both in its academic
and in its lay sectors.

Other, not directly political motifs of intra-cultural antagonism
recurred here, but again in variant forms. The struggle between
Paris and the provinces, between privilege and merit, between the
versatile amateur and the specialized professional, was epitomized
in the hostility between the University and the Academy, between
the schools of the Latin Quarter and the salons of the Right Bank.
A similar deployment of values was apparent in England between
the wars, but here the lines of battle were drawn *inside* the universities, dividing the scholar-gentlemen from the young professionals
whose only resource was talent. The main issue in the struggle was
the cultural authority of the new discipline of English, whose cause
was championed by the Leavises and the writers based on the quar-
terly *Scrutiny*. The campaign was in one central sense successful. By
the end of the Second World War the new generation had effectively
displaced the old guard on their own terrain, and within a further
ten to fifteen years they had extended their influence over much of
the lay literary culture outside the universities. But the profession of

---

14 The first outbreaks of the 'crisis' occurred in the Maoist or semi-
Maoist far-left currents of France and Italy, extending also to the Communist
parties, particularly in the latter case, and involving a number of independents as well. These circumstances were taken—in many cases avidly seized—as
evidence of a general crisis of Marxism. The less sensational but better attested
hypothesis of a crisis of Maoism, or of culpably lingering illusions in Stalinism, was less enthusiastically bruited, being not so flattering to the renegades
or ideologically so serviceable to their new allies.

English, as it took shape in England, was both an occupation and a claim, the one quite inseparable from the other. The claim was, in effect, that English could and must become the organizing centre of an intellectual elite capable of interpreting the general interest to a society structurally incapable of self-direction—the centre, that is, of an intelligentsia of the 'classic', 'French' type. The fortunes of this cultural effort were complex, but to the Leavises it came to seem like an unending defeat. French intellectuals could claim to represent a general interest as if by public statute; the Leavises' attempt to win the same prerogative for their discipline was met with scorn. The underlying paradox of the French intelligentsia was that its corporate independence was seen as a positive warrant of constitutional stability; it was much the same paradox that appeared, greatly exacerbated, in Leavis's increasingly wilful, subjectivist insistence that he, more or less alone, defended the 'real' world of English culture against its actual, degraded simulacrum. Every assertion of intellectual corporatism served only to emphasize the irreducible difference between the two national cultures and their respective types.

The Leavises would occasionally couple the United States with France in favourable contrast with England. There too, in the vast American public education system, careers were open to talent. At other times, they would represent the USA as England's future. It was the historic model of all the changes that were remaking traditional patterns of consumption and recreation between the wars, yet its traditions of intellectual independence were such that it seemed also to offer the most advanced paradigms of opposition to the march of 'industrial civilization'. There was demonstrable point in both suggestions, but neither really registered the historical uniqueness of the US social formation, which fostered a distinctive intellectual stratum and a remarkable national variation on the enigmatic modern phenomenon of intellectual corporatism.

The United States on the morrow of the Armistice contrasted with France and Britain not only in the degree of its economic development (it was now the world's premier capitalist economy); it was also an exceptionally decentralized and in important respects fragmented society. Federal institutions and activity had developed rapidly in the first twenty years of the century, and would acquire unprecedented centrality in the course of the thirties, yet there was no commensurate evolution towards a genuinely national system of political parties or media along familiar European lines. Regional and other particularisms (religious and/or ethnic) remained proportionately strong in US politics and culture.

However, if in this sense US national institutions appeared underdeveloped, in another sense their politico-juridical ground-plan, the Constitution itself, enjoyed a corresponding prominence. The genesis of the modern United States might be said to have inverted the normal historical relationships of nation-state formation, a congeries of small and compact settlements achieving a basic state-form which it then filled with populations and territories many times its own size. The state created the nation, as it were, in a process that continued right into the 1920s. (As late as 1920, fully one-third of US citizens were first- or second-generation settlers.) But the nationalism that arose in these conditions was necessarily different equally from the separatist and the unificationist nationalisms of Europe. Lacking—by definition—that popular prehistory of kinship and custom from which to fashion an effective national consciousness, an inclusive US nationalism could look no further back than the Constitution, before which there was, mythically, nothing but a wilderness and a latter-day project of Creation. Thus the founding texts of the US polity and the themes that cluster around them were internalized, in a kind of para-nationalist constitutional fetishism, as one of the true *longues durées* of American culture.

The US intelligentsia, as it took shape in the early decades of this century, reproduced this para-nationalist thematic in its own dominant collective ideology. This was, in effect, the dominant ideology of its main institutional emplacement, the national educational system, and, in its most elaborated version, the intellectual achievement of one profoundly influential thinker: John Dewey. Dewey's educational thought was radically and expressly functionalist: it envisaged a school system that would produce adequate numbers of young adults trained in the skills and attitudes required to sustain the American economic and political order. It was, in this respect, a creed of active national conformism, and in conditions where the weight of pre-bourgeois educational and other cultural values was virtually nil, its hegemony over the intelligentsia was assured. Yet pragmatism as a whole was more than this, and even in its applied forms could plausibly claim to be more than a policymaker's schema. For the underlying warrant of its conformism was not some ancient *Volksgeist* but a body of postulate and argument, a constitutional rationalism that in principle transcended particular interests. The Deweyan watchword 'education for citizenship' was not only functionalist; it also evoked notions of an order based always and everywhere on free, reasoned participation and valuing critical independence as a cultural norm. Dewey's later career itself showed that these notions were not always and everywhere mere pieties; but only very special cultural conditions could so enhance their power that they became dominant in the ideological formation of a whole segment of the intelligentsia—as was in fact to happen in the milieu of *Partisan Review* and the 'New York intellectuals'.[15]

The nucleus of this intellectual formation was triply marginalized within its cultural environment in the thirties. First, many of its members had come out of the East European Jewish immigration, at a time when that community was only partly assimilated and discriminatory practices—most relevantly the *numerus clausus* in higher education—oppressed their children. Second, the dominant political influence in the group was Trotskyism, here as elsewhere a controversial minority current within the intellectual left. Third,

---

15   Dewey was an important intellectual influence on several at least of the *Partisan Review* circle, most notably Sidney Hook and James Burnham, but also James T. Farrell. The Commission on the Moscow Trials and the Committee for Cultural Freedom brought the philosopher into direct contact with the journal. (See James Burkhart Gilbert, *Writers and Partisans*, New York 1968, pp. 201–3 and passim; and Alan Wald, *James T. Farrell: The Revolutionary Socialist Years*, New York 1978.) Yet Dewey attained a *national* cultural influence that *Partisan Review* could never emulate. It was very much a New York journal throughout and New York's relationship to the US was not at all like that of London or Paris to their respective national settings.

their cultural orientation was defiantly internationalist and avant-garde at a time when the Popular Frontist literary intelligentsia had joined with an older generation of nativist ideologues in an intolerant cult of 'Americanism'. These were not auspicious circumstances for any new, independent magazine starting out in 1937. But the writers around *Partisan Review* embraced their individual and collective vulnerabilities and made them the substance of a programme, an ethos and a style. The 'New York intellectuals' were anti-academic, and even where (as increasingly) they drew their main income from university teaching, they practised a versatile, generalist mode of writing that was at odds with the prevailing 'Germanic' emphasis on specialized scholarship. Their cultural stance entailed outright opposition to the emergent 'mass culture' of the American city, but they were equally firm in their rejection of conservative nostalgia, whether populist or elitist. Their political disinterestedness was the opposite of quietist; only a minority was ever directly politically engaged, but politics was always a central reference for them, and furnished the occasions of their most vigorous polemical sorties. Bohemians in the academy, moralists in the marketplace, intimates of a literature beyond factions yet veterans of the politics of culture: such were the members of what was arguably the 'alienated intelligentsia' par excellence.

Or such, rather, was what Lionel Trilling—the Arnoldian of the circle—might have called their collective 'best self'. For the historical record of the New York intellectuals was one of increasing incorporation and dependence. They may have been alienated from the dominant culture but they belonged to it nonetheless. As Stalinism and the run-up to war drove their politics into crisis, the editors of *Partisan Review* came increasingly to define this alienation as the characteristic state of the displaced, propertyless intellectual. In doing so, they both mistook the real determinations of their original isolation—which had been their minoritarian politics and aesthetics—and misread the cultural affinities of the ideal of 'intellectual' in the American context. This ideal had first emerged in the writings of Van Wyck Brooks and his Westport school as part of an explicitly nationalist cultural programme; and the evolution of the New York intellectuals showed that the association would be a lasting one.[16] *Partisan Review* entered the 1950s utterly transformed. Its political poise had been badly shaken by the war against the Axis and shattered by the Cold War that followed. The journal now supported the US State Department's global effort to contain the spread of Communism. At home, it favoured a pre-emptive ideological strike that would deal with the political menace while averting the risk of an over-vigorous right-wing assault on civil liberties—the political proclivities of America's 'liberal' intelligentsia were the target of Trilling's major post-war intervention, *The Liberal Imagination*. In the outcome, the journal's solicitude did nothing to avert the McCarthy repression or—Philip Rahv's solitary and heavily qualified disquiet notwithstanding—to resist it when it was unleashed. By 1952, alienation was sufficiently assuaged for the *Review* to run a symposium on 'Our Country and Our Culture'.

Thus, a rhetoric of independence coexisted with a record of conformity. 'The intellectual' and the free play of 'mind' became cultic objects in a milieu that, much in keeping with the surrounding culture, was deeply conservative in the fifties, liberal and even radical in the sixties and early seventies, only to swerve rightwards again thereafter. Prominent writers were sharing drinks and ideas at the White House before the Elysée Palace was added to the social map of the high intelligentsia; and Parisian 'Gulag chic' had its tougher-minded equivalent in the New York-Washington 'military-intellectual complex'.

The post-war history of the New York intellectuals is perhaps most starkly illuminated by the career of one of their younger representatives, Norman Podhoretz. Podhoretz studied with Trilling at Columbia (and then Leavis at Cambridge) in the immediate post-war period. Having completed his academic studies, he joined the

---

16 Brooks's programme was the deviant continuation of Randolph Bourne's, which had envisaged a balanced combination of nationalism and internationalism. *Partisan Review* criticized Brooks's nationalism before the war, citing Bourne's position as more acceptable and more radical in its affinities. But cultural cosmopolitanism alone was not a sufficient safeguard against nationalist attitudes, after the subsidence of its own radicalism.

prestigious New York magazine *Commentary*, of which he became editor in 1960. Formed in *Partisan Review*'s 'liberal anti-Communism', he later embraced an idiosyncratic 'radicalism' based on Mailer, Goodman and Norman O. Brown. But by the later sixties this amalgam had disintegrated, and Podhoretz turned towards the neo-conservative politics whose most clamorous publicist he became. The main purpose of his memoir *Breaking Ranks* was to recapitulate and defend these successive allegiances, but its most powerful demonstration is of a whole tradition quite radically blocked. The alienation, or what remained of it, was of a wayward society from the quintessential American standard represented by the 'intellectual'. And that appellation, claimed compulsively on page after page, was no longer primarily important as a reference—to a milieu, say, or a programme; it was now above all the symptom of a measureless self-regard.[17]

6

The purpose of these comparative notes is not to set the scene for general theoretical conclusions; that would presuppose more exacting historical scholarship and finer analytic tools than any utilized here. But it is hard, considering these divergent yet oddly echoing histories, not to feel curious about the sources of Debray's polemical energy, not to inquire what exactly it is that underwrites his freelance oppositionism.

The main impulse in *Teachers, Writers, Celebrities* is undoubtedly political. It is political first of all in the general sense that its inquiry into the development of the French cultural apparatuses is shaped by a strong strategic preoccupation with the forms of bourgeois power and the answering forms of an adequate socialist programme. But Debray's more topical and more intimate concern here is with the political fate of a whole intellectual generation. The strength of this motivation can be measured by its very persistence. In 1967, in the first of what were to have been thirty years in a Bolivian jail, he wrote 'In Settlement of All Accounts', a vivid memoir of his student days at

---

17   Norman Podhoretz, *Breaking Ranks*, New York 1979.

the École Normale.[18] He was already conscious then of a certain unreality in the political attachments of his milieu, and of the rising pressure of careerism and competition inside it. Within a decade his worst fears had been borne out. His *Modeste contribution aux discours et cérémonies officielles du dixième anniversaire*, published in 1978, depicted the May explosion as a functional crisis of development for consumer capitalism in France, and attacked its intellectual notables for their regression to irrationalism and political reaction.[19] The present work is a more ambitious attempt to lay bare the specifically cultural structural mechanisms that led to the all but total collapse of the Parisian left intelligentsia in the later seventies, by one of its few honourable survivors.

However, Debray's politically intransigent Marxism is not his only resource. His mediology produces a 'Frankfurtian' analysis that explicitly denies the presence of politically sufficient contradictions within the cultural order. How, then, is his own position sustained? This is the function of a second level of his text. From time to time Debray will pause to mediate on the trans-generational continuities of the old *lycées*, or to demand 'total support' for the few surviving literary reviews of the old kind, or to brood on the possibility of a world without *Le Monde*. These passages are intermittent and brief, but they are more than rhetoric. They are outcrops of a discourse that underlies the expanse of *Teachers, Writers, Celebrities*: the classic discourse of the French intellectual tradition. The undeclared activity of this discourse is responsible for certain anomalous features of the text, very notably the systematic resort to anatomical and zoological metaphor, as if in compensation for a forbidden ontology. External circumstances also suggest the ambiguities of the association. The fact that a Marxist reflecting on the involution of the French intellectual tradition can spontaneously reproduce the themes of its minoritarian English counterpart of an earlier time is a sign that

18 Debray, *Prison Writings*, pp. 169–207.
19 The bulk of this work was translated in *New Left Review* I/115 ('A Modest Contribution to the Rites and Ceremonies of the Tenth Anniversary', May–June 1979, pp. 45–65) together with a reply by Henri Weber (pp. 66–71).

strong cultural currents are running in channels that remain to be opened for investigation. One can know only what one refuses, says Debray, paraphrasing Goethe. Mediology, with its emphatic commitment to the primacy of explanation, suggests the necessary correction. The maxim is a half-truth whose necessary complement is its inverse: one can refuse only what one *knows*.

ii. Into the Mêlée

The idea of corporatism, in the theoretical tradition of the left in the twentieth century and since, is inseparable from the memory of Antonio Gramsci, for whom it identified a class habitus displaying collective self-assertion of a fundamentally defensive, particularist character, the opposite of the 'hegemonic' disposition that looks beyond the given social order, aiming to remake it as a whole, in keeping with its own interests and general potentials. Trade unionism has been the basic form of working-class corporatism, for which Britain's political Labourism has been one epitome. The corporatism of intellectuals has had a strikingly different appearance, however, and not only because it arises on the other side of the division of mental and manual labour. In this case, to speak in the broadest terms, the particular interest to be defended and advanced is precisely an imputed general interest, a universal value—whatever substance that may be taken to consist in from case to case—transcending the lesser, driven conflicts that disfigure the human landscapes of the time. In a phrase that became canonical in the inter-war period, the defining virtue of the intellectual is to be or to rise *au-dessus de la mêlée*,[20] to assume the subjectivity proper to the habitus of intellectual corporatism. This way of framing the matter follows Gramsci's lead in implying a critical displacement of received notions of the 'traditional intellectual' while also attempting to describe and explain its specific historical reality and efficacy as an objective trend and a topic of discourse in its own right. For what has to be reckoned with is the fierceness and resourcefulness

---

20   See preface, p. vii, above.

with which the corporatist claim—be it scholarly or activist in manner, literary, philosophical or sociological in substance—has persisted down to the present—and with what confusing effects.

Cultural criticism in the tradition of humane letters was a familiar genre, especially in Germany and England. But the political and cultural upheavals of the 1920s renewed its energy and sense of purpose, provoking a Europe-wide rally of the humanist intelligentsia. In Germany, as the First World War neared its end, the conservative anti-bourgeois tradition of *Kulturkritik* was renewed by Thomas Mann, whose *Reflections of an Unpolitical Man,* published in 1918, described and lamented the coming defeat of (German) culture by (French) civilization, the onset of a spiritless modernity given over to politics, rationalism and 'prose', the obsolescence of traditional 'inwardness' and the hegemony of 'civilization's literary man'.[21] In 1925 the Italian philosopher Benedetto Croce, repenting of his early attraction to Mussolini, published his response to the *Manifesto of the Fascist Intellectuals* and embarked on a course of cultural opposition centred on 'the religion of liberty' and a 'true aristocracy' of intellect.[22] Kindred themes ran through Julien Benda's *La Trahison des clercs* (1927), a classic statement of the intellectual vocation, which deplored the misalliance of mind with politics in contemporary mass movements, foremost among them nationalism, and recalled *les clercs* to their sacred duty in the service of perennial values.[23] Then, at the turn of the decade, came F. R. Leavis's *Mass Civilization and Minority Culture* and José Ortega y Gasset's *The Revolt of the Masses* (both 1930): an English literary critic and a Spanish philosopher united in rejecting instrumental reason and the 'democratic' Babel of the modern market in values, in the name of cultural wholeness and authority, an integral 'humanity'.[24]

---

21   Thomas Mann, *Reflections of a Nonpolitical Man* [published English title *sic*], New York 1983.

22   See, for example, Benedetto Croce, *My Philosophy and Other Essays on the Moral and Political Problems of Our Time*, London 1949.

23   Julien Benda, *The Treason of the Intellectuals*, New York 1928.

24   F. R. Leavis, *Mass Civilization and Minority Culture*, Cambridge 1930; Ortega y Gasset, *The Revolt of the Masses* (1930), London 1932.

These works form a historical cluster, not a faction. Their philosophical divergences were, at their extremes, irreconcilable. Leavis's cultural diagnosis associated him with Ortega and the Mann of 1918, but his episodic political sympathies, in the anti-fascist alert of the 1930s, lay rather with Benda, Croce and the later, the official Mann.[25] Croce's vision of history, contrasting with that of his English, German and Spanish contemporaries, was essentially progressivist, while Benda's quasi-platonic vision of 'the eternal' reduced history to degrading circumstance. Yet their affinities were crucial. All of them wrote from and for the presumptive commitments of a received humane culture. Their respective understandings of this culture revealed a shared idealism. For Mann, Leavis and Ortega, all drawing on the German romantic tradition, it was the integral human negative of commercial-industrial 'civilization'; Benda's realm of perennial values was set above and against the to-and-fro of social struggle; for Croce, modern history was in essence the self-realization of liberty, temporary appearances notwithstanding. Politically, they were rather elusive, for, in effect, their options were emergency measures dictated finally by a commitment that was meta-political in character. Their common basic inclination was towards an authoritarian liberalism disengaged from the clashing social interests whose true moral measure it claimed exclusively to be. Croce was directly active in politics, yet his philosophy of practical reason left no space to theorize this course, distinguishing only economics and ethics. Like the others, he dwelt on the critical intimations of culture, reason or spirit, and this led not to a politics of any ordinary kind but to an ethics of intellectuality. Spiritual 'treason' was Benda's theme, and the others echoed the charge; together they assembled a gallery of treachery and default. Croce and Leavis attacked patronage and academicism, Ortega deplored

---

25 It is worth marking the contrast between the earlier and the later Thomas Mann: the book of 1918, ultra-nationalist, inconsolable in the face of democracy and casually racist towards Poles and Irish among others, has been an embarrassment to Anglo-American liberal good sense, which honours the memory of the anti-fascist exile.

the proliferation of technical specialisms, and Benda condemned the pamphleteering 'organizers of political passions', right or left. The positive counterparts were Croce's 'poet militant', Leavis's 'disinterested minority', Ortega's 'man of culture', Benda's *clerc*: so many redemptive images of the genuinely autonomous and hence properly engaged intellectual.

Here, then, is intellectual corporatism as a subject-position, a self-affirming cultural and political identity. In the same period, it began to be focused as an *object* of analysis. The 1920s witnessed not only this late rally of the humanist intelligentsia; it also saw the beginning of a sociology of intellectuals. Karl Mannheim was one of the legendary founders of this branch of sociology. (He also became, in later years, a target of conservative-humanist criticism, drawing fire from T. S. Eliot after the war, and from Leavis's *Scrutiny*, among others.[26]) His consideration of 'the sociological problem of the intelligentsia', in *Ideology and Utopia*—published in 1929, at the height of this cultural episode—is one of the best-known documents of its kind.[27] Its starting point, in Alfred Weber's famous phrase, was 'the free-floating intelligentsia'. How was this phenomenon to be understood and evaluated? Mannheim dismissed all class-ascriptive analyses of the intelligentsia. In his view, neither provenance nor location nor orientation determined them as a part of any fundamental social class. The only thing that unified intellectuals was their high level of education: unified *and separated* them, for while members of fundamental social classes tended to reproduce 'directly and exclusively' the modal outlook of their peers, intellectuals were formed through an educational experience that brought the whole of society and its opposing forces into view. As a result, they acquired a special bent for 'synopsis', for 'synthesis' and 'dynamic mediation'; they were uniquely aware of society as a whole, and correspondingly less prone

---

26   T. S. Eliot, *Notes Towards the Definition of Culture*, London 1948; G. H. Bantock, 'Cultural Implications of Planning and Popularization', *Scrutiny*, 14, 3 (Spring 1947), pp. 171–84. Eliot nevertheless participated in Mannheim's discussion forum, the Moot, as did some of Leavis's collaborators.

27   Karl Mannhein, *Ideology and Utopia* (1929), trans. Louis Wirth and Edward Shils, London 1936.

to sectional partisanship. Two courses were available to them, then. The more common course was to affiliate to a fundamental social class and to serve it by spiritualizing its struggle for advantage, by transmuting 'interests' into 'ideas'. This was not a satisfactory option, Mannheim believed: intellectuals were trained into a highly deliberative frame of mind that made them dubious allies, and in straining to repress this quality in themselves they usually lapsed into an equally unserviceable fanaticism. The other and preferable course was to exploit the potential of their distinctive training; to organize *as* intellectuals in an educational 'forum' that would transcend the particularism of 'the party schools'. In such forums they would seek to fulfil 'their mission as the predestined advocate of the intellectual interests of the whole'.

Mannheim's analysis, with its social-scientific air and peaceably reformist politics, was in obvious ways a departure from the humanist tradition. Yet it surely begins to sound familiar. Indeed its continuities were fundamental. This sociology of knowledge was led by its own relativist logic into a familiar dualism: on the one hand a driven world of 'ideology' and 'interest', on the other, the deliberative exploration of the social whole—or, in terms that he might just as well have chosen, 'mass civilization' and 'minority culture'. The outlines of his social policy are equally recognizable. His personal democratic convictions do not cancel the fact that in proposing a social peace whose cultural foundations were by definition inaccessible to the great majority—workers and capitalists alike—he was updating the claims of a pseudo-aristocratic authoritarian liberalism. Mannheim's sociology was thus a transposition of cultural criticism, not, in theory or in political implication, a break with it. The passage from humanistic to scientific reason occurred within the received discursive convention. However, this convention really was now nearing the point of an important mutation, the decisive condition of which was political.

In the Communist movement, the late twenties and early thirties had been devoted to the assertion of 'class against class', in culture as in politics. Calls for an authentically proletarian or revolutionary literature were flanked with broadside denunciations of bourgeois culture and its representatives. Associations of worker-writers were set up, with journals to serve them: the German *Linkskurve,* or *Anvil* in the United States. Communist intellectuals drew unsparing portraits of the 'decadent', 'social-fascist' culture they had left behind: Dmitri Mirsky's *The Intelligentsia of Great Britain* and Paul Nizan's *Les Chiens de garde* (both 1932) are classics of this phase.[28] With the victory of fascism in Germany came an urgent change of diplomatic posture in Moscow and, as a consequence, in the respective national orientations of the European Communist parties. A scant two years saw the abandonment of the ultra-left 'Third Period' in favour of the militant moderation of the Popular Front. Opposition to fascism and war, organized in the widest obtainable political alliances, now took precedence over specifically anti-capitalist initiatives. The critical tests of the new orientation were political and military, but its most ostentatious novelty was an altered and intensified *cultural* practice. Now, the logic of popular-frontism entailed a depolarization of cultural life. 'Proletarian' activity continued, but with reduced or no official encouragement; the cultural apparatuses of the Comintern parties were henceforward devoted to mobilizing the forces of the 'democratic bourgeoisie'; the symbolic vanguard of the struggle against fascism was to be the 'critical intelligentsia'. The organizations, journals and events that incarnated the new course were typically national or universalist in address: the League of American Writers, *Das Wort,* the International Writers Congress for the Defence of Culture. Marxism and working-class struggle, where they were still urged, were refigured as the most consistent and committed inheritors of shared traditions. So, old hostilities were curbed and new allies courted. In France, for example, Henri Barbusse, the awkward notable who, exploiting the prestige he enjoyed as the author of the pacifist classic *Le Feu,* had hampered the implementation of a sectarian cultural line in French Communism, was now exalted as the very type of the 'progressive writer'; while Paul Nizan, the leftist scourge of philosophical

---

28   Dmitri S. Mirsky, *The Intelligentsia of Great Britain*, New York 1935; Paul Nizan, *The Watchdogs: Philosophers of the Established Order*, New York and London 1973.

'buffoonery', found himself reviewing the works of Julien Benda in articles that were models of forbearance and cordiality.[29] Such were the means and circumstances of the Communist attempt to rally intellectuals in a militant humanist crusade, a 'popular front of the mind'.

Popular-frontism was in its own most urgent terms a failure: the Spanish revolution was crushed, and within two years fascist armies had taken control of most of bourgeois Europe and were moving east against the Soviet Union. In a longer perspective, however, its impact was felt in the politics of war and reconstruction in every affected country. The cultural forces assembled in this period had many destinies. In the best of cases, that of Italy, they were consolidated in a strong, naturalized Communist tradition; in the worst, that of the USA, they were dispersed by repression. But everywhere they bore witness to the necessary, even though unsought, implication of Popular Front discourse. Out of these years came a potent tradition (or legend) of 'the intellectuals and the left'. In a dreamlike condensation of orthodox Leninism and high-humanist disaffection, the intellectual *as such* was figured as a critical agency of political opposition and advance, and even of revolution. This was more than a sentimental inheritance of the left. It was rather the commonplace within which both socialist and conservative reflection on intellectuals was conducted in the succeeding decades.

In 1942, after years of meditation in his native Austria and then in American exile, the economist Joseph Schumpeter published his analysis of the social order in the West.[30] His theses were stark. Unlike Mannheim, he spoke plainly of capitalism and socialism, of the inevitable defeat of the former by the latter, and of the conspicuous revolutionary role of a social group that capitalism had fostered but could not repress unless by fascist means: not, as might be thought, the working class but the intelligentsia. Capitalism was

29 See Annie Cohen-Solal, *Paul Nizan, communiste impossible*, Paris 1980; Paul Nizan, *Pour une nouvelle culture*, textes réunis et présentés par Susan Suleiman, Paris 1971: 'Un clerc de gauche', pp. 275–9.
30 Joseph Schumpeter, *Capitalism, Socialism and Democracy* (1942), London 1954, ch. XIII, 'Growing Hostility', pp. 143–56.

inherently self-destructive, Schumpeter believed, and this in significant measure because it tended to generate a climate of 'almost
universal hostility' to itself. Capitalism created a critical habit of
mind that, once formed, would stop at nothing: 'the bourgeois finds
to his amazement that the rationalist attitude does not stop at the
credentials of kings and popes but goes on to attack private property
and bourgeois values.' The whole social order was at the mercy of intellectuals, in whose interest it supposedly was to 'work up and organize
resentment, to nurse it, to voice it and to lead it'. Although intellectuals
were drawn from among the highly educated, Schumpeter wrote,
their hallmark was the subjectivity of discontent: there is no such
thing as a happy intellectual. He went on to detail the cultural and
social developments that in his view had formed this social group.
These were structural to capitalism and their upshot was inevitable.
The intellectuals, searching for a social mass capable of lending force
to their compulsive 'nibbling' and 'biting', would 'invade' the labour
movement, flatter the workers as once they had flattered princes, and
prepare them for the culminating assault on capital.

Conceived in post-Hapsburg Vienna and completed in wartime
America, Schumpeter's work spanned two centres and two generations
of discourse on intellectuals. The inherited theme of intellectual corporatism was refashioned in his hands. The old humanistic criticism
had posited a transcendent social interest and a kind of social being
who bore witness to it: Benda, Leavis and Mannheim were all devoted
to a vocational ethics of intellectuality. Schumpeter dealt roughly with
this project; the problem of the day was, so to speak, not 'society' but
'culture'—the intellectuals and their irrepressible socialist leanings.

Schumpeter's theses were among the opening statements in a discussion that engaged US culture for more than twenty years, in the
overarching context of the Pax Americana: a long boom and a long
counter-revolution. Anti-communism was the keynote of the time.
At home, the left was hammered; and meanwhile the US state moved
outwards, creating the financial, politico-military and cultural institutions through which it implemented its hegemony over the
capitalist world: Bretton Woods, NATO and (in ironic tribute to the
intellectual crusades of the thirties) the Congress for Cultural

Freedom. Schumpeter's economic pessimism was controversial in these conditions, but his cultural diagnosis seemed apt. In the *film noir* lighting of the Cold War, the shadow cast by intellectuals was socialism. Lionel Trilling, a literary critic working in self-conscious descent from Matthew Arnold, went so far as to claim that the left movements of the 1930s had 'created' the US intelligentsia.[31] His own solution was a feline liberalism committed to 'variousness, possibility, complexity, and difficulty'; and there were many who agreed. But to another kind of liberal—Schumpeter's compatriot and fellow-economist Friedrich von Hayek—the Arnoldian play of mind, the forte of the 'second-hand dealers in ideas', was precisely the endemic favouring condition of anti-capitalism.[32] Little more than a measure of fastidiousness distinguished Trilling's cultural politics from official ideology. But in a world of loyalty oaths and passionate conformism, even that could seem subversive.

The theme of socialism as the new 'treason of the intellectuals' was a commonplace of North Atlantic culture in the 1950s. The Cold War bound the old and the new discursive conventions in a phobic discourse on the irresponsibility of intellectuals. However, the opposite evaluation was possible too. The idea of an essential affinity between intellectuals and socialism had first been promoted by the left, most dramatically in France, where it was a commonplace. Julien Benda—Nizan's *clerc de gauche,* who conceded when the time came that it was 'permissible' to support the Popular Front—was the mannered epitome of this tradition. In post-Liberation France it found a new symbol and a definitive theorist in another philosopher: Nizan's old friend Jean-Paul Sartre.

'What is literature?' was the opening question of Sartre's post-war career.[33] His answer was: *committed* literature. And what he meant by

---

31   Lionel Trilling, *The Liberal Imagination* (1950), New York 1976, p. 8. See also Trilling's biographical study, *Matthew Arnold*, New York 1939.

32   Friedrich von Hayek, 'The Intellectuals and Socialism' (1949), in George B. de Huszar, ed., *The Intellectuals: A Controversial Portrait*, Glencoe, IL 1960, p. 371.

33   Jean-Paul Sartre, *What Is Literature?*, trans. Bernard Frechtman, London 1950.

this was that there was an identity between commitment to liter-ature and commitment to socialism. Literature presupposed free inter-subjectivity, a 'pact of freedoms' between writer and reader. But capitalist class relations negated this condition. To write at all, then, was to oppose the norms of capitalist culture and to prefigure the unalienated order of socialism. An authentic commitment to literature was, logically and morally, a commitment to socialism. The writer *as such* was of the left. Or, as he later put it, in his 'Plaidoyer pour les intellectuels' (1965), the writer was necessarily an 'intellectual'.[34]

So 'what is an intellectual?' Intellectuals emerge from among what Sartre called 'the technicians of practical knowledge', under the pres-sure of an irresolvable contradiction. The conditions of formation of these technicians are in every way functionally associated with capital-ism, yet they are educated in an official humanism (Mannheim's 'synoptic' vision). Their special skills are implicitly universalist, yet they are deployed according to the particular logics of capital and the state. Structurally defined by this situation, the technicians of practical knowledge can do one of two things: they can submit in bad faith, or they can become 'meddlers', dedicated minders of other people's busi-ness—'intellectuals'. Intellectuals are 'monsters', Sartre maintained, a 'lived impossibility'. That is the one and only principle of their social being. 'False' intellectuals try to escape their contradiction by escaping into a bogus universalism devoted to 'constructive' social criticism. (Like the poet Lamartine in the revolution of 1848, they cannot reason beyond the proposition that social conflict arises from 'a terrible mis-understanding'.)[35] 'True' intellectuals, in contrast, embrace their contradiction. They are 'singular universals', embodiments of human values as yet unrealized, and as such they find common cause with the other singular universals of capitalism, above all the working class. The true intellectual is a true humanist and the true humanist is the revolutionary socialist intellectual, the 'guardian of fundamental ends'.

---

34   Jean-Paul Sartre, 'A Plea for Intellectuals', *Between Existentialism and Marxism*, trans. John Mathews, London 1974, pp. 228–85.

35   Cit. Karl Marx, *The Class Struggles in France 1848 to 1850*, Moscow 1968, p. 39.

Sartre's political values were in every way opposed to Schumpeter's. He wrote as a decided Marxist, with express debts to Gramsci. But whereas the main Marxist tradition had always seen the question of the intellectuals as an aspect of the larger strategic problem of political organization, Sartre made it primary. At the centre of his cultural landscape was a figure at once new and old: the independent, the intellectual as revolutionary witness. The negative historical condition of this departure was the decomposition of Stalinism, but it was fuelled from deeper-lying sources, in older cultural formations such that Marxist philosophy could meet conservative sociology in a common idiom. For the parallels in these two analyses are equally strongly marked, and can be pursued in detail. They are the signs of a shared convention and a shared history. Schumpeter's sociology and Sartre's ethics were oppositely but equally interpretations of a single compelling historical image: *le clerc de gauche,* the autonomous intellectual as the herald of socialism.

There is no simple lesson to be drawn from this history; it provokes too many questions to be usable in that way. For now, it must suffice to point to the terms of an ethico-political crux. What I have been trying to describe is the persistence in twentieth-century culture and politics and since of what might be called a 'romance of mind'—a whole set of ideas and images that have not only persisted but actually flourished, becoming as much a part of socialist cultural tradition as of more powerful liberal traditions, with results that are, to say no more, ambiguous. Humanism and its distinctive guardian—the intellectual, the Arnoldian 'best self' of an 'ordinary' world—are living, more vigorously and more variously than many of us like to think.

So where is the alternative? The anti-humanisms of the past half-century, as propounded by Louis Althusser and Michel Foucault, for example, have been either too little or too much: too little, if all they really intend is a consistent anti-essentialism, which can scarcely claim to deal with historical humanism as a whole; too much, if they are pursued to the point where they undermine the notion of a general human emancipation, which is the ultimate goal of any socialism worthy of the name. Indeed, Althusser may have been allowing so much in defining Marxism as a '*theoretical* anti-humanism'. We have to pause to ask whether there actually is an alternative in the clear, expected sense. Sartre used to say that Marxism was the unsurpassable horizon of all thought in our time: one could think against it, certainly, but not beyond it. Perhaps socialist intellectuals are similarly placed in relation to humanism: scarcely the faithful heirs of an old tradition, as the lulling tones of popular-front culture suggested, and scarcely the heroic consciences of Sartre's vision; struggling towards a kind of self-understanding that is consistently historical and materialist, no doubt—but a humanism all the same.

1981–1988

Burke's Way

The name of Edmund Burke has long been a byword for political reaction. In the *Reflections on the Revolution in France* (1790) the young Whig James Mackintosh was quick to see and reject 'the manifesto of a counter-revolution'—a consciously propagandist tract in which Burke summoned his uncommon rhetorical powers for an assault on the principles and policies of the French revolutionaries, to be followed, as he soon came to urge, by actual warfare, wholehearted and prolonged, against the country that had given birth to the '*armed doctrine*' of Jacobinism. That episode alone would have won Burke a place in the pantheon of conservative thought. However, with the October Revolution in 1917, his polemic against democracy was recharged for a new era. Just rewrite 'France' as 'Russia', the English jurist A. V. Dicey suggested within a year of the Bolshevik victory, and Burke's insights would shine forth in all their enduring truth. In the Cold War conditions of the mid-twentieth century, then, the appropriation was solemnized: Burke was elevated to the status of political philosopher, a prophet of the 'new crusade' against Communism. (Conor Cruise O'Brien's *The Great Melody* concluded with a late exercise in this genre, notable as a surrender to an orthodoxy its author had fought against twenty years before.[1]) In this and

---

1   See the Introduction to his edition of the *Reflections*, London 1968, pp. 56–76.

in his defence of custom and trans-generational obligation and 'prudent', piecemeal change, Burke was indeed a conservative for modern times.

Yet it is commonly acknowledged that had Burke for some reason fallen silent in the early days of 1789, before the outbreak of the Revolution, he would have been remembered, less vividly, as a liberal Whig parliamentarian with a record of tenacious effort in the service of causes that brought him no easy benefits: justice, conciliation and eventual independence for the thirteen North American colonies; opposition to the Protestant Ascendancy in Ireland and relief of Catholic legal disabilities there and in Britain; and—a campaign that baffled and wearied even some of those closest to him—reform of the East India Company, 'a state in the guise of a merchant', to name some major instances. Burke was no democrat, at any time, even though he came to admire the temper of the American colonists over the years of their war against Britain; and his field of political action was an inter-continental empire whose essential legitimacy he did not question. Nevertheless, he deplored the government resort to force in dealing with the insurgency across the Atlantic and popular political agitation on the streets of the imperial capital in the period of the Wilkes affair. It was he who held that 'the people' are the only true judges of their oppression; and who wrote to a friend that his sole motive in pursuing the governor-general of Bengal, Warren Hastings, was sympathy with Indians, 'who are images of the great Pattern as well as you or I. I know what I am doing; whether the white people like it or not.'

There are at least the appearances of paradox here, and it is the merit of David Bromwich's long, detailed and learned study, *The Intellectual Life of Edmund Burke*,[2] with its unstinted use of his sub-ject's own words—notes, drafts and letters as well as the published writings and the reports of his speeches in parliament—and those of his contemporaries too, to establish this beyond the reach of conven-ient simplification, even if there remains considerable scope for doubt and disagreement over the character of the questions to be put and the possibility of resolving them. The meaning of Burke's 'return

---

2   David Bromwich, *The Intellectual Life of Edmund Burke*, Cambridge, MA and London 2014 (the first of two volumes).

upon himself', as Matthew Arnold termed it in the 1860s, may be a matter for dismay, as it was for the revolutionary Tom Paine at the time, or for affirmation, as it was for a conservative such as Russell Kirk in a later era. In another perspective again, it may be a touchstone of liberal disinterestedness —so Arnold believed—for its exemplary and most un-English fidelity to ideas. Marx, for his part, assumed simple venality: Burke was 'a vulgar bourgeois through and through'. Bromwich's emphases are manifest in his title, which Arnold would surely have approved. This is a study of Burke as a thinker—though the book contains a lot about eighteenth-century politics both parliamentary and extra-mural, inevitably, and a little about his social and family life—and, then, of the thinking rather than the thought. That phrasing is hyperbolic, granted, but it matches Bromwich's opening statement of purpose, which some may think a little enigmatic itself: 'I have tried to answer the question, What did it mean to think like Edmund Burke?' The question has more than one meaning, in keeping, it may be, with Bromwich's dual character as a writer: a literary scholar specializing in the Romantic period, with books on Hazlitt and Wordsworth and an edition of Burke's speeches and letters to his name, he has made a second reputation for his activist critical writing on US foreign policy and cultural politics today. Appearing in the *London Review of Books* and *Huffington Post, Raritan* and *Dissent* among other venues, work of this kind makes up the collection *Moral Imagination: Essays*.[3] Ranging from reflections on basic conditions of any credible democratic political culture— questions of censorship and self-censorship, for example—to commentary on current developments, during Obama's tenure of the White House, Bromwich was an unsparing critic of the president he once witheringly described as 'the world's most important spectator'— or more summarily, in an election year, as 'a bad president'.[4] In the

---

3 David Bromwich, *Moral Imagination: Essays*, Princeton 2014.
4 See respectively 'What Are We Allowed to Say?', *London Review of Books*, 22 September 2016; 'On Super Tuesday', LRB, 5 March 2020; 'Obama's Delusion: The Presidential Letdown', LRB, 22 October 2009; 'A Bad President', LRB (Letters), 5 July 2012.

arresting words of Samuel Moyn, writing in the *Nation*, he has been a 'Burkean regicide'.[5]

Here, Bromwich pursues his question in more than one direction, starting with his subject's birth into the family of a Dublin lawyer in 1730 (if not 1729: authorities differ) and continuing 'from the Sublime and the Beautiful to American Independence', a span of just over fifty years ending with Britain's final acknowledgement of the accomplished fact, in 1782. The order of treatment is broadly chronological—with one great, seemingly untameable exception, the *Reflections*, anticipations of which are so frequent as to leave that work with an index entry twice as long as some of those to which *The Intellectual Life* is nominally devoted.

In his first adult incarnation, Edmund Burke was a philosophically inclined man of letters. With a distinguished undergraduate career at Trinity College Dublin behind him, the twenty-one-year-old left for London, there to study for the bar. Seven ill-documented years later, that plan had come to nothing, but Burke had published two books and was working to commission on a third. They made a striking trio. The first, *A Vindication of Natural Society*, appeared anonymously in 1756; its thesis, that society as it existed was a corrupting environment for human life, which should properly be guided only by the laws of nature as these were disclosed to unaided reason, was taken up by contemporaries such as Paine—but was in fact parodically intended, in mockery of the apodictic manner and beliefs of the Tory philosopher Henry Bolingbroke. (Another such vindication, unknown to Burke at the time, had appeared the previous year: Rousseau's *Second Discourse*, the work of a thinker he respected as preeminent in his generation but came to loathe as 'the great professor and founder of *the philosophy of vanity*'. Montesquieu was always the more sympathetic point of reference for Burke.)

An Abridgement of the English History, begun the next year, was before long abandoned, but its central perception of English common law as an anti-axiomatic creation whose contingencies ran back into the historical past but not to an originary nature, announced a

---

5   Samuel Moyn, 'The Burkean Regicide', *Nation*, 12 August 2014.

complementary theme that would remain primary for Burke. Much the most important work of the three, the second in time (1757), was *A Philosophical Enquiry into the Origin of Our Ideas of the Sublime and the Beautiful*, which led the field in its area of European discussion for a generation, drawing the attention of Kant and Herder, among others. Burke's philosophy in the *Enquiry* is essentially a psychology, and the dispositions in play in the experience of art are grounded in the senses, not moral life. Pleasure, which turns on 'social affections', and pain, which turns on self-preservation (fear and the ultimate terror of death) and is predominant, are the basic terms. Humans are natural spectators, Burke wrote, and 'terror is a passion which always produces delight when it does not press too close, and pity is a passion accompanied with pleasure, because it arises from social affection.' Only one state is worse than terror and that is apathy; humans, for all their love of custom and habit, are naturally drawn also to excitement, and hence the attraction to what is terrible, or sublime. The 'causes' of sublimity, as Bromwich lists them, include '*privation, suddenness, successiveness* (when irregular) and *obscurity*'. That last is necessary, for clarity drives out the sublime, which consists in the power to 'astonish', to renew the 'ignorance of things' that 'lies at the source of our admiration'. The tenor of the discussion—or perhaps mere habit—may evoke painting or music, but Bromwich makes the case that Burke's favoured medium of sublimity, for its power of abstraction and repeated displacements of context, was in fact that of reason and sociability themselves, none other than language. 'The sublime, in the greatest poetry'—Burke's reference here, as often, was to the Milton of *Paradise Lost*—'is . . . a heightening and bringing to awareness of a state of disjunction or derangement that is a normal condition of language.'

The next seven years brought a second transition in Burke's life, to public discourse of a different order. This was the period of his editorship of the *Annual Register*, a yearbook of politics and related affairs. It also included some time in the private employment of the chief secretary to the Lord Lieutenant of Ireland—a relationship that ended badly, but not before he had drafted an unpublished *Tract Relative to the Laws against Popery in Ireland* (1762). How closely that issue concerned him was illustrated at the turning-point that came soon afterwards, with his appointment as private secretary to the Marquess of Rockingham, a Whig grandee and leader of the proto-party that went by his name. Acting on information from a reputable source, Rockingham sought reassurance that Burke was indeed a Protestant, and not the crypto-papist and Jacobite he was rumoured to be. Burke carried the day, winning confirmation of his post, and the new secretary was soon launched on a second public career as member of parliament for the pocket borough of Wendover, sitting with the Rockingham Whigs. Suspicion and innuendo persisted over the years. As the Irish son of a devout Catholic mother, Mary Nagle, and a father whose embrace of the established church may have been no more than a pragmatic adjustment, the husband of another prac-tising Catholic, Jane Nugent, and an advocate of legal equality for her co-religionists, Burke was always exposed to attack here. However, the fault-lines of politics in his early years in parliament ran other-wise, across the high ground of the constitution itself.

In 1760, George III came to the throne with the firm purpose of regaining the powers that had been lost since 1689, a mission made flesh in the person of his chief minister, Lord Bute, who was a court confidant, not a member of parliament. His nemesis was the radical agitator John Wilkes, whose satires provoked a vindictive government counter-attack that ran for years in the courts and in parliament, often by illegal means and reaching one of its climaxes in the mur-derous repression of a peaceful public gathering in May 1768. Restraint of the monarch was a basic principle for the Rockingham Whigs. Burke was outraged by the evident promotion of force from last to first resort in the calculations of the authorities, seeing it as a deliber-ate 'innovation' of constitutional significance. Innovation (distinct in his mind from allowable reform) and violence were great hatreds of his, and here now was a violent innovation, launched in flat defiance of the truth that the normal medium of popular government must be trust. He responded immediately by forming a parliamentary com-mittee of inquiry into the killings and, in a longer view, writing a pamphlet, *Thoughts on the Cause of the Present Discontents*. This was not a personal production in the way of the *Enquiry*; it was written for the party, and others had share in it. But the draft was Burke's, and he remained its principal author. It is closely involved in recent history, tracing the emergence and operation of an effective 'double cabinet' ensuring the continuity of royal authority amidst the appearances of a parliamentary system, and moves to more general considerations on the proper character of the political order. 'From *Thoughts*', Bromwich rightly judges, 'one gets a clearer idea of what Burke meant by the British Constitution than can be derived from any of his later works'. At the forefront of the Constitution as Burke images it are 'the people', of whom he says, in Bromwich's concise summary, that they 'should not be trusted as advisers on policy or even necessarily as true reckoners of their interests in the short run, but they are always the best judges of their own oppression'.

To this extent, but this only, the presumption of 'good sense' must always be in their favour. For while that principle excludes absolutism or 'austere and insolent' aristocracy as a viable form of polity, it makes no concession to government by popular will: 'I have nothing to do here with the abstract value of the voice of the people', Burke wrote, and good government cannot be simply 'a continued scuffle between the magistrate and the multitude'. Intermediate powers are an essential element of the constitutional formula, and the critical locus of these is the House of Commons. The character of effective representation, in its turn, is not to be mistaken as a dutiful relay of popular 'opinion'—which Burke regularly opposed dismissively to 'interest', a term tacitly qualified as 'real'. Opinion must be guided towards a just understanding of interest. Representation is not the execution of an imperative mandate, therefore: 'The virtue, spirit and essence of a House of Commons', Burke wrote, in a decisive formulation, 'consists in its being the express image of the feelings of the nation': an *image*, not a voice, of the people now remade as part of the *nation*.

Burke rejected Bolingbroke's conviction that the necessary alternative to an ideal political consensus was unprincipled faction; he distrusted political 'independents' as figures whose overweening self-regard led them into inconsistency and practical inconsequence; and he hated neutrality. The best vehicle of representation, in his view, was the political party, 'a body of men united, for promoting by their joint endeavours the national interest, upon some particular principle in which they are all agreed'. A disciplined body aiming for continuity over time and sworn against private deal-making, the party would pursue 'a generous contention for power' quite distinct from 'the mean and interested struggle for place and emolument', in this way working for government of and for the people.

Such was Burke's general thinking at the time of his translation from Wendover—which had been gifted to him by Lord Verney—to the properly elective constituency of Bristol, a great trading port, the second city of the kingdom at the time and a centre of democratic energy. Addressing his electors—some 5,000 in all, or one-tenth of the general population, of whom 904 had voted for him—he explained himself without delay: he was a member of parliament, not of the City of Bristol, and his duty extended to the whole of a great nation and its Empire. By then—this was late 1774—the American Revolutionary War was imminent. Burke's preferences in the developing conflict over the future of the Thirteen Colonies were conservative enough. Ideally, he would have seen the Americans welcomed as partners in Empire. But there was no chance of that, or of any other scheme of conciliation, such as forgoing imperial tax-raising measures while neither surrendering nor emphasizing Westminster's formal rights in such matters. George III and the North administration were bent on a course of provocative and punitive assertion that led inevitably to war. Sooner forfeit the colonies than wage a war to hold them, Burke judged; presumptive entitlements were not worth the moral risk to the British and the Americans alike as 'Anarchy', the political sublime in the forms of protracted revolt and war-fever, became habitual; and thus he went over to the defence of American independence. In doing so, he was courting self-contradiction, for the colonies could be seen as the most advanced outpost of political 'liberty' and the nearest thing to a democracy that the times could show. He disliked American individualism, which was antithetical to his own familialist conception of social being. At other times, his reasoning came to blend his characteristic appeals to precedent with an idiom of 'original rights'. His practical resolution was in itself consistently Burkean. American democracy should be accepted but not copied. This transatlantic creation was 'wholly new' and 'singular' but not a rupture, an 'innovation' of the kind that settled prejudice rightly abhors. It was a legitimate growth from faraway English beginnings, now its own accomplished fact in its proper place—like Britain in its necessarily different way.

Burke's response to the domestic reform agitation that spread at the end of the 1770s was indeed quite different. Demands for reliable public accounting, shorter parliaments—annual, then triennial—and enlarged representation for the counties were taken up in an expanding network of local associations; the example of the armed Irish Volunteers was seen by some to set a new standard for popular self-assertion, as did the anti-Catholic mobilizations that culminated in the Gordon Riots. One Rockingham peer called for universal manhood suffrage and constituencies drawn to a fixed ratio of members to voters. But for the party as a whole the demands of the movement exceeded anything they could support, and its principal role was to moderate the surge of democratic feeling. Burke opposed the demands for reform of representation, warning those who claimed a right to 'new-model' the constitution—an affirmative usage of the day, consciously recalling Cromwell—against hasty interference with the workings of so 'complicated' a device. For on close inspection, the proffered 'remedies' might prove either needless or—and here came unmistakable crocodile tears—insufficiently drastic. In a more practical spirit, he put forward a scheme of 'oeconomical reform' of government finances by which, whatever the intrinsic merit of his proposals, he thought to divert the popular movement from the goal of reformed representation. His argument against the demand for shorter parliaments was summary: elections are distracting, wasteful and a moral hazard, encouraging venality; they are a necessary evil in a representative system, and the fewer there are the better. The argument against reforming the accumulated jumble of constituency forms was of another order altogether. To tamper with that, he argued in a speech to the Commons, was in effect to call into question the Constitution itself, a 'prescriptive' order always already pregiven in each generation,

a Constitution made by what is ten thousand times better than
choice ... made by the peculiar circumstances, occasions, tem-
pers, dispositions, and moral, civil, and social habitudes of the
people, which disclose themselves only in a long space of time.

That being so, his conviction was that 'neither *now* nor at *any* time is
it prudent or safe to be meddling with the fundamental principles
and ancient tried usages of our Constitution'.

In this speech made in the early 1780s Bromwich identifies the
'true beginning' of Burke's counter-revolutionary writings of the 1790s—
to which need only be added the psychology of the *Enquiry*. Burke's
'turn upon himself' was not what Arnold and like-minded readers
supposed it to be. The fears that prompted it were and would remain
domestic, British and Irish. Moreover, the revolution in France was
quite unlike the American in that it could not be rendered back into
tradition by recourse to a precedent such as that of England in 1689,
which Burke had been able to invoke for the Thirteen Colonies; it was
an unambiguous innovation, the work of a people who in their passion
for reason and collective self-making had put themselves beyond all
custom and so beyond shame and fear. Here was the spark that
ignited the great flare of counter-revolutionary passion in Burke's
Reflections. Jacobinism had released the power of the democratic
sublime, an 'astonishing ... wonderful Spectacle', but one without
the corrective urge to familiarity or the saving ambiguity of fiction.
The revolutionaries were 'at war with heaven itself', Burke said; that
this was 'the worst, the second fall of Man' was the view of a parliamentary ally, in the same Miltonic register. Bromwich exaggerates
not at all when he judges that 'the design of the revolution signified
for Burke a surrender of the idea of human nature'.

So, what does it mean to think like that? Phrased just so,
Bromwich's guiding question prompts a counter-question: And what
exactly does that mean? It suggests, first, that there is a distinctly
Burkean way of thinking, which—second—stands as a criterion,
more likely than not to be positive, for those coming after him. It
suggests also that the study set in train in this way will be affirmative
overall, unpacking or varying a judgement that is already basically

secure. In short, it is a believer's question, though not implying defence of a doctrine. Bromwich offers two answers to it: Burke's way is exemplary, and mysterious. The disconcerting thing about these answers is not so much their content as their light-touch, sometimes merely glancing role in the weighty, slow-moving work they are a part of. It is significant that the book is not framed as a thesis and that its question cannot easily be rewritten as one. Scholarly debts are duly acknowledged but disagreement rarely ruffles the surface of the text. Bromwich writes a limpid prose, with an admirable reach for subtlety of expression. Yet too often his positive judgements on Burke are compliments, superlatives belonging to the rhetoric of eulogy rather than critical discrimination: 'Coercion and cruelty never had a fiercer enemy . . .'; 'no writer has seen so comprehensively . . .'; 'every party has been the better for what it learned from Burke'. In a sentence beginning 'The complexity of Burke's greatness . . .', it is the complexity that is in focus: the 'greatness' is a presumptive given of judgement. Significant criticism of the work and the man is not lacking: he must be read with methodic 'suspicion'; and he was virtually incapable of admitting his mistakes—not a good quality in a public representative ostentatiously faithful to high principle. But finally, the compliments weigh more heavily than the caveats, as they usually do in academic ceremonies of this kind, where the first and last duty is one of attendance, acknowledging, in the manner of Burke, a non-dischargeable debt to the past.

What Burke exemplifies, in the normative sense, is 'moral imagination'. Bromwich takes this phrase, which he has made his personal motto, from the *Reflections*, and glosses it as 'the power that compels us to grant the highest possible reality and the largest conceivable claim to a thought, action or person that is not our own, and not close to us in any obvious way'. The exercise of moral imagination is more than mere empathy, in that it brings with it a capacity and a need for self-development: 'the force of the idea . . . is to deny that we can ever know ourselves sufficiently to settle on a named identity that prescribes our conduct or affiliations'. Burke is not one of the writers listed in aid of this, where it occurs in the book called *Moral Imagination*, and this is not the meaning the phrase seems to bear as a passing coinage in the *Reflections*. What is clear from Bromwich's account as a whole, however, is that his subject could bring to his causes strength of sympathetic feeling answering in some measure to these descriptions. America, India and France, together with Ireland and the overlapping question of Catholic emancipation, were the main instances, and there were others: his denunciation of the British navy's treatment of the Jewish traders of St Eustatius, in the Dutch Caribbean, and intervention to spare two men convicted of sodomy from the stocks, were two noteworthy local episodes. Turning to social classes, on the other hand, his moral imagination operated selectively. Even his striking insistence that the people were usually justified in their claims of oppression was buttressed by the familiar and convenient commonplace that ordinary folk want only to be left in peace. And for Jacobins and the Parisian crowd there would be no question of sympathetic understanding at all. No moral disposition operates in a vacuum, least of all one that actually presupposes a field of differences and asymmetrical relations. Moral imagination may be far better than a lack of it, but it cannot sufficiently characterize any critical position.

The Burke imaged in Bromwich's question is the one that fascinates, and it is not in the nature of fascination to reduce its glowing object to ordinary sense. The passion remains, 'finally mysterious', in the last words of the Introduction. Nonetheless, Bromwich's study offers relevant evidence and suggestion for any who care to look. Of Burke's three great campaigns, two were against particular imperial wrongs; the third, by contrast, was epochally reactionary, but also quite deliberately constructed so as to bring conservative fears of revolution into alignment with the unseasonable cause of religious toleration—the piteous condition of the Catholic Marie-Antoinette as she appears in the *Reflections* was the key in this. These two kinds of wrong came together in Ireland, and in the Burke family network. Irish—not Anglo-Irish, as Yeats preferred to think—and historically Catholic, of gentry stock but also, now, including educated professionals, the Burkes and Nagles were the type of an indigenous ruling bloc, or would have been had it not been for the British laws that had diminished people like them and continued to penalize them—old families denied their due place in the greater family of the nation. Edmund himself was a bourgeois in a milieu dominated by aristocrats, the men of 'presumptive virtue' whom he, a 'new man', would at times flatter, at times idealize, while noting the characteristic 'languor' of spirit that came with their titles and estates. A bourgeois, then, but not 'through and through', and still less the 'vulgar' hired pen of Marx's caricature. For some, his speeches 'stank of whiskey and potatoes'. Bromwich makes rather little of Burke's early formation, just as O'Brien, in his long labour of identification, made too much of it. But there is no avoiding the inference that some part at least of the affective charge that fired his political passions had been laid very close to home.

Burke has often been called 'the father of modern conservatism', whether in praise or in condemnation. Bromwich is quick to dismiss this characterization as a 'commonplace' that 'no serious historian today would repeat'—too quick, perhaps because of his wish to claim Burke's moral imagination as a resource for a contemporary intellectual politics whose poles are conscience and power. In any case, he makes too much of a confusing metaphor, taking the statement to be primarily about Burke rather than his readers. Parentage in intellectual history is a status awarded by the children, who may choose the same parent for different reasons, or diverse parents in support of a compounded single purpose. Burke's relation to the Tory principles of his own day is a matter of limited relevance in this. And if 'modern conservatism' is taken in its real plurilineal constitution and as including not only politics but literature and thought as well, then it becomes impossible to doubt that, in another phrasing of the commonplace, Burke's work has long been an important intellectual resource for conservatives. The Eliot of *Notes Towards the Definition of Culture*, a work written in opposition to the gathering expectation of social reform in Britain after the Second World War, comes immediately to mind. However, that Burke is first of all the author of the *Reflections*, and a wider consideration of his writings suggests a more general claim for his political significance.

Bromwich is inclined to treat Burke's politics as personal conscience projected into public space, more than once quoting his dictum that 'the principles of true politicks are those of morality enlarged', and elsewhere characterizing his Burke as 'anti-political' or essentially a 'moral psychologist'. Here again is a figure with particular appeal in a literary-intellectual field where politics is often denied its specificity, let alone its final human significance, except in strongly, conventionally pejorative terms.

But reductive formulations in this spirit do scant justice to the evidence of Burke's political thinking and his place in modern political thought—although this is not of a kind that should lead Bromwich to commend him to democrats. For Burke was the first European thinker to pose the question of popular political representation as, in effect, that of maintaining oligarchic class rule in the conditions of emergent democracy. His formula was exact. Stable and effective rule depends on the trust of the people, with force reserved as a last resort. The strategic work of a party—as distinct from factions and self-styled independents—is to navigate 'that popular humour which is the medium we float in', to 'guide' the transmutation of 'opinion' into 'interest', and so to *represent*: not to express a popular will, which is the aspiration of democrats, but to create 'an express image', an ideo-affective visualization, 'of the feelings of the nation'. As Bromwich observes, Burke's habit was to defend the party as a means of effective opposition, saying little about any constructive function. This was in part a matter of personal context: the historian Richard Bourke has shown in his *Empire and Revolution* that the youthful author of the *Enquiry* was already developing a concept of the party function in the later 1750s, a time well before the encounter with Rockingham introduced the possibility of a political career in a party with governmental prospects.[6] (As the object of a work of ascetic historical scholarship, Burke in this version is a strictly period figure; not also, as Bromwich or O'Brien would have it, something of a *vade mecum* for our times.) The more substantial reason was also temporal, but in a larger, historical sense: Burke continued to think of representative politics as a necessary tempering of initiatives coming from above, in an oligarchic order,

---

6   Richard Bourke, *Empire and Revolution*, Princeton 2015.

not to be confused with the unrestrained impetus of a democracy based on right. The Burkean party would play a decisive role in managing an unstable formula, representing the people not only to their betters but also, and crucially, to themselves, offering them an 'image' of what they felt. This Burke was a pioneering exponent of hegemony as a mode of rule, a thinker not only for modern conservatives but for all bourgeois politics, a kind of Modern Prince for his class.

2016

Afterlives of the Commune

L'imaginaire de la Commune is the title of Kristin Ross's new book in its first, French edition. It is debatable whether this laconic phrasing could have survived the passage into English with its resonances unimpaired. The more elaborate formulation of the English edition, *Communal Luxury: The Political Imaginary of the Paris Commune*, is properly informative, recalling an event and its animating vision, and defining the emphasis of Ross's treatment, which falls on a triumph of political and social imagination.[1] What it surrenders, however, is the great, stirring generality of the simple phrase 'The Commune!'—'the rallying cry' as well as 'the thing itself'—which the author herself insists upon, as she ranges through the experiences of seventy-two days in Paris in the spring of 1871, reconstructing an altogether more extensive and complex time-space, both objective and inward, of communes past, present and to come. The unique military conjuncture of the time is well known: the victorious Prussians camped to the east of the capital, staying their hand, as the defeated government forces, now regrouped at Versailles to the west, began a sustained bombardment of the city's revolutionaries. But in Ross's treatment, even a strict measurement of time reaches back some years, into the later 1860s, which saw a ferment of political discussion among the workers of Paris, as the Second Empire faltered. 'It is the clubs and

---

1   Kristin Ross, *Communal Luxury*, London and New York 2015.

the associations that have done all the harm', was one police official's retrospective judgement. There, in what one anti-Communard author called 'the Collège de France of insurrection', the idea of the 'social Commune' had taken shape well before the collapse of official resistance to Prussia's armies.[2] Its imaginative hold on posterity would be greater and longer-lived, sustained through the '70s and '80s and beyond by those who had survived the bloody repression to make it to the Communard colonies of London and Geneva—and also by such unflagging champions as Peter Kropotkin and William Morris. Only one French veteran, the geographer and anarchist thinker Élisée Reclus, gets as much attention as these two, a Russian gentleman scientist and an English poet and decorator who had neither first-hand experience of the insurrection nor even much initial awareness of what was unfolding—in contrast, say, with Marx, who, in his London exile, was intensely engaged. But that is in keeping with Ross's understanding of the Commune's imaginary, which is not inhibited either by national borders or by the programmed sequences of modernizing reason. It is a four-dimensional network of sorts in which familiar lines of political inheritance criss-cross with new bondings in the present and retrospective acts of affiliation that enrich the significance of the events they look back on. Thus, Jacobin and Proudhonist currents were predictably to the fore from the outset; Elisabeth Dmitrieff, the founder of the Women's Union, opened a key intellectual 'transversal' between Marx and revolutionary currents in Russia; Kropotkin and Morris became a part of the memory of the Commune by virtue of their embrace of its historic promise and their own later individual contributions to the thought-cluster for which it offered the foremost symbol—in a word, its imaginary.

This is a long-standing preoccupation in Ross's work, as readers of her first book, *The Emergence of Social Space* (1988), centred on the poetry of Rimbaud, will be aware; the constructions of social memory and their political implications are the matter of an incisive critical study, *May '68 and Its Afterlives* (2002). *Communal Luxury* bears a close relation to both books, as historical writing in a modernist mode:

---

2   Ibid., p. 14.

Bloch's *Erbschaft* is an explicit presence in it, and the Benjamin of the 'Theses on the Philosophy of History' is Ross's inspiration for the priorities she sets herself. 'I have preferred', she says, to attend to the 'voices and actions' of the Communards themselves, rather than

> the long chorus of political commentary or analysis—whether celebratory or critical—that followed. I have not been concerned with weighing the Commune's successes or failures, nor with ascertaining in any direct way the lessons it might have provided or might continue to provide for the movements, insurrections and revolutions that have come in its wake. It is not clear to me that the past actually *gives* lessons.

However, she continues,

> Like Walter Benjamin . . . I believe that there are moments when a particular event or struggle enters vividly into the figurability of the present, and this seems to me to be the case with the Commune today.[3]

The alternatives mapped here are not so stark, in truth. Ross's arresting declaration implies a different style of learning, not the conclusion that there is nothing to learn. The lessons are in the first place historical, and the procedure, following Henri Lefebvre, involves both 'the lived' and the 'conceptual', retracing the actual words and actions of the insurgents—such as Reclus and Dmitrieff—and also pursuing certain 'logics' arising from them. Her purpose is to return to the Commune as it can now be more easily seen, without interpretive pre-emption by two state narratives that have in her view worked to confine its meaning and force. The first and more insistent has been that of official French political culture, which has represented the insurrection as a convulsive episode in the long march, since concluded, towards the Republic. The second, which has lost much of its authority since the collapse of the powers and the movement that

---

3   Ibid., p. 2.

sponsored it, is the narrative of 'state-communism', in which the Commune became 'the failed revolution of which [the Russian October] would be the corrective'.[4] Rejecting both narratives, Ross disclaims any intention of founding a third, and it is true that the network she traces, with its openness and unprogrammed transversals through spaces and times, does not much resemble the grand narratives of the Fifth Republic and the Soviet Union. What, then, is the specific character of this political imaginary and what is its force, as it 'enters . . . into the configurability of the present'?

1

The Commune was 'an audacious act of internationalism'—that above all, in one veteran's judgement.[5] The first city-wide institutional form of the revolution, the Central Committee of the Twenty Arrondissements, was the creation of the International Workingmen's Association, whose Paris membership at this time was reportedly 50,000. Foreigners were welcomed from the start, and supporters such as Dmitrieff were made citizens in recognition of their engagement. (The Versailles authorities were correspondingly obsessed with the involvement of foreigners in the Commune, circulating ridiculously inflated estimates of numbers laced with the usual xenophobic slurs.) However, Dmitrieff's new-found citizenship was Parisian, not French, and was awarded pending the day when 'the Universal Republic [would] make her a citizen of humanity'.[6] Ross herself chooses as the symbolic point of departure for the Commune a political meeting in the autumn of 1868, when, as one old revolutionary recorded, a certain maker of artificial flowers rose to speak, and, dispensing with the established etiquette of such gatherings, began not with the 'sacramental' *Mesdames et Messieurs* but with *Citoyennes et citoyens!* 'The room erupted in applause.' The sacrament was that of the nation, which the Commune's revolutionaries repudiated, wanting Paris to be, in Ross's

---

4   Ibid., p. 4.
5   Ibid., p. 11.
6   Ibid., p. 29.

words, 'not the capital of France but an autonomous collective in a universal federation of peoples'. This was not the false universalism of the French state, be it imperial or newly republican: anti-colonial and anti-chauvinist sentiment ran strongly in the city, and as one Communard put it, the Republic itself was merely 'the last form, and not the least malevolent', of authoritarian rule.[7] Casting off the illusions and trammels of the nation, the revolutionaries of the Universal Republic, or 'the workers republic', as the International also termed it, also set their faces against the state. For all the radicalism of particular social reforms—the invention of the crèche system, for instance, or the remaking of education—the truly momentous originality of the Commune lay, as Marx declared, in the very fact of its 'working existence', which constituted a blow against the state as such as a mode of social organization. The elected Commune was not a parliamentary body but an organ uniting legislative and executive powers; the standing army was abolished; permanent offices were recast to be occupied in principle by anyone, at a worker's salary and subject to recall; priests were dispatched to 'the recesses of private life'. In the 'simple fact' of itself, as Ross puts it, the Commune discovered the means of working-class self-emancipation, what Engels would call a state 'that is not, properly speaking, a state, but is "what exists in common"'.[8] Within its ranks, however, there were significant differences in understanding of the scope of political practice. Whereas the International's immediate response to the proclamation of a new republic had been to call for elections to a municipal government, months later the members of the Women's Union, 'the Commune's largest and most effective organization', 'showed no interest in parliamentary or rights-based demands', and were 'indifferent to the vote . . . Participation in public life . . . was for them in no way tied to the franchise'.[9]

Education was another matter, necessarily, and the Commune moved quickly to reshape its institutions and practices, with the International again taking a leading part. At this time, one-third of

---

7   Ibid., p. 38.
8   Ibid., p. 99n.
9   Ibid., pp. 27–8.

the city's children were educated in religious schools and the same proportion not at all. Henceforward, education was to be free, compulsory and secular, for girls as well as boys, and its ethos would be integralist or 'polytechnical', aiming at the 'harmonious development' of the person, developing individuals capable of skilled labour and an active cultural life. 'He who wields a tool should be able to write a book, write it with passion and talent', went one statement of the ideal—or at least 'take a break from his daily work through artistic, literary or scientific culture, without ceasing for all that to be a producer'.[10] Manual labour itself was to be valorized. One Jesuit institution was repurposed as a technical school for adolescent boys, while the École des Beaux Arts now housed equivalent provision for girls; teaching positions were open to any skilled worker aged forty or over. In the thinking of the Commune's boldest educational theorist, the poet, fabric designer and Fourierist Eugène Pottier, these initiatives embodied a radical and consequential egalitarianism and a deeply optimistic pedagogy whose first principle was 'everything is in everything': any knowledge offers a good place from which to commence new learning.

Art too was drawn into this process, with outcomes ranging in implication from the necessary but limited to the socially visionary. The painter Gustave Courbet, speaking from a position in the fine arts, urged complete independence for artists as a cultural estate, unconstrained by either censorship or subsidy. However, as Ross emphasizes, the Commune was strikingly rich in artists—alumni of the schools who had not made good but also practitioners of the decorative and other applied arts, fine woodworking and shoemaking very conspicuous among them—and here again old divisions were to be superseded. The Manifesto for an Artists' Federation, proposed in response to a call by Courbet—and drafted by Pottier—aimed to rally 'all artistic intelligences', and ten of the forty-seven representatives elected at a founding meeting were from the decorative disciplines. Most significantly, as Ross notes, the Federation made no attempt to specify the nature of art or to determine criteria for evaluating works

---

10   Ibid., pp. 42–3.

claiming that title: its purpose was to create conditions 'assuring the liberty of all'. Here too it was the 'simple fact' of itself, a collective gesture overturning the received social order of culture, that was important. The Manifesto had 'enormous' impact, according to one contemporary, not because it raised 'the artistic level' but because it 'spread art everywhere'. As Ross writes, its concluding statement envisaged 'transforming the aesthetic coordinates of the entire community' as one moment in the making of the Universal Republic. This gives something of the flavour of what came to be known as 'cherry time', after a popular song of the day, *Le temps des cerises*: or in the phrase that gives her book its title, 'the birth of communal luxury'.

2

Ross's accounts of the Commune's 'working existence', rendered with economy and ease and an engaging array of portraiture that can only be noted here, take up the first half of her book. In the second, her focus shifts to its afterlife in the revolutionary emigration—following, among others, Reclus and one of his most salient political interlocutors, Gustave Lefrançais—and the 'web' of associations that the memory and example of 1871 soon wove. An impassioned loyalty was just one of the ties that bound Kropotkin and Morris to the Commune, and Ross rightly dwells on this moving reflex of fellow-feeling and its inventive symbolism. (The Morris of *News from Nowhere* re-enacted the insurgents' levelling of the Victory Column in the place Vendôme in his decision to have Trafalgar Square reborn as an orchard.) But her main emphasis lies in the plane of historical vision: both thinkers rejected progressivist understandings of revolution that reduced it to a culmination of modern historical tendencies. Thus, Morris was critical of the 'unmixed modern', seeing in 'communitarian or tribal societies of the past'—above all medieval Iceland—'clues to the economic forms of a free life in the future'. Evolutionary biology rather than romantic art led Kropotkin along a convergent line of thought, persuading him of the adaptive value of cooperation in harsh, thinly populated spaces such as Siberia or the outlying Nordic territories and illuminating the social potential of Russia's ages-old system of communal agriculture, the *obshchina*. (Reclus shared Morris's fascination with Iceland, and was to recruit his fellow-scientist Kropotkin to write for his great *Nouvelle géographie universelle*.) Marx too can be claimed for this school of revolutionary 'anachronism': Ross sees in the writing of his last decade a significant re-evaluation of non-capitalist social forms. We should not be too afraid of the word 'archaic', he wrote to Vera Zasulich, explaining that nothing in *Capital* implied the necessary supersession of the *obshchina*, which might or might not survive as the social basis of a post-capitalist agriculture. Everything would depend on the historical circumstances. 'The new, for Kropotkin as for Morris, could only be modelled on anachronisms land-locked in the present', Ross writes. 'Being attentive to the energies of the out-moded was one way to think oneself into the future.'[11] 'Decentralizing the flow of history' is her bold metaphor for the kind of historical thinking practised by Morris or Reclus, and it is apt, inasmuch as 'centralism' is the recurring value in a pattern of negative association to which the Commune stands as the exemplary opposite.[12] It represents the dominance of the capital over the provinces, the city over the countryside, the metropoles over the colonized world, the imperatives of progress against the faltering stubbornness of 'outmoded' ways, the seemingly illimitable scale of the cities and factories draining the life from older, more modest kinds of workplace and settlement. Above all else, it represents the state itself, with its standing army, police and bureaucracy as the institutional antitheses of popular autonomy—and not only the Imperial regime and the bourgeois Republic now raised over the dead bodies of the Communards but any state, actual or envisaged. This, Ross maintains, was the sense of the only amendment that Marx thought it necessary to make for the new, 1872 edition of the *Communist Manifesto*, the categorical declaration from *The Civil War in France* that 'the working class cannot simply lay hold of the ready-made state machinery and wield

11   Ibid., p. 116.
12   Ibid., p. 74.

it for their own purpose'. In this, he indicated 'clearly the distance
that the Commune made him take toward his earlier thoughts about
state centralization'.[13]

Élisée Reclus was one of those to live that correction in their personal experience of the Commune. A 'socialist republican' at the
outbreak of the insurrection, he emerged an advocate of the world
federation of autonomous communes, a vision which, by 1880, had
acquired the name 'anarchist communism'. As a variety of anarchism, this differed from the 'collectivist' strain associated with
Proudhon in its demand for 'the complete extinction of exchange
value', an end to money and markets, and a disalienation of labour
of which the Commune had given a foretaste.[14] In the spectrum of
communism, it stood for an immediate and categorical liquidation
of the state as a social form, a point of principle shared by Kropotkin—
though not, for example, Morris, who, as George Bernard Shaw
recalled, 'would not countenance Anarchism on any terms'. Fifty
years on, and for much or all of the twentieth century such differences would be so many calls to schism, sometimes with deadly
outcomes; the fate of Barcelona's commune is an inescapable reference here. However, in the revolutionary culture of the 1870s and
after, Ross sees a non-purist model that is perhaps worth the effort of
emulation:

> The post-Commune period was, I think, like our own, not a period
> of great theoretical purity. And William Morris was not alone in
> thinking that an obsession with such purity frequently gets in the
> way of the task of making socialists.[15]

Passages like this remind us that for all its rich interest and value as a
work of historical retrieval and remembrance, *Communal Luxury* is
a book with designs on the future, even if Ross has a way of deflect-
ing close scrutiny in this respect. In it, or rather by virtue of it, for

---

13   Ibid., p. 78.
14   Ibid., p. 106.
15   Ibid., p. 108.

this is a self-aware work of construction, Reclus, Marx, Morris, Kropotkin and others such as Lefrançais come together as the constituents of an informal canon, diversely shaped and self-identified, politically, supporting a distinctive vision of revolutionary communism, a 'social transformation predicated on a large voluntary federation of free associations existing at the local level', a commune of communes.[16] Ross holds out the immensely appealing prospect of an integrally green communism in a society freed from capital, state and national passions, a general instance, perhaps, of her preferred intellectual orientation, which she presents as an undoctrinaire exchange between Marxism and anarchism. However, this takes us a long way from the Commune, as fact or vision, and the Marx of this dialogue is already something of an anarchist. Ross makes a good deal of his late reflections on the *obshchina*, and the change of perspective she sees in it. But his judgement there seems broadly consistent with his early scepticism about the prospects for successful 'local' communism, and he certainly did not accord any strategic weight to this communal form. Isolated and technically primitive, the *obshchina* might turn out to be a beneficiary of revolution, he believed, but would not be its agent. Its fate would be largely decided, one way or the other, by the great social forces concentrated in the cities. As for the Commune itself, the lesson confirmed in its short lifetime was both older and, crucially, more specific than Ross allows. It is the actually existing state that cannot 'simply' be taken over 'ready-made', not the state-form or centralism as such. Marx reported and endorsed the Commune's view that its own working constitution should be the model for all public authority countrywide; but he rejected as a deliberate misrepresentation the suggestion that the non-repressive functions of central government were all to disappear along with the army and officialdom—he was with Lefrançais in this—and as 'mistaken' the belief that the general spread of communal self-government would mean the end of the territorial nation. The revolutionary process that the workers of Paris had embarked upon was necessarily protracted and fallible, Marx insisted; 'they

---

16   Ibid., p. 111.

have no ideals to realize', only 'their own emancipation . . . to work out'. His writings on the Commune embody that belief, finding a register that was unavailable in principle to Reclus, for all his great personal distinction, as an absolutist of the Universal Republic. Here, contrary to an old stereotype, it is not Marx who seems the doctrinaire.

3

However, it may be that the point of this rather awkward association of Marx with anarchist communism lies in the more familiar association that is thereby weakened and made marginal. The name of Lenin occurs just three times in *Communal Luxury*, once as that of the man who is said to have danced in the snow outside the Winter Palace to celebrate the seventy-third day of Soviet power—the lifespan of the Commune plus one—and twice identifying an author with a ready eye for a borrowable book title, such as *What Is to Be Done?* (Chernyshevsky) or *The State and Revolution* (Arnould). There is no acknowledgement that this light-footed, light-fingered character might have shared in the political imaginary of the Commune in anything more than a petty, rivalrous spirit, with Petrograd as the corrective to Parisian failure.[17] Yet the memory of the Commune was at the heart of Lenin's political advocacy in the spring of 1917, after the fall of Tsardom, as the all-important revolutionary-democratic precedent to follow—in fact, a reality already coming into being in the Russian capital, where the army and police no longer held sway over the people. At the same time, the agrarian politics of the revolution pass without recall, leaving the impression that between the debates over the *obshchina* and the investigations of Gramsci and Mariátegui four decades later, the record of Marx's posterity is a strategic drought.[18] As it was, the key texts of that time showed a striking attentiveness and flexibility in their assessment of changing political conditions in the countryside, subject to the principle that new

17   Ibid., p. 4.
18   Ibid., p. 85.

dispositions on the land, which would be nationalized, must be decided by the peasant soviets themselves. But these considerations and others like them involve seeing the second Commune as Ross insists on seeing the first, in its unfolding as a process and an idea with unspent claims on the future. It is only with a rigorous and reductive effort of hindsight, from a vantage-point well beyond 1989, that it can be set aside as a relic of the punctured triumphalism of 'state communism'.

'The Commune *state*' was Lenin's characteristic phrasing, for he had no doubt that the work of revolution involved more than dismantling the old agencies of class domination and recreating social relations on a new footing. In Paris, the hope of common luxury had been shadowed from earliest days by the threat of subversion and defeat. Spies and reactionary conspiracies were a problem from the beginning. There was an explosion of popular sentiment in the scores of newspaper titles that now appeared; but others sympathetic to the Versailles government, including *Le Figaro*, were ordered to close. Above all, there was the military outlook, which quickly darkened and then got far worse, the city's isolated and ill-coordinated defenders facing an army eight or nine times their number. All these called for exceptional measures in more or less painful tension—if not flat contradiction—with the norms of 'the democratic, social Commune', yet were demanded in the interests of collective self-preservation, as many came to agree, in the controversies that arose as Thiers's army drew nearer. And to that extent, the public authority would retain at least some of the characteristics of a state. Paris was reduced, after just ten weeks of freedom, in a government massacre that left some 25,000 men, women and children dead—a median estimate—and this before the onset of a merciless judicial repression that continued for years. The scale of official barbarism was overwhelming, so much so that the idea of it nearly drowns the point it nevertheless conveys. If we are drawn to the imaginary of the Commune, with its lyric air and unquenchable spirit, this is not least because, unsurprisingly, imagining was a large part of what it could actually do, in the time available to it. The wonder is that it achieved so much. Granted a longer term, it would have had to cope more systematically with the other side of the lengthy process it had embarked upon, imagining the exigencies of self-preservation in an implacable capitalist environment just as resourcefully as it had imagined the forms of freely associated life. The lessons were drawn just the same—and lessons is what they inescapably are, all of them, whether inspirational or cautionary, however they may be refigured—by Marx and Morris, and by Lenin too, as he worked for the birth of an unexpected second Commune state in another fallen empire, in 1917.

2015

Forever Orwell

Eric Blair began by taking the name of England's patron saint and ended up assuming his role. When it finally arrived, 1984 was the year of St George. This way of putting it risks understating the sheer scale of Orwell's celebrity, the worldwide currency and talismanic power of his name since his death in 1950. But it recalls attention to what many have said about him over the years, usually in sympathetic or admiring tones: that in him Englishness was not merely one provenance among others but a touchstone, a matter of moral constitution. Thus, Rob Colls's intellectual portrait *George Orwell: English Rebel* joins an already substantial body of commentary—his introduction lists some twenty predecessors, who themselves are only a subset of the much larger corpus of writing devoted to the man, the works and their afterlife.[1] Where he differs from these is in his particular interest in Englishness, in particular that of the working class, which has been his speciality as a historian over the past thirty-odd years. That too has been a busy field, and the result is a book of conspicuous learning, more than a quarter of its length given over to the scholarly apparatus. It is also, within its simple chronological scheme, a digressive book, here taking off to explore some aspect of a general situation, there pausing over some circumstance or consideration, as if wanting to find room for everything. In this, Colls is

---

1   Rob Colls, *George Orwell: English Rebel*, Oxford 2013.

faithful to his general understanding of Englishness as a historical
formation: the title of his principal work on the topic, a loose-limbed
discussion ranging from the Middle Ages to the present, is an
awkward, telling epitome of his position. *Identity of England* (2002)
finds its form by negation of the more obvious and fluent phrasings
to hand in the book itself. (Omit the essentializing or stipulative
definite article while avoiding an easy, evasive plural or the deceptive
calm of *English Identity*: national character is a singular not a plural,
yet indeterminate and changeful.) Colls's understanding of Orwell is
of a piece with this. 'I am not saying that Englishness is the key to
Orwell . . . There is no "key" to Orwell', he writes in his introduction,
'any more than he is a "box" to open.'[2] And then, in a parting sentence
whose placing and manner are worth noting for later consideration:
'His Englishness, though, is worth following through.'

This is the optic through which Colls reviews the familiar course
of Orwell's life: private schooling and service in the Imperial Indian
Police (1911–28); the rejection of Empire and return to England with
the aim of becoming a writer; living hand to mouth in Paris, hop-
picking and tramping in the South of England, a self-styled Tory
anarchist discovers the poor (1928–31); the early novels and the decisive encounter with the North of England working class (1932–36); a
socialist fighting in Spain, fighting at home, against fascism,
Stalinism and war (1937–39); the herald of revolutionary patriotism
(1940–43); the fabulist of political betrayal (1943–50). The turning-
point in the sequence comes in 1936, and its significance, as Colls
reads it, is that during his two months of fieldwork for the publishing
commission that became *The Road to Wigan Pier*, Orwell 'for the
first time in his life found an England he could believe in', a popular,
proletarian Englishness that would serve him as a political stimulus
and test from then onwards, inspiring his wartime advocacy of revolutionary patriotism.

The test applied in two ways. It served to justify Orwell's unrelenting campaign against the left intelligentsia, whom he portrayed as a
menagerie of grotesques, rootless eccentrics with a fatal weakness for

---

2   Ibid., p. 7.

abstraction and hard-wired doctrine, gullible in the face of Soviet boosterism and nihilistic in their attitude towards English institutions. Colls relays these themes in a kindred spirit, as contemptuous as Orwell if not so inventively abusive in his treatment of abstractions, systems, 'set-squares and equations', dogmas asserted in disregard of personal experience and what is 'reasonably assumed to be the case'—everything that is suggested to him by the word 'ideology'. However, he goes further and applies the test to Orwell himself. The 'ludicrous' anti-intellectualism, as he sees it, was at least in part a projection of the feelings of deracination that Orwell recognized and feared in himself. The Gordon Comstock figure in *Keep the Aspidistra Flying*, from 1935, the year before the journey north, can be read as George Orwell's mocking appraisal of Eric Blair the writer. The powerful appeal of the Englishness that he found in working-class Lancashire and Yorkshire lay in its promise of belonging. But this Englishness was itself sustained and made articulate by the organizational form and culture of the labour movement, its unions and their party—which, until late in the 1930s, seemed not to feature in Orwell's political perception and reasoning.

Colls's political meridian is 1945. He concedes the ineffectuality of Labour in the later 1920s and 1930s, dismisses its purely gestural policy towards the Spanish war, and has bitter words to say about the party of recent times, but the upward path from the promulgation of the Immediate Programme in 1937, across the popular radicalization of wartime to the landslide victory in the first summer of the European peace, is in his eyes numinous. Orwell's outlook was quite different. Colls chooses to make nothing of it, but *The Road to Wigan Pier* concludes with a call for the formation of a popular socialist movement based on an expanded conception of the working class (including non-manual occupations) and ready to resort to 'revolutionary' violence in the struggle against fascism, which Orwell saw as an inherent potential of industrial capitalism. His leading slogan, *Justice and Liberty!*, echoed, perhaps not accidentally, the name of the Italian resistance organization led by Carlo Rosselli, the theorist of 'liberal socialism' and soon a volunteer in the anarchist militias in Spain. It was an eclectic scheme, coming after Orwell's philippic

against left intellectuals and owing much to his experience of the
marxisant circles of the Independent Labour Party, in which he had
moved for several years. Certainly there were better-judged assess-
ments of impending probabilities. But it stands as a vivid indication
of Orwell's imaginative distance from the official thought-world of
the Labour Party.

1

Colls is correspondingly qualified in his attitude towards Orwell's
Spanish period, both the fighting itself and the polemical episode
that followed back in London, including *Homage to Catalonia*. He
hates Stalin's Comintern quite as much as Orwell came to hate it, but
has no positive political sympathy with the revolutionary militiamen
of the POUM. He applauds the achievements of Rojo's centralized
army and, resisting Orwell's claim that the Republic was turning
'fascist' in its slanderous, brutal assault on the revolutionary left,
defends the Negrin government for its realism and competence in
desperate circumstances. Orwell eventually reconsidered the thesis
that defence of the Spanish revolution was a condition of winning the
war, but only after a period of years during which, in starkest contrast, he held on to it as a truth of wider application—in Colls's
words, seeing 'Spanish lessons as English lessons'.[3] That is to say,
rather, that errors abroad gave rise to errors at home, as Orwell the
anti-fascist persisted in his belief that the European war now
threatening, like the one twenty years past, would be a strictly inter-
imperialist conflict, which the left should oppose on principle.

War came; Orwell resigned from the ILP and volunteered for
active service, eventually finding roles in the Home Guard and the
BBC Empire Service India Section. Now the incompatible urges of
the past two years were resolved, Colls tells us; 'Orwell's great recon-
ciliation with England, his England', begun in Wigan in 1936, would
soon be complete. The defining work of this period was *The Lion and
the Unicorn: Socialism and the English Genius*, which reinvented the

---

3 Ibid., pp. 74–9, 106.

strategy of the POUM on the terrain of the national war effort, arguing that only a socialist revolution could make good the failings of capitalism and Britain's political elite, creating the psychological and material conditions of success in the struggle against fascism. The great difference in this case was the centrality of the idea and imagery of nationality. The English were a family, but one 'with the wrong members in control', Orwell wrote. The revolution would be 'fundamental', pressing far beyond what he called the 'timid reformism' of the Labour Party, but not less English in its means and outcomes because of that. For England—it is always England, not Britain—is, in Orwell's own words, 'an everlasting animal stretching into the future and the past, and like all living things, having the power to change out of recognition and yet remain the same'. Colls expresses his warm admiration for Orwell's statement of the national theme but is quick to lodge a claim on behalf of the Westminster parliament for its role in forwarding the revolutionary programme, and likewise to claim him as a supporter of the Atlee government for the rest of his life.

The culminating moment was short-lived. By the later 1940s, and arguably sooner, Orwell's English preoccupations had been overlain by international politics, above all the geopolitics of the new Cold War. In this rather more than in other respects, Orwell was indeed at one with the Labour government, seconding Bevin's foreign policy and even offering the Foreign Office Information Research Bureau the benefit of his political assessment of fellow writers. Anti-Communism had been a constant in Orwell's political thinking since 1935 (the dating is his own) and now it was assuming a new and inescapable objective significance. This, whatever Orwell may have intended and however dismaying to him the upshot, was the conjuncture into which *Animal Farm* (1945) and *Nineteen Eighty-Four* (1949) were released. The earlier of the two novels, in Colls's reading, offers a radically pessimistic assessment of both the traditional working class and the new middle class, the teachers, technicians, journalists and other non-manual workers who had long been central to Orwell's vision of a popular socialist bloc. His beast fable does not say why the animals allow themselves to be robbed of their gains or why the pigs act as they do. It all unfolds as if to show that nature will out. This satire on the Russian revolution, as Orwell described it in one of his several statements of purpose, is also, in Colls's estimate, 'against revolutions in general'. *Nineteen Eighty-Four* projects the outcome of one revolution in particular, it might be said: the one announced in *The Lion and the Unicorn*. The novel 'envisages the end of England', the name, the history, the identity and the language. What survives of Englishness is to be found among the proles, from whom, however, the Party has now abstracted itself entirely, creating a parallel reality. The O'Brien figure is intellectuality taken to its anti-English extreme of 'idealist solipsistic nonsense'. Colls does not quite say as much, but the inference to be drawn is that in the end the fundamental opposition in Orwell's political imagination was England versus Communism. Speculating on the futures that the novelist of *Nineteen Eighty-Four* did not live to define for himself, he writes: 'the signs are he would have been a Cold Warrior'. By 1949, the signs were he already was.

3

Orwell is a difficult critical study. The familiar problems of accuracy and balance are rendered acute in his case in part because of his own debatable critical habits, including a deep contrarian reflex that should not be idealized, and his many changes of mind; in equal part because of the historic gravity of the situations in which he found himself at decisive turns in his life, and the fateful character of the causes he upheld or resisted. Viewed in a certain light, 'George Orwell' has long been a bundle of conventional topics, a repertory of period pieces awaiting their next performance. Robert Colls acknowledges such difficulties and makes them a principle of his historical procedure. 'Almost all general statements about who or what [Orwell] was can be matched by equal and opposite statements', he writes. 'For all his gifts of clarity and precision, and for all his seriousness, [he] is difficult to pin down—a writer who held many points of view, some twice over.' The critical imperative, then, is not to reduce or totalize but to assume Orwell whole, in all his self-contradictoriness, and to take him 'a step at a time'. Thus, Colls reviews all that Orwell, 'a literature and liberty man at heart', had in common with the traditions of liberalism while being 'not really a liberal'.[4] He considers the tastes and reflexes of the young man who introduced himself to the *Adelphi* magazine as a 'Tory anarchist' and who, in the opinion of many of his friends and acquaintances, never wholly became anything else. He traces the paradoxes of the intellectual who wrote phobically about the intelligentsia, the self-exiled son of the upper middle class who 'never really left Eton', the 'godless Protestant' who pondered the significance of a general loss of belief in personal immortality, and, above all, the socialist who discharged so much of his polemical fire against the left. Orwell was all of these things, Colls insists. There is no consistent politics to be found in his work, only one of 'time and place and conviction'.

Colls's discussion teems with judgements, his own and Orwell's, and is certainly not hospitable to familiar resolutions of the tensions it restages. Indeed, his procedure can make for difficulty in reading (and paraphrasing). A book that moves one step at a time, in a kind of parataxis, risks losing in overall proportioning what it gains in local life, and there are times in *George Orwell: English Rebel* when it seems that its claims are short-life, as context-bound as their author takes Orwell's politics to be. The results of the discussion are uneven. Colls is hugely knowledgeable and informative about Orwell's writing, but at critical points open to challenge in his reports of it. ('Where would I be without my prejudices?' he asks, in a self-indulgent moment, and the unsought answer is, 'Somewhere else.') His undoubted pleasure in his own eloquence leads too often to performances in which clarity and balance of judgement, and even sense, play second fiddle to a showily balanced phrase. (One example among numerous: 'The old left could never forgive Orwell for being so wrong, and the new left could never forgive him for being so right.') The standard he urges in reading Orwell is suspended when he turns to Marxist theory, in passages that are simply unworthy of his book at its best. (Similarly, it is unnerving to learn that the

---

4   Ibid., pp. 181, 185.

revolutionary Victor Serge was a 'dissident conservative', that the Italian Ignazio Silone was East European, and that Jurgen Habermas [b. 1929] was a prodigious mentor to the 'new Marxist sociology of the 1930s'.) Of greater significance for the book as a whole, however, is that Colls's preferred procedure is a substantive argument in itself, one whose purpose is not merely to acknowledge Orwell's self-contradictoriness but to valorize it. The procedure is the thesis, which in its turn calls forth a serviceable rhetoric. The closing sentence of the Introduction illustrates it, re-presenting the major claim of the book as a tentative, qualifying afterthought: again, 'his Englishness, though, is worth following through'. The opening sentences offer a second example: 'George Orwell was what they used to call a "Socialist". He shared also some of the attitudes to life that used to be called "Tory".' 'They' still do and still are, in truth, but in this droll overture a habit of naming and classifying is momentarily interrupted, as if challenged, and that is the point. Here is a rhetoric whose key purpose is to disarm.

Colls's manner may be thought of as cautionary, hesitant, dubitative, and certainly preferable to the 'ideological' style he so liberally castigates.[5] 'On the other hand' is the wry subtitle that opens his final chapter. Alternatively, it may be thought of as methodically elusive, a work of purposeful evasion. Colls is protective of Orwell, in a specialized sense. He is quite free in his own criticisms of his subject, and not censorious, even though irritable and perfunctory in his concessions when faced with the strictures of others, notably feminists. But what he resists, as a matter of non-negotiable priority, is any attempt at classification, any critical gesture that would reach for conclusion, draw a line or indicate an order, and in so doing limit the play of 'on the other hand'. Colls's Orwell cannot 'really' be any of the political or cultural beings he was or appeared to be. He must retain his indefinite variousness, or, as we might say, change while staying the same, rather like the everlasting animal in *The Lion and the Unicorn*. This Orwell is not merely English: he is Englishness itself.

---

5   Ibid., pp. 91f.

4

This Orwell had come to 'listen to England', to 'believe in the people', the working class, and Colls takes pains to moderate such differences of implication as there might have been between the character of this belief and that represented in the government of 1945. He makes little of Orwell's political disagreements and disappointments, preferring to emphasize his continuing critical support for the Labour government (a position he would have shared with most of the Marxist left); and manages to obscure the qualitative difference between his 1941 programme of action, which urged a general nationalization of capitalist property and a radical reduction in income differentials, with the limited measures of the Atlee years. The socialist who emerges from this controlled representation was, in Colls's echoing phrase, 'a Labour man', understanding at home and primed and vigilant abroad, in the face of an imagined Communist menace.

Indeed, this would have been a banal enough outcome, had it not been for the pathos of a slow, early death and the oracular status that came with the publication of *Nineteen Eighty-Four*. For it is easy to forget just how far Orwell was typical of English literary intellectuals in his time. Although never the stereotypical 1920s aesthete, his fervent, self-punishing admiration for James Joyce's *Ulysses* reveals someone keenly aware of the unmined potentials of literary form. His earliest political passion was his revulsion from Empire, in which he followed a path opened up by Leonard Woolf and E. M. Forster, whose novel *A Passage to India* appeared during his time in Burma. Social questions moved to the centre of his concerns as the capitalist economies slumped, inspiring the missions of discovery that informed *Down and Out in Paris and London* ('district-visiting' was Q. D. Leavis's scornful name for the genre). The legendary preoccupations of the literary 1930s, associated with the names of W. H. Auden and Stephen Spender, among many others less well known, were poverty, unemployment, the threat of fascism and another European war, all making for a more or less pronounced turn leftwards and a spirit of resistance captured in the rally to the defence of republican Spain.

With the eventual outbreak of war and the military crisis of 1940 there began the work, variously intended, variously pursued, to create a new, social-patriotic consensus in support of what was hailed as a 'People's War' for a reconstructed Britain—an effort in which the writers now assembled in the BBC's talks department assumed the representative role once assigned to the Thirties Poets. The Second World War reached an end: or rather, 'ground to a halt right in the middle of Europe', Colls tells us, with 'no clear winner': an extraordinary judgement on a conflict in which the Axis had suffered 'clear' defeat, but, in its way, a verbal replay of what actually occurred as the clear winners turned to confront their Soviet allies, whose survival, Colls seems to say, was not among the desiderata of the victorious imperialist powers. Now began the struggle against 'totalitarian' Communism, and an intellectual mobilization without precedent, continuing over decades, as the CIA bankrolled so-called Non-Communist Lefts in the international Congress for Cultural Freedom and in journals such as the London-based *Encounter*. The leading intellectual patsy in that particular case, it would one day be revealed, was the emblematic poet of the Communist 1930s, Stephen Spender. But the hero of the hour was the author of *Nineteen Eighty-Four*, who, indeed, had written the role years before, in his essay on Dickens:

> To this day, to the average Englishman, the French Revolution means no more than a pyramid of severed heads. It is a strange thing that Dickens, much more in sympathy with the ideas of the Revolution than most Englishmen of his time, should have played a part in creating this impression.[6]

---

6   George Orwell, 'Charles Dickens', *Collected Essays*, London 1961, p. 43.

5

Seen in the successive general politico-intellectual conjunctures of his career as a writer, framed in long or medium shot, Orwell was not quite the lonely voice of legend; close-ups can mislead. But although he was in his way typical, that way itself was not usual. His distinction was his extremism. Schooled for loyal public service, he signed up to police the farthest outposts of the Indian Empire. Back in England and concerned now to learn more about the social majority from whom he had been quarantined as a child, he 'went native in his own country' (in V. S. Pritchett's famous words), insisting on primary contact with the poorest and least secure, the invisible and the discarded. To him, opposition to fascism, which he shared with many thousands, intellectuals or not, meant leaving for Spain within days of finishing *Wigan Pier*, not to report but to fight and kill political enemies. Reflecting on the needs and potentials of a popular war against Hitler, he radicalized the canons of the Communist-inspired Popular Fronts to urge a programme fusing patriotic unity with the overthrow of a bankrupt ruling class and the system of property it defended. He had good reason to be impatient of official Marxism (over and above his romantic recoil from all abstraction except his own) and to reject the politics and culture of the Russian party dictatorship and its regimented International. He would come to have his personal reasons to loathe and fear Stalin's enforcers. But his last novel exceeded any of these in its vision of a bureaucratic-collectivist caste psychotically self-propelled towards the perfection of its own rule, in which, in Colls's words, 'the object of power is power and the object of murder is murder'.

This extremism had its accompanying thematic constants. One of these, perhaps surprising in someone capable of impulsive activism, was an imaginative conviction of probable failure. Orwell could affirm the possibility of liberating transformation in his recollections of revolutionary Barcelona or his prospectus for a socialist England, but every one of his six novels narrates the failure of an attempt at fulfilment or release, be it private or public, individual or collective,

temporary or long-term. Another, associated feature of the writing is
a vein of sadomasochism. This is a delicate topic in Orwellian circles,
and Colls's concessions in the matter are ambivalent. When he writes
in a testy aside that his subject did not need Isaac Deutscher to tell
him how to be 'a Trotskyite', he is presumably referring to an essay
on *Nineteen Eighty-Four*, dating from 1954, in which the Polish
Marxist, a one-time colleague at the *Observer* newspaper, in fact said
relatively little about Trotsky but rather more about Orwell's 'mysti-
cism of cruelty', the great abstraction of 'power-hunger' that served
him as a pass-key to modern history.[7] 'If you want a picture of the
future,' Orwell wrote, 'imagine a boot stamping on a human face—
for ever.' This cannot be written off as a statement internal to the
invented world of Ingsoc. It had first been drafted a decade earlier, in
the last of the novels of the 1930s, *Coming Up for Air*. The protagonist, another George, has been listening to a political talk:

> I saw the vision that he was seeing . . . What he's *saying* is merely
> that Hitler's after us and we must all get together and have a good
> hate . . . But what he's *seeing* is something quite different. It's a
> picture of himself smashing people's faces in with a spanner.
> Fascist faces, of course. I *know* that's what he was seeing. It was
> what I saw myself for the second or two I was inside him. Smash!
> Right in the middle! The bones cave in like an eggshell and what
> was a face a minute ago is just a great big blob of strawberry jam.
> Smash! There goes another!

The event is not a Hateweek rally: it is a discussion of anti-fascism at
a local meeting of the Left Book Club. The irruption of this fantasy of
extreme violence is gratuitous and surely symptomatic, suggesting a
compulsion that was partly formative of Orwell's late political vision,
with its radical abstraction of power from property relations.

The conviction of probable defeat was another shaping presence,
in this case taking the form of the nearing extinction of Englishness,

---

7 Isaac Deutscher, *Marxism, Wars and Revolutions*, London 1984,
pp. 60–71.

which had long—or perhaps always?—been Orwell's reserve currency of moral evaluation. Colls is right to give the question of national identity a crucial role in Orwell's constitution and it is precisely for that reason that the critical hesitation seems called for. Can it be that 'in the beginning Orwell did not have much of an Englishness to believe in'? It may be, on the contrary, that he had too much. The young Blair was a child of colonialism on both sides, the family including a public administrator, a timber merchant and a clergyman in India, and a Caribbean planter who married into the English aristocracy. He was himself born in Bengal. At the age of eight he passed into the privileged English network of preparatory and public schools, where the regime included military training, and remained in it until he went to Burma, another Blair in the service of the Raj. This was indeed an upper-middle-class formation, involving strict forms of social segregation. But in colonial conditions its binding term, its master-signifier, would have been national: British, or more likely, invoking the ideal country that breathes life into the practical machinery of Britain, 'English'. That single word would say it all. However, the corollary was that once the colonial class relationship was rejected as unjust, the identification would be rendered incoherent. Englishness would be reduced to a meaning without a referent. Resigning while on leave at his parents' home, Blair would no longer be the Englishman he had been trained to be, but knew no other way of being what he could only be: that is, English. This was the crisis that he began to work through, with results that came some years before Wigan. 'A tramp is only an Englishman out of work,' he declared in *Down and Out in Paris and London*, signalling that the privilege of normativity had been extended, if not wholly transferred, to the popular classes. With that shift, which was confirmed in the years following, the national identification regained its old fullness of social implication; Englishness was reconfirmed as the test of public virtue.

6

This condensation of values was Orwell's personal utopia, which he defended with a passionate single-mindedness in which he never recognized the fanaticism he was so quick to denounce in fellow socialists. His hyperbolic Englishness inspired his characteristically wrong-headed, simplistic excursions on behalf of 'plain' language, licensed an uncritical attachment to the good sense of the nation and a phobic anti-intellectualism to match. It was also the small miracle that founded his post-mortem cult, a community of observance embracing every intensity of adherence from missionary ardour to conventional good form, and a spectrum of political allegiance extending from right to far left. Colls brings his book to a close with a brief survey of some of this, rehearsing the litany of Orwell's attributes and the variety of his incarnations—'a Society, a Trust, a Fund, and a Memorial Prize . . . a National Treasure' and (nearly) a statue.[8] The manner is ironic, sometimes playful, in the way readers will have come to expect after three-hundred-plus pages, with a dusting of nostalgia for an England and a social democracy now past. But irony is all it is, and the memories are vicarious: Colls was born in 1949. This is Orwell for postmoderns, a particular mode of adherence to the cult.

Deep Labour, as it might be styled, has a hold on Colls's imagination as a phase in the political history of the working class and more fundamentally as the embodiment, in institutions and strategic bent, of a lasting disposition towards what is concrete, familiar, tested and shared, and a corresponding distrust of abstraction and system. That historical formation, based on the northern industrial working class into which he was born, is past tense—though not the commitment to 'local knowledge', the habitus that, true to rhetorical form, he would probably decline to call 'the English genius'. But what vectors might now be available to it, for a politics of the aftermath? The indications are ambiguous or worse. If Colls's reflections have their

8   Colls, *George Orwell*, p. 235.

beginning on the ground of the (non-Marxist) left, it is not at all clear that they will reach conclusion in the same political quarter. His brief survey of Orwell's successors closes on a tableau with two figures. One is Christopher Hitchens, who played the part of 'a second Orwell' more fully than he could have foreseen, ending his days estranged from the left. The other, 'today the major exponent of prime Orwell political writing', in Colls's judgement, is a fellow Tynesider of working-class origin, his schoolmate John Gray. A philosopher of the right committed to ideas of local knowledge, a liberal critic of liberal enlightenment, a canary in the cage of British political culture, deserting Labour for the Conservatives in the 1970s, then returning in the 1990s, it is Gray whom Colls, himself to the last, 'refrains' from nominating as 'an Orwell for our times', another avatar of what changes but always stays the same.

2014

Good Sense and Sensibility

'By the time Margaret Thatcher became Prime Minister,' Ferdinand Mount has reported, he 'had long ago abandoned any thought of a political career and had happily settled for a life of writing anything that came to hand or mind'.[1] *English Voices* is the book of that prospectus: only one among the score and more he has published, including novels and works of history and political advocacy too— for as it turned out, politics had not altogether done with him—but the one that answers most readily to this light sketch of a career in the world of letters.[2] Ranging across thirty years from 1985, it gathers up some fifty-three substantial book reviews, half of them from the *Spectator*, where Mount has written since the 1970s, most of the rest coming from the *Times Literary Supplement,* which he edited for much of the '80s and early '90s, and the *London Review of Books,* which bulks larger in the more recent work. A compilation on this scale does not lend itself to conventional synopsis—the number of books discussed is greater still, totalling more than sixty. The title and subtitle of the volume are designed more to accommodate its diverse materials than to define them or to indicate binding themes.

---

1 Ferdinand Mount, *Cold Cream: My Early Life and Other Mistakes*, London 2008.
2 Ferdinand Mount, *English Voices: Lives, Landscapes, Laments*, London 2016.

An introductory discussion of Englishness stresses the mongrel historical constitution of its people, taking a cue from Defoe's well-known satire—and motivating the indefinite plural 'voices'. But the appeals to shared legacies of common law, and a language both rich and loose-limbed—with echoes of Tennyson and Orwell respectively—have no follow-through in the preambles that subdivide the contents, or in the essays themselves. However, there are other ways of characterizing it.

Life-writing is by far predominant here: letters, biography and autobiography, memoirs and diaries, with a little history and some studies in architecture and landscape. The lives themselves are mainly political and literary, with extensions into ecclesiastic affairs, the architecture of villages and suburbs, and some tennis; nineteenth- or more often twentieth-century in time, with some survivals into the twenty-first, they include parliamentarians from Robert Peel to Roy Jenkins and writers from Coleridge to Kingsley Amis. (Shakespeare and Pepys are the two exceptions in this scheme.) All are English by virtue of birth or residence or adoptive belonging, though Scottish connections are not rare (William Ewart Gladstone, for example, and the novelist Muriel Spark); the gathering also includes two ex-colonials, one from the old dominions (Germaine Greer), the other from the Caribbean (V. S. Naipaul), and there is one Jewish intellectual refugee, now naturalized, from Hitler's Vienna (Elias Canetti). It is not difficult, then, to nod at the publisher's suggestion that the book is 'like a national portrait gallery of the English mind'. The temporal construction of the volume is more interesting than the simple chronological index '1985–2015' suggests. Nearly two-thirds of the essays come from the later half of that time span, most of those from the last ten years; the '90s, by contrast, have only three to show. In this sense, *English Voices* is a more recent body of writing than its self-presentation allows. However, a comparative chronology of its subjects looks quite different. Of the eleven now collocated as 'voices of our time', fewer than half are young enough to be classified as contemporaries of Mount's (*b.* 1939), and only one in the entire book is younger than him—though, nearing seventy, Peter Ackroyd is hardly a newcomer. The disjunction internal to 'our time' pitches the book as a whole towards retrospect.

Mount's retrospects can be simple, whether he is discussing Gladstone, whom he regards as a living presence, or A. J. Balfour, whom he dismisses in a withering recollection of *Brideshead Revisited*: 'In the end, I am afraid, the charm is all that remains.' Sensible of decline all around, he is nevertheless resistant to the evasions of conventional nostalgia, as he shows in his appreciation of Ronald Blythe, the author of *Akenfield*, while not letting go of the values it promotes. But at times his approach to the past is less a backward look than a form of time travel. The discussion of Blythe closes in that mode, which he amplifies in concluding a visit to the ancient forest of Hatfield in Essex:

> Wandering back to the car in the twilight through a grove of hornbeam pollards (to the twentieth-century forester as strange a sight as date palms), I caught sight of the ice-blue lights of Stansted airport only half a mile away and for the first time remembered exactly where I was. No municipal park of cherry and lime could confer such solitude.[3]

Then there is this arresting moment, coming at the end of a passage in which Cardinal Basil Hume has been commended for having ended a four-hundred-year cultural estrangement between Englishness and Roman Catholicism:

> [Hume] was the witness ... to a possibility of life that seemed no longer available, and his voice was like the whistle of a train that stopped running years ago but which you can sometimes hear at night on the far side of the valley.[4]

This is not a retrospect or even time-travelling; it is a haunting. 'Real ghosts' are not obliging, Mount declares, confronting the English

3   Mount, *English Voices*, p. 224.
4   Ibid., p. 170.

writer M. R. James with the example of the American namesake who wrote *The Turn of the Screw*: 'They do not go away when they are told to.' He is talking about disruptive revenants, but his implication is general. 'For me, these bones live', he writes, referring to the manifold material traces of human activity in old landscapes, in a preamble with the title 'In Search of England'.[5] The past is everywhere, even if often only in the form of its pastness, as in a haunting.

Indeed, such time bends can be commonplace, as any reader of Mount's *Cold Cream* (2008) will be aware, and indisputably corporeal. What emerges from this memoir of an upbringing in 'Hobohemia', a 'raffish sub-division' of the English upper class, is a demonstration of the enabling power of privileged family networks and their institutional mediations—even where money is short and prudence is just more good advice for the incurably raffish. Born into junior branches of the Anglo-Irish aristocracy on one side (his mother, Julia, was a Pakenham) and the titled gentry of Berkshire on the other, Mount has been, by his own account, one of those beings to whom things just providentially happen, who are always 'bumping into' this or that significant person. The phenomenon sets in early— in the womb, we are told, in a humorous aside that is no more than the plain social truth—and becomes routine. On holiday in Florence, he is received by Harold Acton, a friend of Uncle Tom (sixth Earl of Longford). Uncle Tony, married to another of the Pakenham girls, is better known to the world as the author of *A Dance to the Music of Time*, Anthony Powell. On the other side of the family, young David, son of cousin Mary (now Cameron), has the 'cheek' to take the leadership of the Conservative Party. One lasting semi-familial tie is that with Isaiah ('Shaya') Berlin, who has been sweet on Julia since Oxford. Other recreational encounters include, in no necessary order, Donald Maclean, George Orwell, Oswald Mosley, Siegfried Sassoon (a neighbour) and 'the occasional Mitford'. An Eton schoolfriend brings him home to parents who turn out to be Celia Johnson (she of the deathless *Brief Encounter*) and her husband, Peter Fleming, 'explorer' and brother of Ian. Back at college he is taught

---

5 Ibid., p. 210.

German by the future John le Carré. As with individuals, so with institutions. Mount's temporally mobile first-person narration, with its 'self-indulgent' selectivity, has the effect of backgrounding or even seemingly undoing ordinary causal sequences, so that he appears to find himself at Eton without ever having applied, and then at Oxford (Christ Church), again without the usual preliminaries. Illustrating the self-deprecating habit of the memoir, he notes this narrative roving as a sign of deficient 'personal growth'. But we might also see in it a rhetoric of the always-already, the defining condition of hereditary entitlement, here signifying the redundancy of focused effort.

The subject that speaks in *English Voices* is recognizably the older self of Ferdy Mount in *Cold Cream*, at ease and engaged across a wide range of matters, convivially learned, with a sharp eye and an attentive ear and a particular knack for correcting the blunders of writers less inward than he is with the usages of the titled classes. The novelist is never very far away. Mount is droll, affectionate at times, with a mild suggestion of decadence—the word *delicious* has an improbably wide range of attachments in these pages, most of them not normally edible. 'Sheer delight' was the response of the *Times Literary Supplement,* pursuing the metaphor of consumption; 'lovely', said the London *Evening Standard*. Yet it cannot be a great surprise to find him, in the early '60s, working in the Conservative Research Department, on the way, he hoped, to a parliamentary seat, without any evident prior process of political acculturation; or to find him, twenty years later, in 10 Downing Street, where he had been invited— just like that—to head an independent policy unit for Margaret Thatcher. True to form, it seems, he had been always already a Tory, and by 1979, after an instructive stay in the United States, he was done with 'convictionless, wind-blown politicians'. Writing in the *Spectator* in the days after Thatcher's electoral 'triumph', he hailed her 'individualist and populist Toryism' and concluded: 'A cautious half-glass of good ordinary claret may safely be raised to the future.'[6]

Mount's spell in Downing Street, his 'holiday from irony' as he later called it, lasted less than two years, and *English Voices* belongs

---

6   Ferdinand Mount, 'Mrs Thatcher's Triumph', *Spectator*, 12 May 1979.

entirely to the decades since. These essays are not the work of a stock
party doctrinaire. Personalities (always) and policies (sometimes)
take precedence over ideas. Nearly all Mount's titles obey a simple
formula: a personal name, then a thematic phrase ('John Osborne:
Anger Management?'). The only 'ism' discussed in its own right is
that of John Wesley's followers ('The Rise and Fall and Rise of
Methodism')—whose 'cheerful activism' forms a salutary popular
alternative to Canetti's monstrous 'crowds', themselves phobic pro-
jections of an intellectual narcissist. There are available reasons for
this emphasis, both occasional and philosophical. Biography is the
matter of most of these essays, which are weekend book reviews, and
it follows as if naturally that the 'quiddities' of individual lives rather
than transferrable abstractions will have first consideration. For
Mount, besides, the beginning of political wisdom is Berlin's idea
that 'diverse and incommensurable goals are endemic to the human
condition', from which it follows that no theory can be both coherent
and comprehensive. So, away with anything that smacks of 'unad-
justed dogma'. But such reasoning sits too easily in the cultural
landscape from which, arguably, it takes its justification—its obvious
'good sense', as they say—in the first place. The ease of discursive
passage from entertainment to contestation and back, that social-
stylistic fluency sometimes called 'civilized', is itself a political
resource very unequally distributed. A near-monopoly of the dominant classes and their specialized elites, it is a kind of 'exnomination'
(Barthes), or a politics of no politics.[7]

This is not quite Mount's way, in spite of contrary appearances. It
is not that he lacks the inclination to negative capability, to borrow a
phrase from a favourite poet, Keats. Writing about religion, he is by
turns 'intemperately Protestant', appreciative of the enlivening power
of Methodism, reverent in his tribute to Basil Hume, while deliberately emphasizing that one of the shared qualities of his 'old
masters'—Shakespeare, Coleridge, Keats, Dickens and Hardy—is
their distance from Christian belief. (He will add, on another occasion, that those who dwell on religion as a matter of 'belief' are

7   Roland Barthes, *Mythologies*, London 1993, p. 138.

anyway missing the point: you don't question tennis at the moment
of service, he points out, obscuring what had seemed a simple enough
proposition.) In literary matters, his admiration for the Virginia
Woolf of the feminist essays is unforced, yet manages to be both fresh
and crusty in its conclusion, remembering 'a woman brimming with
wit, malice, common sense, imagination and caprice rather than . . . a
plaster saint for a godless age'.[8] But in the simpler case of W. G. Sebald,
'a master shrouded in mist', the crustiness becomes the inspiration of
a portrait that is too much the familiar metaphysical German as
looked upon by an empirical Englishman. And the thought, incited
by a multilingual version of *A Midsummer Night's Dream*, that 'those
who prefer to hear stuff in their own lingo' might be considered
'imperialist racist fascists' is an alert from the golf-club bar.

The great politico-ideological contests of the twentieth century
ranged Mount on the side of the bold Western David, of course. The
closing words of his appreciation of Hugh Trevor-Roper, from 2005,
recall a once-mighty ideological adversary:

> The causes for which he battled with such ferocious glee have
> come out on top, in the Cold War no less than in the English Civil
> War. In politics as in historiography, the Marxists and the marx-
> isants have been routed. It is easy to forget how their premises and
> arguments were once taken for granted and how quirky and
> perverse seemed those who spoke out against them.[9]

And indeed such moments are a reminder of the voices that go
unheard in Mount's whispering gallery. With just a few idiosyncratic
exceptions (Greer, Alan Bennett, Le Carré, Arthur Ransome, author
of the children's classic *Swallows and Amazons*, and the philo-Soviet
ecclesiastic Hewlett Johnson, Dean of Canterbury), here is a spectrum without a Left. Of course, what is not published cannot be
reviewed. But even a very short list of eligible-but-absent voices—
salient authors or subjects of the kinds of book Mount chooses to

8   Mount, *English Voices*, p. 113.
9   Ibid., p. 38.

write about—is telling for what it says about the national imaginary as mediated by him: Richard Hoggart, Jack Jones, Eric Hobsbawm, C. L. R. James, Dorothy Thompson, Angela Carter, Tony Benn. Mount's local party loyalties are more ambiguously framed. No great admirer of politicians in general, Conservatives included, he is damning in his judgements of Harold Macmillan, whose premiership he thinks was an anachronism and a historic mistake, and Edward Heath, the technocrat; the mock-heroic Lord Hailsham he dismisses as an exhibitionist. Among his contemporaries, two of his three touchstones are legends of the Labour right, Denis Healey and Roy Jenkins (the other, as always, is Margaret Thatcher); and the plainest statement of political inspiration in the whole collection comes aslant, in a sub-section nominally devoted to religion, in a portrait of a Liberal leader, Gladstone. For an uncomplicated Tory loyalist, Mount's intellectual presence must be about as reassuring as Matthew Arnold's higher journalism was for party Liberals in his own time. But Arnold's free play of mind had a brake, which he applied in a motto from the French conservative thinker Joubert: 'Force till right is ready.' Mount's equivalent statement of limits deserves the same notoriety. 'There are times', he wrote in *Cold Cream*, defending the domestic programme of the Thatcher governments—including the premeditated fight to the finish against the miners—'when what is needed is not a beacon but a blowtorch.'[10]

Mount did his bit to fuel the blowtorch, and would have done more had not the bearings of the Thatcher government shifted during her second term, now giving priority to the formulation of a new *Östpolitik* for the last days of the Cold War. As it was, he returned to full-time journalism and writing. If, more prosaically, the ratios of intellectual engagement in public affairs—the exercise of shadow authority—can be calculated from a scale ranging between the extremes of prophecy, or moral leadership, and policy, the formulation of practical goals for duly equipped institutions, Mount's readings show a continuing pull towards the latter end. This practical bent, in the centre-right zone marked out by Thatcher and Blair, has

10   Mount, *Cold Cream*, p. 347.

been most obviously displayed in the book-length works he has written over the past thirty years: *The British Constitution Now* (1992), *Mind the Gap* (2004) and *The New Few* (2012), an attack on the spread of oligarchy in British political and economic life. But it is present too even when, as often in *English Voices*, the occasion is not primarily political. Mount's Gladstone is a working fusion of the two modes, a seer and an effective reforming politician in one. He is, moreover, a figure who defies the reductive polarizing terms of the given 'political creeds' and party shibboleths. He is 'reverent' among utilitarians, a communitarian in his own day, but tolerant—eventually—in the face of narrow confessional demands, and liberal in his sensitivity to popular conditions of life. There is something in him of Berlin's philosophy and also Michael Oakeshott's, two figures whose mutual hostility was unrelenting.

This Gladstone is 'not merely . . . a brilliant relic' of his own time but 'an unstilled voice in the conversation of ours'.[11] He is unmistakably actual. Since the mid-1980s, Mount judged in 2005, all 'the three main parties'—that is, the all-British Westminster parties—had 'experienced a Gladstonian moment', a time of 'revisions and recantations': Labour coming to reconsider its faith in 'state socialism', Conservatives remembering that they had never really believed in all that 'crude Manchester liberalism', and Liberal Democrats being led to reconsider 'the vapid tax-and-spend policies they had drifted into'. The spirit of 'the Grand Old Man' was politically alive, it seems, in the numinous persons of Blair, Brown, Cameron and Cable, and their agenda was one that he 'would have recognized as his own': devolution of power in the multinational UK; defence of Burke's 'little platoons' (of which the family is the prototype) and of local government discretions; the conjoint 'shrinking of the overblown state'—and 'the most ticklish question of all', undoing 'the disadvantages of the poor without denting their self-respect and damaging their independence'.

All these headings are in effect variations on one: that is, 'self-reliance'—'Thatcherite rhetoric', Mount notes, but also, in his assessment

---

11   Mount, *English Voices*, p. 121.

of a changed ethico-political climate, 'the common political language of the twenty-first century'. Social solidarity is necessary, he insists, but will only be supple enough as a binding value if it can tap the deep resources of family and nation—without at the same time weakening the means of individual self-reliance, as British political 'managerialism' has done. 'Opportunities for the masses to make their own lives have been sparse and cramped.' This is Mount in the character of one-nation Tory, the wettest of the wet, as Conservative Central Office judged him in the days of his parliamentary ambitions—someone 'so wet you could shoot snipe off him', said Conrad Black, dipping into the linguistic dressing-up box that a Canadian press magnate keeps to hand for English country-house weekends. More precisely, perhaps—for Disraeli is barely present in *English Voices* and never as the author of *Sybil*[12]—this is Mount in the role of Tory tribune or as the intellectual precursor of one: not a paternalist in the vein of Disraeli's aristocratic fantasy and no populist in anybody's book, rather a Gladstone figure both visionary and activist, with the gift of making 'the people' believe they have not been 'forgotten'. But it is clear that the 'holiday from irony' has lasted far longer than Mount imagined; negative capability now begins to look more like a schizoid disorder. For in this tribune-like figure we have a chimera shaped in the encounter of an undoubtedly humane self

---

12   [However, Mount has since given us a gripping non-fiction counterpiece, in his forensic investigation of 'the many lives of Aunt Munca' (*Kiss Myself Goodbye*, London 2020). There is little future in arguing for a general parallel here, even if echoes of Disraeli's romance are hard to overlook. But these are both stories of transfigured social destiny, in one case (Sybil's) through genealogical discovery, in the other through an opposite, tireless and ingenious career of lying including bigamy and perjury—both concluding in the revelation that, in one way or another, these women have always been what they latterly become: Sybil, the Chartist 'daughter of the people', is in fact of noble blood and heir to a fortune in urban property; Munca, the putative daughter of a Sheffield scrap dealer and now a woman who can afford a permanent reservation at Claridge's, or 'The Pub' as she calls it , has all her life had the silent support of the millionaire who is her biological father. Mount's extraordinary aunt (this is one of the very few relationships she properly claims or admits to) looks not unlike Sybil in travesty.]

with the other self that helped to prime Thatcher's blowtorch. Mount rejects the 'radical individualism' of the neo-liberal turn and the 'equality of opportunity' that is its only—spurious—mitigation. He urges the development of an ethos and a policy agenda combining solidarity with popular self-reliance in a strategy for reducing the dizzying inequalities of social life in Britain today. And he does this, apparently, in serene unawareness of the part he played in a political war against the only social agency that has fought consistently and with some effect for those general goals: the organized labour movement. But this is not a voice that can be easily admitted to the island conversation, from which, likewise, all consequential anti-capitalist politics and thought have been shut out—'routed', as he says. Opportunities for the masses to make their own lives have indeed been sparse and cramped, and only more so in the past forty years, under the political stewardship of Westminster's latter-day Gladstones. The social condition Mount rightly deplores is, morally speaking, one of his own making. His problem is the artefact of a foregoing 'solution'.

If the appeal to Gladstone marks a high tide of post-Thatcherite illusion, the example of Walter Bagehot prompts reflections of a more sombre kind. Bagehot was a 'brilliant' journalist, Mount agrees, and significant as a pioneer of 'the higher journalism'. But that English institution has had its 'downside', in a disregard for deeply held popular feeling. Thus, Mount writes,

> the most potent resentments at work in Europe today are those provoked by inequality, mass immigration and the incursions of the European Union. And they are precisely those with which the elite media are most reluctant to engage.[13]

Bagehot held the masses in contempt, and believed in taking the world 'lightly', Mount tells us, adding: 'The trouble is that so many people will insist on taking it seriously.' Quite. And at a time when the politics of immigration and Europe have demonstrated their

---

13   Mount, *English Voices*, pp. 346–7.

power to confound liberal expectations, he might do well to look to his own higher journalism, in which the first—the oldest and most pervasive—of these resentments has long been a special cause, to reconsider the realism of his own nostrums for the redress of inequality, perhaps even to imagine what unexpected turns 'the most ticklish question of all' may yet hold in store. *Tu quoque*, as the old tag goes, or, in common parlance, 'You said it!'

2017

William Empson, Nonesuch

Seven is the number of types of ambiguity that William Empson announced in the book he published in 1930, aged just twenty-four, winning immediate and lasting recognition as a pioneer—or vandal—in literary criticism. It is also the number of chapters in his successor volume, *Some Versions of Pastoral* (1935). A third book, *The Structure of Complex Words* (1951), varied the pattern a little, including, as well as literary studies, a set of theoretical chapters that runs—by Michael Wood's reckoning—to seven. In truth, Empson's first count remained unconfirmed, even in *Seven Types of Ambiguity* itself: an object-lesson in the irony that was a central preoccupation of his critical writing and his poetry. As for the rest, he was after all a mathematician who loved pattern, a poet skilled in rigorous prosodic schemes—someone with a bent for what he called 'trick-work'. There is no reason to grant the number seven any special significance, beyond remarking, perhaps, that human cultures have counted so many things in sevens—the days of the week, the stages of life, oak groves, brides and brothers—and that the word itself is then an exemplary growth in the linguistic 'shrubbery' that Empson came to see as more important in our ordinary processes of interpretation and judgement than what he called 'official' knowledge. Here and now, however, in Wood's book of seven chapters, the symbolism is surely unequivocal: it is an emblem of affiliation, or attachment.[1]

---

1   Michael Wood, *On Empson*, Princeton and Oxford, 2017.

The reader approaching *On Empson* for the first time does well to begin with its publishing context. The book was commissioned for a series named Writers on Writers, in which Empson is preceded by Arthur Conan Doyle, Walt Whitman, Elizabeth Bishop, W. H. Auden and Susan Sontag. This is a miscellany suggesting enthusiasm as a governing consideration rather than any impersonal continuity of theme or field. Its authors, whatever their practical association with the academy, are projected as 'writers', not scholars. Of course Wood has been a career academic with a distinguished institutional record in Britain and the US, and literary interests extending from Yeats to Nabokov, as well as writing for and (especially) about film over many years; the generic term 'scholar' would not be misapplied here. But the design of the occasion calls for another kind of performance, and this is not the place to look for a conventional monograph duly robed and hooded. 'The Empson I would like to conjure up in this book', he says, and the choice of verb is already a declaration, 'is a *writer*, both as a critic and a poet'—not because he practises in more than one mode, that is, but because of the way he inhabits both, in 'a long intimacy with language, a feeling that you have to care for it and can't go anywhere without it'. Wood's book is an introduction to this Empson, and a highly appreciative one: 'celebration' is a recurring word in the jacket copy, as is 'wonderful' in the prose of the book itself.

For all its relative brevity in the range of commentary on Empson—John Haffenden's biography, at the far end, comes out just short of 1,500 pages in two volumes[2]—Wood's study offers a comprehensive sweep across the writings, including two detailed chapters on his strange, haunting poetry, with its syntactic compressions and transpositions, and learned analogies pursued in the manner of his acknowledged master, John Donne. Empson was as precocious in this as he was in the interests that led him to *Seven Types of Ambiguity*, earning himself a place in two of the defining anthologies of the time, Michael Roberts's *New Signatures* (1932) and *Faber Book*

---

2   John Haffenden, *William Empson: Among the Mandarins* and *William Empson: Against the Christians*, Oxford 2005, 2006 respectively.

of Modern Verse (1936)—in which his allowance of poems, it happened, was seven. But the major emphasis necessarily falls on the
critical prose, and in particular the three books Empson had written
by the early '50s, the point at which he settled to live and teach in
England, after significant spells in Japan and China.

The encounter is one of performances as much as or more than
abstracted ideas. The Empson manner is bluff, matter-of-fact,
'grand casual', in Wood's happy phrase, and radically awkward.[3] He
acknowledges the poetic in its customary setting, but only to
announce an analytic move against the 'irritation' of 'unexplained
beauty'; the judgement of value, which is commonly thought to be
the primary business of the critic, 'comes either earlier or later' than
the work on which he himself was bent, 'whose object is to show the
modes of action of a poetical effect'. Disdainful of imagistic and
symbolist poetic programmes, believing that poetry belongs to a
common world of debatable statement and counter-statement, he is
committed to 'puzzling' and to the morality of 'argufying', as he
would say—not merely engaged but disputatious where need be. 'My
attitude in writing [*Seven Types of Ambiguity*, he explained,] was
that an honest man erected the ignoring of "tact" into a point of
honour.'[4] The manner comes with a social history: Empson was the
Winchester-educated son of Yorkshire gentry, and elements of the
old common touch mingle in his personal register with schoolboy
usages and ingrained habits of hyperbole and euphemism that
contribute to the effect of a form of sociability not quite at ease with
itself.

Wood's conversational tone is different. The prose is feline, by
turns quick and slow, focused but alert to what might turn up along
the way, prizing subtlety. In this too there is a history, one less
squarely social—though Wood marks his distance from the 'grandee'
Empson—than professional. The decades of devotion to close reading,
as brilliantly practised by Empson and hardened into doctrine and

---

3   Wood, *On Empson*, p. 71.
4   William Empson, *Seven Types of Ambiguity*, third ed., Harmondsworth
1973, p. 8.

pedagogy by the New Critics—of whom he was by fierce avowal not one—nurtured a widespread habit in Anglo-American literary criticism of fictioning the critical presentation as a process of discovery, the written record of a naked encounter between reader and poem. Wood's modus operandi shares in this tendency, and projects it a stage further. 'All along [Empson] has been doing what good critics do', he tells us at one point: 'trusting his own sense of the words and the writer's gift'. And the encounter is not only bare; it is live, as if streamed from the classroom. Empson was capable of ending a chapter with a list of the texts he had meant to discuss but must (now, so to speak) leave aside; Wood's performance is similarly staged. 'I want to glance at . . .', 'I want to pause over . . .', or, taking leave of the real temporality of reading a printed book, 'a month or so ago I was trying to work out . . .'. This is critical writing modelled as interaction in real time.

1

It makes for a style of discussion in which qualifications seem at times more in evidence than substantive claims. But what is clear, nevertheless, is the centrality—or rather, to take an active metaphor, the unceasing pressure—of the idea of ambiguity in Empson's thinking, as it extends its range from (some) poetry to language use generally over the twenty-odd years between *Ambiguity* (Empson's own familiar name for his first book) and *The Structure of Complex Words*, with a corresponding procedural development from the verbal analysis of local or small-scale effects to a concern with entities of a quite different kind and scale. Wood begins with a passage from the first book, in which Empson analyses four lines from *Macbeth*, balancing his case on a single word. *Some Versions of Pastoral*, in contrast, takes a whole literary mode as its object, and with a minimal outline characterization for guidance (the work of the form is 'putting the complex into the simple'), proposes new instances of pastoral and a sketch of its modern development.[5] At the

---

5   William Empson, *Some Versions of Pastoral*, London 1935, p. 23.

heart of the book, as Wood rightly judges it, is the trope of irony, which marks the uncertain relation of the speaking subject to what is said—and in particular a long analysis of the double plot and the 'double irony' that Empson himself was inclined to claim as 'somehow natural to the stage'. Like its predecessors, *Complex Words* returns to canonical literary texts; and it presents its linguistic inquiries as serving the interest of literary criticism: 'even a moderate step forward in our understanding of language would do a great deal to improve [the pursuit], and in any case to improve our general reading capacity.'[6] But the throwaway closing phrase points to a rather different balance of interests and priorities. Here was an untilled field of semantic inquiry: the 'rich obscure practical knowledge' that, as Wood too benignly puts it, 'language holds in trust for us', the ideo-affective 'shrubbery' of everyday communication.

It is in good part by conventional licence rather than any more stringent test that Empson is called a 'critic'. Compared with his Cambridge contemporary Queenie Roth and the teacher she married, F. R. Leavis, he came both earlier and later than the critical moment itself. His work in its textual detail is often redolent of philological styles rather than the ingenious feats of close verbal analysis for which he is best remembered. And for all his distrust of general theories, it was towards such conceptual horizons rather than the more common pursuits of the mid-twentieth-century literary critic that his main intellectual energies were normally directed. He was out of tune with the anti-intentionalism of the New Criticism, without ever venturing a considered critique of it or upholding a coherent alternative, as Wood shows; the late essay collection *Using Biography*, which he lived to see nearly into print, was a gathering of disparate studies with no general framing material bar a snorting reference to 'the Wimsatt Law' forbidding critical recourse to the life and its recorded purposes. The exception to this constitutional pattern was itself exceptional in the critical field: his decades-long crusade against 'neo-Christian' critics and their conforming fellow-travellers in the academy. Beginning early, with unorthodox readings of poems

---

6   William Empson, *The Structure of Complex Words*, London 1951, p. 145.

by George Herbert and Gerard Manley Hopkins, and a defence of a
sceptical John Donne against the High Church Eliot, and continuing
up to the time of his death in an egregious, unfinished reinvention of
Marlowe's *Faustus*, Empson's war reached its greatest intensity in
Milton's God (1961), a work single-mindedly devoted to the thesis that
'the reason why [*Paradise Lost*] is so good is that it makes God so bad'.

Empson's divine 'torture-monster', the father who demands the
sacrificial killing of the son, must be the scariest of all the bogeys in
the repertoire of English critical controversy; even an admirer as
creative as Wood finds reason to pause. But there are less lurid,
more familiar reasons for this resistance to Christian privilege: 'It
strikes me', Empson observed, writing now with approval about
Henry Fielding,

> that modern critics . . . have become oddly resistant to admitting that
> there is more than one code of morals in the world, whereas the
> central purpose of reading imaginative literature is to accustom
> yourself to this basic fact.[7]

Here is the cardinal value of Empson's writing as Wood depicts it, in
one encapsulating figure after another. He enlarges 'our repertoire of
human possibilities', and 'will always be there when we try to understand the kinds of adventure that reading can afford'. Or again, 'the
great gift . . . of Empson's open sense of ambiguity is the challenge of
unexplored verbal territory . . . of worlds we thought we knew.' And
in irony we have the exercise of what Empson called 'a generous scepticism', and what Wood, now following Henry James, calls the 'gap
between meanings' that is 'the home of the possible other case'. These
figures also domesticate; the image of critical virtue that takes form
in them is far from strange. If anything, Wood's beguiling phrases
refresh an old stereotype: that of the liberal critic bravely affirming
'the value of individual existence in all its variousness, complexity,
and difficulty'. The words are Lionel Trilling's, from his *Liberal
Imagination* (1950). They are widely revered as a classic formulation

---

7   Empson, *Some Versions of Pastoral*, p. 112.

of cultural liberalism in the decades of the Cold War, and if, after all, they have to be rejected as a statement of position, it is not because the conditions of life they identify are trivial. Empson's essay on proletarian literature is emphatic about this, and the book from which it comes, it so happens, reveals the trick. It is that in its abstraction and ill-concealed tendentiousness such rhetoric offers the simplistic opposite of what it purportedly upholds: an exercise in the higher sentimentality, an intellectuals' version of pastoral.

2

There was much more to Empson's work on literature and language than a benign ethics of the literary imagination—and more to his political thinking too, about which Wood has very little to say. There were obvious good reasons for brevity of treatment in the matter, but the near silence is misleading. On the left since his schooldays, Empson shared the main orientations of Communist policy in the middle and later '30s, though remaining, as he put it, 'shaky in the faith'. He expressed admiration for the political poetry of his *marxisant* contemporaries, especially Auden, while declaring an inability to follow their lead. (The thinking aloud of his poem 'Autumn on Nan-Yueh', from his first stint with the National Peking University in the late '30s, suggests that his diffidence may have been a sign of his better judgement in this.) The bond with China proved durable. Back in London in wartime and working in propaganda at the BBC, he used his position to raise awareness of the Chinese as allies in an integral struggle against the Axis powers. A second, five-year period in China coincided with the civil war and the early years of the People's Republic. The Empsons were strong supporters of the new order (William's wife, Hetta, a white South African artist, was a member of the British Communist Party), and, in the face of glowering hostility in US diplomatic quarters, proudly joined the crowds celebrating Mao's victory. Empson's solidarity with revolutionary China was empirical in scope and significantly conditioned by his personal loyalty to his students and colleagues; there seems never to have been any thought of his following Hetta into the CP. In the same way, his qualified defence of the Chinese party's policy of intellectual 'thought reform'—'teasing' or 'nagging', as he would say—in which he persevered until the unwinding of the Hundred Flowers campaign in 1956–57, was sustained at least as much by his belief in the rooted integrity of his old colleagues as by the political optimism to which he was temperamentally inclined. No later cause took the place of China in his political affections. A visiting appointment in newly independent Ghana left him still hopeful of African socialism but disturbed by Nkrumah's authoritarian reflex. He marched in the Campaign for Nuclear Disarmament from its earliest days, and joined public protests against the British Labour government's support for the American war on Vietnam, turning what was by then a famous signature to good account in the letters pages of the press. In someone who was not principally concerned with politics, inhabiting an intellectual culture in which, as he once waspishly remarked, a want of political opinions was commonly taken for 'depth', this was an admirable record of engagement.

It is perhaps surprising, then, granted his willingness to expose himself to public controversy, that Empson's most passionate engagement should also have been his most narrowly focused—but that is one of the lesser oddities of his protracted *Kulturkampf* against Christianity in the field of literary scholarship.[8] Empson had long been critical of recuperative Christian readings of poems in which he himself saw and insisted upon irreducible contradiction, and by the middle '50s he had identified a 'neo-Christian movement' that had succeeded in altering the canonical terms of reading for a whole range of authors and must now be countered. A decade later he was still preoccupied by a Christian 'revival' to be resisted with due polemical force, as not merely mistaken but immoral and dangerous to human well-being. (Indeed, he asserted, claiming the authority of personal acquaintance, that George Orwell's *Nineteen Eighty-Four* was driven as much by revulsion from Christianity as from the fearsome secular novelties of twentieth-century politics.) Empson was strong in his beliefs, and it was

---

8   Haffenden, *William Empson: Against the Christians*, p. 432.

claims like this that led his professional colleague John Carey—a characteristically unbuttoned witness—to mock him for a proneness to 'crack-brained', 'loopy seizures'. The best that can be said for this one is that it was a delayed and eventually fixated reaction to a current of thought that had welled up, then abated, some ten years earlier than Empson's observations suggested. Christian Discrimination was one of its literary-critical forms and Leavis's *Scrutiny* had fought it in the later '40s, which were also the years of T. S. Eliot's apotheosis. The fact that Empson was abroad for about half of the relevant span of time, and not merely abroad but working in non-Christian (Buddhist) cultures, can only have accentuated the difference between the atmosphere of England in the early '50s and the free-thinking milieu of his undergraduate days, and whetted the edge of his judgements, in which the habit of exaggeration was already pronounced. (The imaginable impact of his sudden expulsion from Cambridge, for possession of contraceptives, would not have depended on any such rhetorical inflation.) Still, by the later '70s, he had concluded that the neo-Christians had 'melted away'. The main enemy now was 'Inhumanism', or the regime of Wimsatt's Law.

The surprise in this case, given the vehemence of his opposition to the critical decree that authorial intention is neither available nor admissible as a measure of success in literary creation, is that Empson was not more concerned to develop a clear, consistent argument against it. As a general position, anti-intentionalism was not so much less vulnerable than the naiveties it outlawed—and which he was not defending, at times indeed appearing to have more in common with the reigning Inhumanism. But if, at the same time, Empson was willing to go so far as to affirm that invented biographical information was preferable to none at all, this was because the stake in this battle, for him, was something not manifest in the title of the famous programme essay 'The Intentional Fallacy'. W. K. Wimsatt and his co-author, Monroe Beardsley, devoted most of their space and emphasis to the question of authorial intention as a criterion of value, and in this they inverted Empson's intellectual priorities. Valuing, as he said, came before or after the work that interested him, which was verbal analysis of literary effects. This was not a technicist prospectus: Empson was not indifferent to matters of relative value. But, like his moral hero Henry Fielding, he trusted his intuitions and hoped they would be good enough. The motivating concern of his work was *interpretation*. Empson's first principle was that there was a fundamental continuity in all language use, however rarefied or low, as a giving and taking of meaning among the social subjects inhabiting it. The self-sufficient literary object posited in Anglo-American modernist poetics was an illusion; the critical dogma of 'the intentional fallacy' was the reflex of an iconicist fantasy; and it was inconceivable that biography—including discoverable intention, in all its mutually irreducible senses—should not be recognized as a necessary structuring and controlling context of communication, which would otherwise risk dispersal in a field of linguistic ambiguity that, in principle, seemed limitless.

3

Biography, here, is not the exclusive, narrowing methodological path it can sometimes be; it is one of the varieties of history, which, in fact, would be the more informative frame of reference for Empson's procedure as it develops towards *The Structure of Complex Words,* a work in progress, in effect—and like its two predecessors in that— for which the term 'literary criticism' will hardly do, even for want of a better one. The life in question now was trans-individual, that of words and their meanings in time. Some of the book's component studies could pass as literary criticism: Wood's samples, concerning 'fool' in *King Lear* and 'honest' in *Othello,* are of this kind. But others ranged far away in their pursuit of historical meaning and its modes, engaging with anthropology, philosophy and linguistics. A second chapter given to 'honest' was contrastingly lexicographical in character, using the occasion to propose a wholesale reconstruction and extension of the Oxford English Dictionary's established methodology; another, more logical and grammatical in bent, unpicked the four (or more?) 'equations' purported in the verb 'be'. Each came with a system of notations tailored for the judgements of

Empson's bluff, mercurial prose analyses—stylistically alien elements that Wood passes over in his own account.

Wood's Empson is too much the literary critic that Empson was not. The object that comes into view in the twenty years of work beginning with *Seven Types of Ambiguity*—focused, it is true, through a largely conventional literary corpus—is language in use, language as historical, socially determinate communicative practice. If Empson's practice is to be given a conceptual name, it is as a variety of literary pragmatics. His inspiration in this, he always emphasized, was his Cambridge teacher I. A. Richards, the author of *Practical Criticism*. But the more suggestive comparison, limited though it must be, is with the work of a younger member of Richards's generation, the Russian thinker Mikhail Bakhtin and his collaborator Valentin Vološinov.[9] Initiatives such as Bakhtin's studies of dialogism, speech genres and heteroglossia and Vološinov's theory of the 'multi-accentual' linguistic sign opened the ground of language as social practice that Empson would later enter from another quarter as he pressed forwards with his investigations of ambiguity and irony. However, the difference was crucial. For while Empson was committed to the historical and social as parameters of semantic analysis, he lacked concepts of the kind that could have assisted theoretical advance in those terms. Bakhtin's 'dialogism' was a property of the individual utterance, not merely a registration of the empirical fact of interlocution, and thus implied the constitutive priority of inter-subjective relations in discourse; Vološinov worked in an established tradition of Marxist thinking about ideology—however under-developed that might be in the field of language. Empson, in contrast, moved among the abstractions of 'mind', 'language' and 'world', and only *Some Versions of Pastoral*, with a single historical cultural mode as its topic, indicated an alternative course. In so far as he owned up to any theoretical allegiance at all, he continued in the liberal–individualist path of his old mentor, the utilitarian Richards.

This intellectual dislocation was one of several, metaphorical or literal, that gave Empson's career its character note. A Westerner in

9 See M. M. Bakhtin, *The Dialogic Imagination*, Austin, TX 1981.

the heartlands of the Buddha and a pantheist (of sorts) among Christians; an English gent among Chinese Communists and a fellow-traveller among Cold War *pentiti*; a linguist among critics, with a sideline in drastic textual editing: the most important of these relations for his general cultural outlook was his experience in Japan and China, which left him with an abiding dislike of the West's presumptuous universalism, above all in the form of Christianity. Settling in England in his later forties, taking up his first and only teaching appointment in an English university after an absence of some twenty years, he was in some ways a stranger. The dislocations were not only contextual: his intellectual inquiries came with their own kind of destiny, it seemed. Empson himself held that the ironist—particularly the practitioner of the double irony that he associated with the stage—must sooner or later reach a place of unknowing, and it is hard to set aside the testimony from so many of Empson's readers and listeners (Michael Wood among them) that they had wondered, on this or that occasion over many years, not simply whether he spoke truly—the standard reservation—but whether he quite believed what he was saying. This is perhaps Empson's inmost curiosity. A brisk rationalist with no time for illogicality passed off as theological 'mystery' or highfalutin 'paradox'—he was dismissive of Oscar Wilde—he was nonetheless fascinated by ambiguity in all its degrees from homophony to contradiction, to the extent that it could seem to be a feature of what he himself thought and actually was: a nonesuch.

2017

About Roberto Schwarz

Roberto Schwarz is the foremost literary and cultural critic of his generation in Brazil and the most significant Marxist inheritor of the Frankfurt School tradition writing anywhere today. These joint distinctions are intimately associated in Schwarz's constitution as a thinker, which is complex. Frankfurt Critical Theory came to him as one element in the constellation of German Marxist aesthetic theory in the earlier and middle twentieth century. 'My work would be inconceivable', he has written, in a characteristically nuanced formulation, 'without the tradition—itself contradictory—formed by Lukács, Benjamin, Brecht and Adorno, and the inspiration of Marx.' 'Equally' inconceivable, that is—to restore a missing word—for Schwarz preceded this statement with another acknowledging a debt to his teacher at the University of São Paulo, one of the outstanding intellectual personalities of the left in Brazil, Antonio Candido.[1]

The fundamental theoretical insight of the German tradition, for Schwarz's purposes as a literary critic, is the idea of the objectivity of form. Forms, whose substances are those of practical life, emerge as part of the historical social process, and may then be worked over to create the 'structural reduction' that is the literary work itself, the

---

1 Roberto Schwarz, *Um mestre na periferia do capitalismo—Machado de Assis*, São Paulo 1991, p. 13. The whole phrase reads: 'Meu trabalho seria impensável igualmente sem a tradição . . .', and so on.

proper object of an integrally dialectical criticism in which form and social process are indissociable. Form is 'the fatal element' of such criticism, as the young Lukács believed—or as Franco Moretti puts it now, 'most of us open a book and see words on a page: Schwarz sees forms—often more than one, pulling in opposite directions'.[2] Schwarz is emphatic in referring this dialectical formalism to the Hegelian-Marxist tradition and to Marx himself.[3] And yet, he insists none-the-less, its inspirational precedent in Brazil was precisely not Marxist: rather, it was the achievement of a socialist—Candido—who, with all his great international breadth of literary culture, was contrastingly 'national' in feeling and focus.[4] In this circumstance there were the signs both of convergence and of possible crux. The Frankfurt School was preoccupied with 'the character and destiny of bourgeois civilization as a whole', Schwarz explained, in an interview given to mark Adorno's centenary in 2003; Candido's commitment, on the other hand, was to 'the peculiarity of the Brazilian experience, be it literary or social'. And what he concluded was that 'the categories of the countries that serve as our models are not convincing as universals, and their direct application in our case is a mistake'.[5] The transition from feudalism to capitalism, the spreading dominion of the commodity form, the great arc of bourgeois development and decline, and the forward march of labour; these and the specifically literary-historical and cultural narratives they undergirded—the classic accounts of the historical novel, realism and naturalism, the competing evaluations of modernism, the transition from liberal

2 Franco Moretti, 'A New Intuition: On Roberto Schwarz's Critical Work', *New Left Review* 131, September-October 2021, p. 87. Lukács's phrase is from *The Soul and Forms* (1910).

3 Roberto Schwarz, 'Conversa sobre *Duas meninas*', in *Seqüências brasileiras*, São Paulo 1999, pp. 236–7.

4 See in English the selection of Candido's writings, *On Literature and Society*, ed. and introd. Howard S. Becker, Princeton 1995.

5 From *Cult*, 72, 2003, pp. 8–12, quoted in Jorge de Almeida, 'Pressupos tos, salvo engano, dos pressupostos, salvo engano', Maria Elisa Cevasco and Milton Ohata, eds, *Um crítico na periferia do capitalismo: reflexões sobre a obra de Roberto Schwarz*, São Paulo 2007, p. 49.

to administered civilization, the steady permeation of the principle of exchange—all were vulnerable to critical check, and even rejection, as authoritative patterns for the world outside the heartlands of capital.

Candido had already studied the working of this antithesis in its most general terms as a conflict between universalism and localism in the Brazilian literature of the eighteenth and nineteenth centuries.[6] His preferred solution, in his own time, was to refuse the lure of polarization, instead upholding the value of spontaneous trans-migrations between the cultures of Brazil and the metropolitan centres, while taking a cautious view of the likely balance in the exchange—of what a country like Brazil might be expected to bring to the cultural ecumene, or see embraced by its more prestigious members.[7] Schwarz was no less keenly aware of the incongruities of Brazil's dependent cultures. 'In the process of reproducing its social order', he wrote in his best-known essay, 'Misplaced Ideas', 'Brazil unceasingly affirms and reaffirms European ideas, always improperly.'[8] This was a rule of perversity from which Marxism was not automatically exempt, either in its official manifestations or, for that matter, in the leading forms of heterodoxy. Schwarz's solution, a subtle dialectical displacement of Candido's, was to pose 'the question of Brazil' (*a matéria brasileira*) as a problem internal to Marxism and to seek a satisfactory resolution in coherent historical-materialist terms. If Marxism appeared intellectually brittle in the face of the palpable realities of Brazil and the rest of the non-metropolitan world, the deficiency lay in its own underdevelopment, which it was necessary to put right. It was not that the country was simply aberrant in its relation to the canonical schemes of historical development, let alone essentially different in the sense of the cultural-nationalist

---

6   Above all in his classic *Formação da literatura brasileira (momentos deci-sivos)*, dealing with the period 1750–1880 (1959; 2 vols., Belo Horizonte 1975).

7   See Schwarz, 'Literature and Underdevelopment', in *On Literature and Society*.

8   Roberto Schwarz, 'Misplaced Ideas: Literature and Society in Late Nineteenth-Century Brazil', in *Misplaced Ideas: Essays on Brazilian Culture*, trans. and introd. John Gledson, London 1992, p. 29.

picturesque. The secret of Brazil's uniqueness, Schwarz maintained, lay in its formation as part of the world system of capital, its historical specificity as a slave-owning economy structurally integrated with the liberal order of international trade.

In this lie the originality and significance of Schwarz's initiative within his parent intellectual tradition. The compelling attraction of Hegelian-Marxist cultural theory was also its notorious weakness: its confident dialectical narratives offered to decipher bourgeois society and culture as an integral, dynamic whole, but seldom with more than passing acknowledgement of the deep discrepancies of history and situation that structure the world of actually existing capitalism. This schematic historicism was troubling enough in the metropolitan zone, where it did much to enhance the philosophical counter-attraction of Louis Althusser and his co-thinkers, in the later 1960s and after. In more dramatically contrasted conditions such as those of Brazil at the end of the 1950s, it provoked a concentrated critical initiative, at once highly specific and—for just that reason—quite general in implication. Assimilating the theoretical resources of his direct inheritance from the culture of the German left and bringing them to bear on the question of Brazil, in the formative environment of the legendary *Capital* seminar at the University of São Paulo, Schwarz began to develop a variety of Marxist critical practice that was unmistakably Lukácsian and Frankfurtian in its bold dialectical ambition, yet rigorous in its fidelity to the distinct shapes of Brazilian history and culture, which were now seen as specific local forms of an articulated world order of capital.[9] Here, to paraphrase one of the

---

9   Schwarz was born to leftist Jewish intellectual parents in Vienna in 1938, and brought to São Paulo, in flight from Nazism, as a baby. He speaks at length about his intellectual relationship with Lukács, from his student days onwards, in an interview given in Eva L. Corredor, *Lukács After Communism: Interviews with Contemporary Intellectuals*, Durham NC and London 1997. For the *Capital* seminar, see Schwarz's retrospect, 'Um seminário de Marx', in *Seqüências brasileiras*; and for more anecdotal recollections, two contributions to Cevasco and Ohata, *Um crítico*: Michael Löwy, 'Ad Roberto Schwarz', and Fernando Henrique Cardoso, 'Roberto Schwarz, seminarista'.

presiding spirits of the seminar, Jean-Paul Sartre, was a Marxism willing and able to find out something new.[10]

The character, logic and significance of that practice are the substance of *Two Girls and Other Essays,* whose contents speak persuasively on their own account. Here we may simply pick out its most important defining characteristics. At the heart of Schwarz's critical achievement are his studies of Joaquim Maria Machado de Assis, Brazil's greatest novelist. Extending across three books and numerous short texts, these develop a sustained account of Machado's historical intelligibility as a student of his own society in the later nineteenth century and make a strong case for his historic originality in the international culture of the novel as well as his continuing actuality as a critical force in Brazilian culture.[11] Given this central concern and the fact of his commitment to artistic realism, it is tempting to identify Schwarz as a Lukácsian of a kind. This would be misleading. Machado's narratives are very remote from Lukács's canons for realistic writing—which, indeed have no counterpart of any kind in Schwarz's work. His realism is much closer to Brecht's in spirit, evaluating novels and plays according to their yield of illumination, without prior judgement of artistic means, always centrally engrossed in questions of form but not in the manner of Lukács's formal academicism.[12] The difference is important, and the more so because Schwarz's Brechtian commitment to realism goes together with his conviction, which he voices with all possible clarity, that literature is capable of discovering new knowledge. This is not the old

---

10   Both Schwarz (p. 93) and Cardoso (p. 330) cite Sartre's *Question de méthode* (first published in 1960) as a key text for the group; Lukács's *History and Class Consciousness* was another.

11   The books are *Ao vencedor as batatas* (1977; partly translated in *Misplaced Ideas*, which also contains several short studies of Machado), *Um mestre na periferia do capitalismo* (1990; *A Master on the Periphery of Capitalism,* trans. John Gledson, Durham, NC 2002), and *Duas meninas* (1997), the heart of *Two Girls and Other Essays,* London 2012.

12   See Bertolt Brecht, 'On the Formalistic Character of the Theory of Realism', in Theodor Adorno et al., *Aesthetics and Politics,* London 1977, pp. 70–6; in the same volume cf. Lukács's critique of Ernst Bloch's defence of German Expressionism ('Realism in the Balance').

Romantic claim of privilege for poetry: capability is not an unambiguous guarantee of outcomes, and there is no suggestion that the
knowledge is of a special order. But it is far bolder than the conventional proposition that artistic realism can aspire to present, in its
own way, what theory always already knows—the effective limit of
Lukács's acknowledgement. Candido had shown how Manuel
Antônio de Almeida, in the form of his novel *The Memoirs of a
Militia Sergeant*, discovered a dialectic of order and disorder that
made possible the reinterpretation of an existing body of knowledge
of Brazilian society. Likewise, what Machado knew about Brazil he
knew before anyone else in any other mode, and the articulation of
his discovery was a formal innovation, the device of the tendentious
narrator, a figure given to caprice or mendacity—if not outright
delusion—and this by virtue of his distinctive class constitution.[13]
This is the meaning of Schwarz's declaration that 'a good novel is a
genuine event for theory'.[14] Or better, perhaps, a genuine opportunity, not yet, or necessarily, an event—as the history of Machado's
reception itself suggests. Franco Moretti has made the appropriate
dialectical correction:

> Literary knowledge is deposited in Machado's texts, yes—it is,
> remember, an *objective* form—but is just as clearly *encrypted* in
> them: it is indeed an objective *form*. To become truly visible, it
> needs to be liberated by the catalyst of critical work. Or in other
> words, the 'new knowledge' of *Brás Cubas* is the product of
> Machado *and* of Schwarz.[15]

The emancipating possibilities of such literary events are inseparable
from the responsibility they presuppose. Schwarz's general critical
position implies an ethics of reading. If the experience of literature is

---

13 *'Narrador parcial'* is Schwarz's phrase. In his interpretation, Machado's narrators are a historically and socially specific form of the figure usually
known in English as the 'unreliable narrator' (the term introduced in Wayne
C. Booth's *The Rhetoric of Fiction*, Chicago 1961).

14 Schwarz, 'Objective Form: On the Dialectic of Roguery', *Two Girls*, p. 22.

15 Moretti, 'A New Intuition', pp. 96–7.

to lead to the discovery that may be there to be made, it behoves us to read well, with due care and patience. 'Close reading' has long been upheld as the special virtue of Anglo-American traditions in literary criticism, with 'dialectical' interpretation featuring as perhaps the outstanding case of its sorry opposite. Schwarz outplays this received dichotomy, combining his dialectical commitment to totality with tireless, micro-fine attention to the detail of the texts he reads, be they Machado's novels or the tiny poems of Chico Alvim or the adolescent Helena Morley's diary.[16] 'Daring' comes high on his list of the virtues, as readers of *Two Girls* learn, and it is a conspicuous feature of his own analyses, as he opens out the data of story and language to disclose the lines of a whole characterology of Brazilian society, the most general matters of the historical social order in the smallest inflections of a text.

These studies are the centrepiece of his work, which, taken as a whole, is impressively diverse. Not only a critic of poetry and drama, Schwarz has also written in those forms, notably in the collection *Corações veteranos* (*Veteran Hearts*, 1974) and the theatrical 'farce' *A lata de lixo de história* (*The Dustbin of History*, 1977). He has also contributed critical insight into their cultural history, in searching studies such as his essay on the Tropicalist singer-composer and musician Caetano Veloso.[17] The retrospective 'Culture and Politics in Brazil, 1964–1969', written in Parisian exile and first published in *Les Temps Modernes*, brought political judgement to the fore, as Schwarz assessed the failings of the Brazilian Communist Party's Marxism, a variety that 'specialized in discussing the invalidity of capitalism' but 'took no steps towards revolution', leaving an open door for the military coup.[18] Commending Chico de Oliveira's essay

---

16   *Minha vida de menina* (1971); *The Diary of 'Helena Morley'*, trans. Elizabeth Bishop, London 1997.

17   Roberto Schwarz, 'Political Iridescence: The Changing Hues of Caetano Veloso', *NLR* 75, 2012.

18   Schwarz, *Misplaced Ideas*, p. 132. Schwarz's scathing judgement on the left intelligentsia was summarized in a fable from a novel of the time, *Quarup* by Antônio Callado: 'an intellectual, in this case a priest, travels round the country in a geographical and social sense, rejects his profession and social position, in

The Duckbilled Platypus, on the formation of a strange new ruling bloc in the unprecedented circumstances of twenty-first-century Brazil, the condition that he calls 'neo-backwardness', Schwarz evoked a Frankfurtian precedent. 'In the style of a dialectic of enlightenment,' he wrote, 'the threshold of changes is not determined by any doctrinaire construction but plotted within a provisional and heuristic totalization that seeks to track the actual course of events.' But the yield of this 'contemporary gaze, without optimism or illusions', was hardly so remote: 'a deep and complex realism' with tangible political implications, a possible gain for the strategic imagination of the left in Brazil.[19] In such moments, the critic is operating as an integrally political thinker.

Schwarz's preferred critical form is the essay (much of his work has been produced for non-academic venues, such as newspaper supplements), and he intends this choice in a sense he takes from Adorno: the essay is a kind of text finding its occasions in 'culturally pre-formed objects', moving somewhere between science and art, though always in the medium of concepts, and not intending to illustrate a received theoretical system, let alone elaborate a new one.[20] His disdain for elaborate methodological prospectuses is of long standing,[21] and it is in keeping that his own most focused statement of theory and method, 'Objective Form', should be a nuanced reflection on the work of someone else, an essay mostly devoted to another essay that moves from structuralist diagramming at one end of its rhetorical range to paraliterary merging with rural folklore at the other.[22] (His title, in the Portuguese, is itself a mime of sorts, though

---

the search for the people, whose struggle he will join—a certain literary wisdom comes in here—in a chapter after the last one in the book' (p. 158).

19 Roberto Schwarz, 'Preface with Questions', *NLR* 24, 2003. See also Roberto Schwarz, 'Neo-Backwardness in Bolsonaro's Brazil' (interviews with Claudio Leal, Bruna Della Torre, and Mónica Gonzáles García), *NLR* 123, 2020.

20 Theodor Adorno, 'The Essay as Form', *Notes to Literature*, vol. 1, New York 1991, p. 3.

21 See his satirical '19 princípios para a crítica literária', *O pai de família* (1976), São Paulo 2008.

22 Schwarz, *Two Girls*, pp. 10–22.

also a summons to theoretical self-examination.[23]) Above all, with its embrace of provisionality and hesitation, and its magpie curiosity, the essay is a critical mode especially well suited to the purposes of a Marxist criticism morally committed to the value of being surprised.

It is a token of Roberto Schwarz's standing in his own country that key phrases from his writings have for years circulated in semi-self-contained form as high-speed versions of his theses; 'misplaced ideas' is one such phrase, 'objective form' is another. It is a further token, this time of gratitude and esteem, that he should at length have been given the mantle he wove for Machado: *um mestre na periferia do capitalismo*.[24] This is a warm compliment but not a simple one, as Antonio Candido had already explained, as if by way of premonition, in an essay on literature and underdevelopment in Brazil. 'We always recognize our inevitable dependence as natural', he wrote:

> Besides, seen thus it is no longer dependency, but a way of participating in a cultural universe to which we belong, which crosses the boundaries of nations and continents, allowing the exchange of experiences and the circulation of values. And when we in turn influence the Europeans through the works we do (not through the thematic suggestions our continent presents to them to elaborate in their own form of exoticism), at such moments what we give back are not inventions but a refining of received instruments.[25]

What, then, is a master on the periphery? Candido's words are a counsel of caution, and many would be guided by them. Rights of audience in the prevailing global cultural order are brutally differentiated. But Schwarz has emphasized the value of daring, and it may be that a little of it is in order here. For if what he has accomplished in

---

23   In literal translation, 'Presuppositions, if I am not mistaken, of the "Dialectic of Roguery"'.

24   A recurring motif in the conference proceedings and associated texts published in Cevasco and Ohata, eds, *Um crítico*.

25   Schwarz, 'Literature and Underdevelopment', p. 130.

and for his inherited tradition of German Marxism is valid on his own national ground, then it implies a general lesson that cannot be passed off as a mere refinement. It is not merely that the general schemes of Hegelian-Marxist cultural history had to be modified, more or less dramatically, to accommodate hard cases such as Brazil; the logical implication of Schwarz's turn to a rigorously historical practice of dialectical criticism is that they were in some way wanting even on their own metropolitan ground—the concatenation of nation-states from which the master-narratives of capitalism and the bourgeoisie were elicited and projected on the screen of world history.[26] What is called for, then, is not refinement but correction or reconstruction, and that is a task for which one commanding model is given in the pioneering work of Roberto Schwarz. As they say, rightly, a master.

2012

---

26 Neil Larsen makes a similar suggestion, referring particularly to the United States: 'Por que ninguém consegue entender Roberto Schwarz nos Estados Unídos', Cevasco and Ohata, *Um crítico*, pp. 20–1.

Hobsbawm's End Times

Eric Hobsbawm was a historian and a lover of the arts, a Marxist–Communist for as long as there remained a party of that name to take his subscription, then a professed social democrat—and an Englishman who was also a Viennese Jew of a certain age. These are the subjectivities at work, in varying combinations, in the twenty-two lectures, book reviews and other essays that make up *Fractured Times*.[1] The matter of the book, in Hobsbawm's opening words, is 'what happened to the art and culture of bourgeois society' after 1914, when the characteristic social class formations of the European bourgeoisie in the previous century had passed way. In fact, the book is more diverse and more varied in its emphases than that flat singularizing pronouncement encourages readers to believe, and could hardly be otherwise, given its temporal span (1964 to 2012) and the occasional character of most and perhaps all of its constituents, half of which began life as spoken performances at museums, galleries and festivals. Another force of diversification was the matchless curiosity of the author. The 'culture' of the title touches all the important current meanings of the term: the classic high traditions of the arts and literature in Europe but also the historic avant-gardes of the early twentieth century and mass forms such as rock music or the

---

1 Eric Hobsbawm, *Fractured Times: Culture and Society in the Twentieth Century*, London 2013.

Hollywood western; the ethos of science at the mid-century, as differently embodied in the careers of Joseph Needham and J. D. Bernal; the everyday phenomena of generalized commodity production; the mingling and remaking of symbolic behaviours of all kinds in the great migrations of the twentieth century, and the significance of globalization today; the changing patterns of public authority instanced in the contrasting destinies of the interventionist 'free' intellectual in the metropolitan world and the zealots of 'public religion', fundamentalist and disciplinarian, since the 1970s.

With great range and the generalizing requirement associated with guest lectures for occasional, non-specialist audiences, inevitably, come selectivity and strict economy of illustration. Europe is the main location of the book, and especially its German-language heartland. The culture that is its chief concern is aesthetic rather than conceptual, involving the pursuits of concert halls, galleries and theatres rather than universities and libraries. Within this bias towards the arts, there are further strong gradations of emphasis. Thus, opera is vividly present here, but there is little about literature or non-musical drama, even though a brilliant portrait of Karl Kraus and *Die Fackel*, his 'lifelong monologue addressed to the world', makes a large exception. Music is everywhere in the book, but not so composers or performers, who are sighted relatively infrequently, and then sometimes only indirectly: Beethoven is named, but only as a 'name', a scrap of general knowledge unlikely to disappear from the cultural database of the twenty-first century. Cinema is a key exhibit in Hobsbawm's general argument, but seldom brought to the foreground, while television has an improbably minor part to play. In all, nevertheless, together with more closely focused studies of European Jewry and of class, gender and the significance of 'youth' in the late nineteenth century, these texts make a book rich in cultivation and learning, predictably strong in general assertion and sprinkled with arresting detail. It is also a book with a definite unity, though not quite in the terms that Hobsbawm's overture proposes. For if we note that the earliest of these texts, a book review in the *Times Literary Supplement*, dates from as long ago as 1964, we then need to add, for clarity, that the next-oldest came fully three decades later, and that the greater part of the collection (two-thirds) was written after the turn of the century. This is late work, much of it post-dating Hobsbawm's memoirs, *Interesting Times*, and late in a sense that goes beyond chronology, entering the substance of the writing.

The 'fractures' of the title are multiform. They include the estrangement of painting from its historic function of representation, with a consequent loss of significant audiences; and the twofold isolation of the devotees of the classical concert repertoire, who have been deserted by younger generations while themselves continuing to resist new and unfamiliar work in favour of a small catalogue of eighteenth- and nineteenth-century favourites. Other fractures are evident in those artistic disciplines where artisan craft traditions have not been adjusted for an environment geared to large-scale reproducibility. The apparent incommensurability of achievement across disciplines and, more so, registers of artistic practice is a fracture of the most general kind. However, for all its privileged status and aptness as a metaphor for observable cultural conditions, fracture is not the master-trope of the book it names. That distinction belongs to the overwhelming natural power of water. Hobsbawm's language is insistent: 'the present creative flood is drowning the globe'; it is 'uncontrollable', an 'engulfment', a 'spate', an 'inundation'; a succession of 'tsunamis' past and to come. This new deluge is the spontaneous culture of developed capitalism today.

Hobsbawm framed his analyses as a social historian rather than a critic or theorist of culture or any art—not even jazz, which he wrote about for the *New Statesman* in the 1950s. His primary interest is in producers and their audiences, and in the changing articulations of technology and market that structure their histories, and all this in a spirit of comparative empirical inquiry. *Fractured Times* is a Marxist book about modern European culture that has no index entries for Adorno, Marcuse or Williams. Georg Lukács appears once, but only as a new kind of bourgeois: the son set free by parental subsidy to pursue a higher calling. Walter Benjamin appears in several guises, however, and most relevantly as the theorist of art in the age of mechanical reproduction and an inspiration for Hobsbawm's reflections on the mixed fortunes of the arts in the twentieth century and since. His general case is straightforward. Technological reproducibility in the arts creates the possibility of mass markets, which, in turn, become the means of artistic viability in any given case. Where these conditions are well matched, the cultural environment is favourable. Thus, literature in its broadest sense, which has for five hundred years been adapted for the large-scale reproducibility inherent in moveable type, has flourished and continues to expand. Music of all kinds and vintages has been well served by the development of recording and broadcasting technologies, while film is the creation of mechanical reproduction and, despite the challenges posed by successive extra-cinematic forms of screening—television, home video and now digital and web-based innovations—has survived, the most successful art form of the twentieth century, into the new millennium.

Big architecture thrives on special terms as signature or legacy, in the *grands projets* of politicians and the tower-building mania of. chief executives in the new centres of capital, though not sculpture, now that statuary has lost its place in the symbology of public spaces. Painting is worst off, having flailed, faltered and lost its way since the late nineteenth century. Objectively at risk of functional redundancy since the invention of photography, easel painters and muralists launched successive departures from the received forms of pictorial representation, with diminishing returns. After all, 'a camera on a footplate can communicate the sensation of speed better than a Futurist canvas by Balla.' Painting clung to artisanal norms of production and associated conceptions of the lone artist in historical conditions where mass reproducibility and collaborative work processes were becoming ever more widely the norm, with the paradoxical result that it now survives mainly as an art of homage or self-regard, the commissioned portrait in oils. In the visual arts more broadly defined, Art Nouveau showed what could still be achieved, especially when aesthetic principles were associated with strong social commitments, as in the creative lineage that ran from William Morris to the Bauhaus. However, this was not the typical case, and art nouveau failed because of its resistance to industrialism and its techniques—which the Bauhaus came to embrace on programmatic grounds, as did the assorted practitioners of Art Deco in a spirit of commercial realism. The musical avant-gardes of the past century have fared no better than their counterparts in painting, in Hobsbawm's judgement. Schoenberg and his disciples failed to win over the existing audience for the central tradition of classical music and never assembled a significant new following for their innovations; jazz forfeited its popular audiences when it made a turn towards art music; the preference of the great majority of younger enthusiasts is rock and pop.

1

This is a mixed report, discipline by discipline and tradition by tradition, and characteristically hard-headed in manner. It is accompanied by a synoptic assessment, a background report quite general in reference and not at all mixed. Hobsbawm's theme now is the historic dissolution of the conditions of artistic experience in the sense handed down from the nineteenth century as 'culture'. That culture was a call to high seriousness:

> The enjoyment of art led to spiritual improvement and was a kind of devotional activity, whether in private, like reading, or in public, in the theatre, the concert hall, the museum, or in the acknowledged sites of world culture, such as the Pyramids or the Pantheon.

Culture entailed a virtuous self-segregation or social askesis, a kind of 'separatism', in the phrasing of this book: a turning away from the everyday and from mere entertainment that is no longer possible in the conditions of developed capitalism. Technological dynamism and the consumerist drive for undeferred gratification come together 'in the spate of words, sounds and images in the universal environment that once would have been called "art", but also vanished in this dissolution of the aesthetic experience'—or a self-annihilating excess of the aesthetic that abolishes 'art'.

The epitome of this aesthetic condition, for Hobsbawm, is the immersive, polymorphously hedonistic culture of rock music festivals and raves; and the epitome of how art may learn to live with its own dissolution as normative 'art' is the 'strange and disagreeable figure' of Andy Warhol, the 'great' mock-Dadaist of his time:

> Warhol and the Pop Artists did not want to destroy or revolutionize anything, let alone any world. On the contrary, they accepted, even liked it. They simply recognized that there was no longer a place for traditional artist-produced visual art in the consumer society.

Warhol's 'troubling' oeuvre nevertheless came close to fulfilling the classic 'modern' ambition to 'express the times', in a visual equivalent of 'the great American novel'—'but it was not achieved by creating works of art in the traditional sense'. And by the 1970s, in Hobsbawm's view, conceptual art was demonstrating that the very idea of a *work* of art had been lost.

The redemptive precedent of the Bauhaus was set aside, leaving only the embrace of commodities, or 'post-art'. Again, the orienting values of these essays are those traditionally affirmed in artistic practice: individual craft, effort, absorption, the disciplines of the stage and recording studio, virtuosity in performance. This emphasis owes something to Benjamin, but a lot more to the predictable priorities of a devotee, in this case one with particular commitments to classical music, opera and jazz. And it is in this capacity rather than that of aesthetician that Hobsbawm interleaves his historical analyses with strong judgements of artistic value. A few examples give the flavour. Classical concert audiences subsist on 'a dead repertoire', which nevertheless constitutes 'a wonderful heritage' that must not be lost. A Billie Holiday in pop music is 'a greater freak' than a Rimbaud composing verses for greeting cards. These forthright evaluations are not what they may appear to be at first sight, yet another exercise of the stock opposition between the properly 'critical' (self-styled) and the 'populist'. The collocation of 'wonderful' and 'dead' in the first case and, in the second, the asymmetry of register in the comparative judgement are indications of a greater complexity of attitude. So, surveying the proliferating international festival culture of the new century, Hobsbawm has no difficulty in acknowledging the greater interest of the rock and pop menu at Roskilde in comparison with the more prestigious programme of legacies available at the Verbier Festival: 'while classical forms stagnate, non-classical ones are striking out on new paths.'

What general criteria might there be to elicit from such moments? Many years before, in a review of Stuart Hall and Paddy Whannel's *The Popular Arts* now collected here, Hobsbawm had rejected the standard view that there are basic terms of commensurability that enable comparative judgements, if not across the whole range of art then certainly within its main modes and across its major registers. The invitation to compare Keats and Dylan (to take a notorious instance not of his citing) is simply misconceived. Yet he also declined the standard alternative, the relativist appeal to the qualities proper to a given 'kind' as 'question-begging'. In truth, any attempt to distinguish 'good' from 'bad' art in the traditional way is misconceived, because radically anachronistic. The matter is quasi-ontological:

> The essential weakness of both these approaches to the mass art is a determination to discover the values of humanity before mass production in a situation in which they are at best marginal. There is no horse trying to look out from under the engine bonnet.

This chilling general judgement rests alongside the avuncular praise for Roskilde, and by virtue of its generality alone may be thought to have the greater weight. Mass art is post-art. There are no 'works' in the relevant sense (unless 'incidentally'), only the 'flow' of word, sound and image giving 'a heightened stylization of life' in which considerations of 'personality', real or fictional, and 'star quality' take the place of what used to be thought of as 'criticism'.

2

Criticism in its relevant senses was the essential practice of enlightenment, the other major commitment of bourgeois *Kultur*, and Hobsbawm's book includes two general surveys, each devoted to one of the two emblematic cultural categories in the history of Enlightenment: priests and their anti-types, 'free' intellectuals. His survey of religion in the past one hundred–odd years starts from a basic distinction between the personal and public aspects of religious affirmation and practice, and these in their turn are differentiated internally. He doubts the common suggestion that there has been a renewal of religious belief in recent decades. Certainly, there have been 'spectacular transfers' of denominational allegiance, above all within Christianity, where Pentecostalism has won the allegiance of millions in the Americas and Africa, but whether aggregate religious belief has become more widespread is open to question, as indeed is the meaning of 'belief' itself, which may or may not include subscription to supernaturalist cosmology or other kinds of bad science and may be largely a mode of communal identification or a valued means of access to rites of passage. What is clear, in contrast, is the steady progress of secularization, that is the protocol by which public affairs are conducted as though gods did not exist. But what is also now clear, he continues, is that the extent of secularist, not to say atheist, conviction was for a long time exaggerated by observers—or rather, obscured by the unrepresentative character of the political orders within which the cause advanced. It was a minority passion, and this would become clear with the progressive enfranchisement of contrastingly traditional social majorities. The result was an increase in the 'public presence' of religion, with significant political effects in nominally secular polities as various as the United States, Turkey, India and Egypt. A further aggravating condition since the 1970s has been the neo-liberal turn in the international capitalist order, with its widespread disruption of customary identities and relationships. These are the conditions in which fundamentalist tendencies have come to flourish in Christianity, Islam and Hinduism, availing themselves of communications technologies such as their ancestral world-views could never have conceived, in their struggle against the politics and culture of the Enlightenment.

   This recrudescence of obscurantism is just one of the general conditions bearing negatively on the historic function of the free intellectual, in Hobsbawm's account. Another is the currency of nationalism and the concomitant weakening of universal values, the indispensable reserve of critical authority in public affairs. Intellectuals as a social layer have their origins in the late Middle Ages, which saw the emergence of an educated stratum not predestined for the literate offices of church and government and in that sense 'free'. It was only in the later nineteenth century, however, in Russia from the 1860s and in France from the 1890s, that the classic figures of the *intelligentsiya* and *les intellectuels* acquired their distinctive profile, uniting occupation ('mental' work of some kind) with dissenting intervention in politics. Formed amid the crises of late Tsarist Russia and the Dreyfus Affair, the intellectuals hit their stride in 'the "short twentieth century" of revolutions and wars of ideological religion', attaining greatest momentum between the end of the Second World War and the collapse of the European Communist bloc. Thus, their role was most vivid in Hobsbawm's 'age of extremes', when social futures were globally in question and where ideas assumed correspondingly resonant forms. (The exaltation of science and its pioneers, in the heyday of Haldane and Bernal, was a specialized case of this.) Their fading came with a new period, characterized by the depoliticization of the electorates in the societies of achieved consumerism. In Hobsbawm's memorable words, 'the road from the democratic ideal of the Athenian agora to the irresistible temptations of the shopping centre has shrunk the space available for the great demonic force of the nineteenth and twentieth centuries: namely, the belief that political action was the way to improve the world.' Intellectuals are still with us, he writes, more numerous than ever before as an objective social category and with an unextinguished potential for oppositional thought and action, as the Occupy movements serve to show. But they can easily be isolated by political enemies and may come to be resented for their advantaged position in the labour market—as 'educated' social superiors. Their role in changing the world is indispensable, yet foredoomed in the absence of a 'united front' with 'ordinary people'. While the outlook for secular reason is uncertain, the prospects for that front are perhaps less good than they have ever been. 'That is the dilemma of the twenty-first century.'

3

In sum, an ever-widening social process, driven by the logic of commodity exchange and the dynamism of technological innovation, has fractured an achieved world of culture. Artists in the traditional high disciplines have either lost their established audience or turned to embrace the commodified art world and the riches it channels to a gilded few. The new mass arts thrive overall, but on terms that are unintelligible to the aesthetic criticism of the past. The great projects of social renewal of the last century have dissipated their promise or failed outright. It is the time of surging post-art, faltering enlightenment and darkened political horizons: a time in which we blunder 'mapless and guideless' into 'an unrecognizable future'. Small wonder that Hobsbawm's choice of motto for *Fractured Times* comes from Matthew Arnold's poem 'Dover Beach'. If this is not the familiar pessimism of *Kulturkritik*, it is something strangely like it. Traceable not only in the high manner of that metaphor of a desert without a prophet or a sign, it is there too in such disfiguring extravagances as the general assault on conceptual art, and in the lament for the passing of the twentieth-century intellectual *maître* and the rise of celebrity advocates like Bono. These instances occur in general surveys, and they acquire a more than simply generic tone through their collocation with the more specialized treatments of Jewish intellectual achievement in the age of emancipation, the Jews in Germany, the fate of *Mitteleuropa*, and a portrait of Karl Kraus written for a Frankfurt book club edition of *The Last Days of Mankind*. The binding theme in these chapters is the fate of the secular Jewish middle class of central Europe, its identification with the German language and culture as a universal medium of emancipation, and its dispersal or destruction under the joint impacts of expulsion and mass slaughter, the spread of nationalist particularism and—the ironic *coup de grâce*—the relegation of German, once the linguistic gateway to the universal, to secondary, regional status. Hobsbawm's historical judgements are inevitably complex, but the prevailing tone is now poignant rather than plangent, conveying the loss of a milieu and the fading of its memory. The great, far-flung bequest of high symphonic and chamber music is suddenly reframed as a local achievement, largely owing to a small number of men working within 'a few hundred square kilometres' of Vienna. Kraus is a still more intimate spiritual presence: 'For Viennese of my generation . . . *The Last Days* is simply a part of our lives. The copy of the first edition, which I constantly reread, bears on its title page the name of my mother.' The verb-tense is deceptive, however, for this is a culture that 'no longer lives'.

Still, Hobsbawm's book is not best viewed as a work of *Kulturkritik*, first of all for the simple reason that it remains open to an undecided future, not as a rhetorical ruse but in virtue of its central categorical commitments. Benjamin's investigation of the work of art in the age of mechanical reproduction, with its critical distinction between auratic and non-auratic art, was conceived as a contribution to a revolutionary aesthetic. In borrowing from the argument for his own purposes, Hobsbawm has altered its internal balance and scaled down its political ambition, but not so drastically as to shut down the passage to a contingently alternative state of affairs. Thus, he is able to produce a significantly differential account of the course of the arts over his chosen span of time—never the forte of *Kulturkritik*. That is not to say, of course, that the account is not vulnerable to challenge on empirical and other grounds. Thus, for example, it is hard to agree that sculpture subsists in a marginal, abject condition, or that the visual art of the past forty years can be seen off with a scattergun denunciation of 'charlatans' who cannot draw or paint and a solitary reference to Damien Hirst. In broader historical terms, the relations between the handicraft skills of picture-making ('painting' is a tendentiously narrow focus) and processes of reproduction have been more various than Hobsbawm's account allows. Etching, mezzotint and lithography are among the pre-photographic processes that enabled artists to create directly in a reproducible form or transpose painted and drawn images for multiple copying. Painters, reciprocally, have done more with photographs than take flight into abstraction and beyond, using them for research and preparation, incorporating them in mixed-media compositions, over-painting them or, at the limit, producing hyperrealist simulations of the photo-graphic effect. The motives for the emergence of avant-gardism must be sought somewhere other than in simple technical rivalry—a situa-tion with no parallel in the coeval patterns of innovation in music and literature.

Hobsbawm is happy to acknowledge productive unions of artisan primary production and large-scale reproduction, even if, as in the case of visual art, he exaggerates the difficulty and limitations of the available choices. However, such initiatives have normally entailed an increase in the factor of collaboration and, crucially for him, a struc-tural redistribution or rearticulation of creative powers, such that it becomes difficult or even inappropriate to speak of the outcomes as art. Although conceding that some arts have always entailed high levels of collaboration (the performing arts especially), he declines to acknowledge the historical reality of many hands at the highest level of auratic art, the studios of the Renaissance, where 'masters' were masters because they were judged worthy to train apprentices, who would execute work they had not designed themselves or assist their teachers directly. Symmetrically, he makes little of the emergence of new individual craft skills—those of the recording studio or the film editing suite, for example—and less of the new patterns of artistic mastery that the demands of complex cooperation have called into being. This is just what Jerry Leiber and Mike Stoller, the legendary words-and-music team who went on to create the role of the modern studio producer, had in mind in claiming that they wrote records, not songs. There is more art in the 'mass arts' than Hobsbawm was willing to grant, and if most of it is bad, this is mainly because, as he claims, it assumes and ministers to 'a closed world'. There is also a great deal more socially rarefied space in which to appreciate it than he assumes. The idea that festivals and concerts, Dionysian or not, are at the heart of popular music today is mistaken. The principal, and perhaps the defining mediation is the personal music player, which allows the filtering out of family, neighbours and fellow-passengers, not to mention the flooded semio-aesthetic environment itself, to create sequestered audiences of one, for command perfor-mances of whatever kind of music is preferred: Beyoncé, *Don Giovanni*,

a Breton harpist, Mahler, a medley created by a friend—it might be
any of these . . . Some find this mass public isolationism disturbing,
but all concentration requires some procedure of detachment, and
this kind is not self-evidently less pure in spirit than the older practice
of reading on the metro or the customary proprieties of the concert
hall.

4

Hobsbawm the historian would not have been the last to accept this,
for if his regard for the high arts (or some of them at least) seems
nearly absolute, there is no associated tendency to idealize their audiences. The essays of *Fractured Times* are demarcated from the general
run of pessimistic cultural commentary by their steady awareness
of the difference between the various arts themselves, as abstract
activities involving making, offering and receiving specialized
objects of different kinds, and 'culture' as the *idée-force* that bound
them in concrete historical formations with more or less settled
social meanings and purposes, as 'the arts'. Thus, for example, the
centring of 'culture' that Hobsbawm discerned in the bourgeois
milieux of the late 1800s, and the valorization of 'youth' that went
with it, presupposed a certain level of capital accumulation and was a
way of signifying it and reaping its yield of prestige—a conjunction of
interests that neither nullifies the achievements of its most talented
beneficiaries nor is redeemed by them. Seen in this way—and it is
Hobsbawm's book that prompts the thought—the ideal that the arts
might be taken to embody, the point of vantage for critical evaluation
of the way of the world, was always already compromised in spite of
itself, and for that reason insecure as the ground of *Kulturkritik*. (By
1894, when George Gissing published *In the Year of Jubilee*, the
bourgeois pursuit of 'culture', so named, was already an object of
mockery.) Indeed, it is arguable that the topos of 'culture' was intrinsically collusive in its semantic formation: homogenizing literature
and the various arts in a shared substance as if to facilitate comparisons and transfers among them, it was the exchange-value of the
spirit. The special authority of culture, which supposedly came from

higher, older things, was in this sense dependent on the commodity form, which it was to have saved from its own insufficiency. Anxiety is inherent in this, and it may be that the high ritual practices of classical concerts and opera in the past century, with their endless compulsion to repeat and continuing resistance to the new and untried, are its golden symptoms. Here is another 'closed world' to set beside that of 'industrialized culture', a world in which the only remaining surprise is the one in the title of Haydn's best-known symphony, and which, in so far as it is closed, as 'heritage', is no better than the rest.

Against such closures, Hobsbawm strikingly sets the example of festivals, especially those dedicated to music, which have been proliferating in the twenty-first century. In 2006, when he lectured on the subject at Salzburg, Britain had seen a near-doubling of the number of music festivals to 221 in just three years, while jazz alone could boast at least 250 scattered across thirty-three countries. Hobsbawm accords these institutions a crucial role in the artistic cultures of the future. They are a formula for assembling minority audiences in economically viable masses, on a national or international scale, and so protecting them and their arts from fatal exposure to everyday market conditions. Artistically, the newer festivals in particular enjoy the advantage of having few if any 'classics'. They are correspondingly open to 'discovery', to 'developing forms of artistic communication' and 'aesthetic experience', to 'adventure', and in so far as they remain so will have an important place in the globalizing culture of the decades ahead. The stakes may not be only artistic, he adds, instancing the multi-centred World of Music and Dance: 'As so often, behind these journeys of discovery lies a cultural or subversive, even a political, impulse.' In a book so preoccupied with endings of all kinds—including the one that, 'alas', did not happen, as revolutionaries believed it would—moments such as this are equally characteristic, both in their uncomplicated expressions of hope and in their transience. Others of the kind are wishful, as when Hobsbawm celebrates the popular apotheosis of Zinedine Zidane, the *beur* football star voted 'greatest Frenchman', as the warrant of a civilized future; or strategic in the paradoxical mode of remembrance, as when he recalls the idea of a union of intellectuals and 'ordinary people'. But these are cadences, both of them, and not surprisingly, for they are remnants of a politics of social transformation in which, by the time he was writing these essays, Hobsbawm could no longer believe—embers fanned briefly into life at the approach of the flood.

2021

Caution, Metaphors at Work

Serious noticing is fundamental to the work of significant writers; it is how they 'save life from itself', James Wood maintains, in the essay that gives a recent compilation of his criticism its title and foremost emphasis.[1] But the phrase has a dual reference, also denoting what Wood would say he does himself in much, perhaps most of his own writing: reviews, not of the ephemeral kind aptly called 'notices' but relatively long, considered critical pieces better designated 'essays'. His subtitle makes the claim without hesitation, and it is not irrelevant that it echoes one of the most distinguished examples of the genre, T. S. Eliot's *Selected Essays*, from 1932. It is easy to make too much of this sign of affiliation, but equally to overlook it, in a writer for whom titles have always been important. Wood joined the *Guardian* in 1992—aged twenty-seven—in the role of lead literary reviewer with the grand public designation of Chief Literary Critic. A quarter-century later, after a spell as Senior Editor at the *New Republic*, during the reign of Leon Wieseltier, he divides his working time between the *New Yorker* and Harvard, where his academic style is Professor of the Practice of Literary Criticism. These assorted authority-claims are matched in the design of *Serious Noticings*, which is more than just his fifth collection of reviews and other occasional texts. In one light it is actually less than that: twenty-two of its

---

1   James Wood, *Serious Noticing: Selected Essays*, London 2019, p. 72.

twenty-nine pieces, more than two-thirds, have already been reprinted in earlier volumes. But in another light, this is not the short measure it might seem. Spanning the twenty years from his leaving the *Guardian* in 1995, with very few blank years on the calendar, the book is in effect a super-selection: *The Best of . . .* perhaps, or *Wood on Wood*, complete with an introductory account of his formation and general understanding of the practice of criticism. The inclusion of two confessional texts, one meditating on the condition Wood calls 'homelooseness', the other on his 'becoming' his parents, relays a notable feature of the essays, amplifying the signs of critical personality as well as—or simply *as?*—a position.

In the practice itself, as evidenced here, what is immediately striking is its spread. The earliest work discussed comes from the early seventeenth century, the most recent from 2015 (Cervantes and Erpenbeck respectively). English-language originals, most of them from the US, make up the greater part of the reading, but there are also translations from seven other European languages (and eight countries: Albania, Austria, former Czechoslovakia, Germany, Hungary, Italy, Russia, Spain). The works discussed at length are joined by at least as many more, familiar or not, receiving anything from a passing mention to several paragraphs of commentary. The emphasis of Wood's critical treatment is variable too, ranging from stylistic analysis, as in a sustained argument concerning Melville's 'atheistic' (or 'polytheistic') pursuit of metaphor or Austen's innovation in the representation of inwardness, to the polemical genre study on 'hysterical realism', from 'reviews' in more common acceptations of the term to autonomous texts. Heading all this, in an unexpected token of his personal history and interests in music (he was a boy chorister, learned piano and trumpet at school, and taught himself rock drumming), is a 'homage' to the Who's legendary drummer, Keith Moon.

The constant throughout these essays is Wood's insistence on judgement, the evaluations he regards as the defining work of the critic. He has a notable capacity for articulate enthusiasm and a withering tongue to balance it. Here he is in full affirmative flow, celebrating the comedy of a favourite novelist:

Saul Bellow is probably the greatest writer of American prose of the twentieth century—where greatest means most abundant, various, precise, rich, lyrical . . . The august raciness, the Melvillean enormities and cascades . . . the Joycean wit, the lancing similes with their sharp American nibs . . . the happy rolling freedom of the daring uninsured sentences, the prose absolutely ripe with inheritance, bursting with the memories of Shakespeare and Lawrence, yet prepared for modern emergencies, the Argus eye for detail, and controlling all this, the firm metaphysical intelligence—all this is now thought of as Bellow's, as 'Bellovian'.[2]

And here he is, in 2009, on the 'cinema-speak' of 'America's best-known postmodern novelist': 'While Auster clearly shares some of [postmodernism's] interest in mediation and borrowedness—hence, his cinematic plots and rather bogus dialogue—he does nothing with cliché except use it.'[3]

The ebullience of judgement is overwhelming in that eulogy to Bellow, no less so the high-troping prose, and even Auster's literary death sentence is given a witty turn: Wood is an ostentatiously writerly critic, one who cultivates metaphor not as mere embellishment but as his essential procedure (he is a novelist as well as a critic). Elsewhere, in a book entitled with some finality *How Fiction Works*, he has set down his understanding of this commitment by way of a contrast with his 'two favourite twentieth-century critics of the novel'. Viktor Shklovsky and Roland Barthes were 'great', he maintains, 'because, being formalists, they thought like writers: they attended to style, to words, to form, to metaphor and imagery'. However, both 'thought like writers alienated from creative instinct, and were drawn, like larcenous bankers, to raid again and again the very source that sustained them—literary style'. Wood's reasoning at this juncture turns opaque—as it often does in such generalizing passages—but his point of arrival is unambiguous. Concerned with basic theoretical questions but without forgetting general audiences—Woolf's

2   Ibid., pp. 74–5.
3   Ibid., pp. 132–5.

'common reader'—he 'asks a critic's questions and offers a writer's answers'.[4]

Wood's ideal critic is 'a triple thinker' (a phrase borrowed from Edmund Wilson, who took it from Flaubert): a writer, talking about fiction 'as writers speak about their craft'; a journalist, writing 'with verve and appeal, for a common reader'; a 'scholar' open to two-way traffic in and out of the academy—and the most important of these identities, not fully captured in Wood's light reference to 'craft', is the first.[5] For his culminating claim is that any critical practice is an attempt to encourage in the reader an experience of the object corresponding to the critic's prior experience of it, a 'sameness' of disposition in relation to the work in question. Thus, criticism is in its inmost constitution a practice of metaphor, and in the unique case of literary criticism, which shares the medium of its object, is itself always already writing. 'So we perform', Wood concludes.

> And we perform in proximity, exulting in the fact that, dolphin-like, we are swimming in the element that nourishes us . . . We write as if we expect to be read; we write like the roses Eliot describes in 'Burnt Norton'—roses 'that had the look of flowers that are looked at'.[6]

While the aestheticist suggestions of this passage are not altogether misleading, they scant Wood's interest in historical formations of sensibility. His 'Wounder and Wounded', on V. S. Naipaul, is a study in postcolonial ambivalence, the novelist's restless union of 'a conservative vision' with 'radical eyesight'. Returning to *The Lion and the Unicorn: Socialism and the English Genius* to consider its idiosyncratic leftism, he places his central emphasis on Orwell's England, 'a place both real and fictional, with its own narrative conventions'. And in a fortuitous parallel essay, he explores Joseph Roth's fascination with an Austro-Hungarian Empire both overweening and

---

4   James Wood, *How Fiction Works*, London 2008, pp. 1–2.
5   Wood, *Serious Noticing*, pp. 5–6.
6   Ibid., p. 9.

unreal, 'magnificent and absurd', and anyway now gone.[7] Still, as he says about the author of *The Radetzky March*, 'you begin—and end—with the prose', and that priority is characteristic,[8] though here again there is a qualification to notice, for with the priority comes a caution: everything has a way of turning into everything else. 'When I talk about free indirect style', he advises his readers in *How Fiction Works*,

> I am really talking about point of view, and when I am talking about point of view I am really talking about the perception of detail, and when I am talking about detail I am really talking about character, and when I am talking about character I am really talking about *the real*, which is at the bottom of my enquiries.[9]

So the prose—his own, this time—makes its looping metaphoric descent into the really real, or 'life'.

'What Chekhov meant by life', how he signified it, is the subject of one of the earliest essays in *Serious Noticing*, about one of the story-tellers Wood most prizes. Its point of departure is the negative example of Ibsen. Ibsen, Wood charges, 'is like a man who laughs at his own jokes . . . He is always . . . making everything neat, presentable, knowable. The secrets of his characters are knowable secrets . . . the bourgeois secrets: a former lover, a broken contract, a blackmailer, a debt, an unwanted relative.'[10] For Chekhov, on the other hand, life is 'enigmatic', 'random', and rendered in a correspondingly 'accidental' style. A detail, here, is 'a reticent event', with a miraculous capability that Wood captures in a hyperbolic turn from Adorno's *Negative Dialectics*: 'If the thought really yielded to the object, if its attention were on the object, not on its category, the very objects would start talking under the lingering eye.'[11] In some similar way, as in Chekhov,

---

7   Ibid., p. 118.
8   Ibid., p. 109.
9   Wood, *How Fiction Works*, p. 3.
10   Wood, *Serious Noticing*, p. 35.
11   Ibid., p. 73.

characters can 'forget to act as *purposeful*' creations like Ibsen's 'envoys', in a reverse identification such that 'Chekhov's very narration disappears' into his character's discourse.[12]

There is life and then there are the hyperactive simulations of life that Wood a few years later denounced in a clutch of mainly US novels of the 'big, ambitious' kind, for which he created the rubric 'hysterical realism'. (The works in question were Salman Rushdie's *The Ground beneath Her Feet*, Thomas Pynchon's *Mason and Dixon*, Don DeLillo's *Underworld*, David Foster Wallace's *Infinite Jest* and Zadie Smith's *White Teeth*, all published between 1996 and 2000.) With due discriminations made within and among these novels and their authors, Wood felt able to announce that 'a genre is hardening'— a new genre characterized by its proliferation of storytelling, improbability, coincidence and parallelism, its displays of specialized information and attraction to ideas of universal inter-connectedness. In writing of this kind realism is being 'overworked', driven to a limit: 'It seems to want to abolish stillness, as if ashamed of silence.' These novels evade reality even as they avail themselves of realist conventions, Wood believes. And what they evade is 'an awkwardness about character and the representation of character in fiction'. The prevalence of caricature is one index of this unease and another is 'an excess of story-telling' that 'has become the contemporary way of shrouding, in majesty, a lack . . . That lack is the human', and hysterical realism is the attempt at a 'cover-up'. [13]

Wood's novelistically human—that is, 'fully human'—has various avatars, including 'strong feeling' and 'consciousness' and 'life' itself, and their opposites include 'information', 'spectacle', 'general messages' and narrative relations that are 'conceptual' rather than vital. 'Lifeness' is Wood's portmanteau coinage (*life* + *likeness*) for the representational qualities, principally those of characterization, that give access to the human. Zadie Smith's *White Teeth*—a novel that Wood holds in high but mixed regard—illustrates for him what happens when that value loses out to its contraries. Young Irie Jones

---

12   Ibid., pp. 47–8.
13   Ibid., p. 146.

(mixed-race parentage, Jamaican and white English) is pregnant, and has no idea which of the Iqbal twins (South Asian parentage) is the father, but then has a vision in which before long 'roots won't matter any more because they can't because they mustn't because they're too long and they're too tortuous and they're just buried too damn deep. She looks forward to it.'[14]

This construction is a non sequitur, as it happens; since the boys are siblings, the child's 'roots' will be the same whichever one is the parent. But Wood's objection to Smith's words is of a different order: it is that—in a move antithetical to Chekhov's—she has here taken over Irie's inner speech, and this as the last act in a tendentious subplot:

> It is Smith who made Irie, most improbably, have sex with both brothers, and it is Smith who decided that Irie, most improbably, has stopped caring who is the father. It is quite clear that a general message about the need to escape roots is more important than Irie's reality, what she might actually think. A character has been sacrificed for what Smith called, in [an] interview, 'ideas and themes that I can tie together—problem-solving from other places and worlds'. This is problem-solving all right. But at what cost?[15]

It is difficult to read passages such as this without taking note of a special kind of metaphor, one instanced in the seemingly redundant phrasing 'character and the representation of character' and the equivocal verb *make*, meaning both *create* and *compel*. This is the family of metaphors in which literary constructions and their authors begin to act and interact like real people. Smith as writer 'made' Irie, as she made everything else in the text of her novel, but the note of compulsion involves a category mistake. And while the status of her word-choice as pun may be urged in mitigation of this apparent confusion, as it might, there can't be much doubt about the references to 'Irie's reality', 'what she might actually think', and her 'sacrifice' on

---

14   Ibid., p. 163.
15   Ibid., p. 163.

the altar of problem-solving. Smith is taken to betray this quasi-existent person, in the same reordering of being that has Chekhov's narrative 'disappear' into the discourse of one of its own characters. Wood may not actually believe that characters are people, but in passages such as these the thought persists, like one of Freud's 'unsurmounted' cultural traces. He builds his arguments on a slope that leads down to what his favourite critic of the novel, Shklovsky, dismissed over a century ago as 'ontological naivety'.

The emergence of hysterical realism marks a crux in literary representation: 'Which way will the ambitious contemporary novel go?' Wood asks. 'Will it dare a picture of life, or just shout a spectacle?'[16] The form of the question recalls Lukács's, in *The Meaning of Contemporary Realism*, no less insistently for all the difference in its substantive terms of engagement.[17] (In the earlier case the relevant life was capitalism and the 'reasonable question' of socialism as an alternative to it, while the 'spectacle' was the modernism typified by Kafka.) The form of the response is divergent, within a common allegiance to figuring the real—and a shared admiration for Thomas Mann. Lukács's preferred 'critical realism' came with a set of formal canons, the what and the how of a valid practice of the novel in his time. There is no strict equivalent in Wood. The list of his positives is various and open, surprisingly so in a critic better known for his 'takedowns', as etiquette has it, than for his enthusiasms. Comedy and secularism are prevailing values: he pairs and praises Cervantes and Proust as 'comic writers, properly snagged in the mundane, whose fiction has too often been etherealized out of existence'.[18] Hrabl is singled out in the same spirit. Wood commends Krasznahorkai's avant-gardist work in the long, seemingly interminable sentence, 'reality examined to the point of "madness"', but also the 'usefully prosaic, . . . almost managerial present tense', of Jenny Erpenbeck's *Go, Went, Gone*, an instalment in her novelistic investigation of 'the domestic interiority of [German] history'.[19] This

---

16   Ibid., p. 162.
17   Georg Lukács, *The Meaning of Contemporary Realism*, London 1955.
18   Wood, *Serious Noticing*, p. 325
19   Ibid., pp. 486, 461.

is the archive of the novel as resource rather than backdrop to a canon.

Wood is nonetheless as judgemental as Lukács, more so if anything because more detailed in his discriminations (at times his close readings, in which he excels, take on the manner of comments in a creative writing workshop). But whereas Lukács's evaluations were grounded in an explicit and ordered understanding of historical actuality and possibility, Wood's have no comparable sanction, be it ethico-political or for that matter aesthetic. His relationship to the theorists he cites—Shklovsky, Barthes, Bakhtin, Adorno, Benjamin, Genette—seems 'accidental', not to say opportunist. Psychoanalysis is a steadier reference-point (and indeed there is more of Freud than Derrida in his summary of deconstruction, to which he allows a fluctuating inclination), but hardly an anchorage. The appeal to 'life' and the really real can hardly fail to summon the spirit of a critic who goes unmentioned: F. R. Leavis. Yet even he, the 'anti-philosopher', rooted his Lawrentian vitalism in a romantic theory of modernity. His conviction of self-evidence in judgement was not self-enclosed. Wood, contrastingly, has seemed bent on a course like that enjoined by Remy de Gourmont and relayed by Eliot in his essay 'The Perfect Critic', turning his intuitions into laws (*ériger en lois ses impressions personelles . . .*), and it may be, then, that these observations are beside the point, too much taken with critics' questions to notice a writer's answer. In this school of thought, the warrant of good judgement is charismatic.

Criticism, in Wood's understanding, is not 'writing about'; it is what he calls 'writing through', and its aim is not best thought of as suasion, 'producing a *reason* in support' of a judgement. The process is one in which the critic is 'describing an experience and trying to stimulate in the reader an experience of that experience';[20] the goal is 'sameness of vision' and that, in the special case of literary criticism, which shares with its object 'the language of metaphor', is 'in some ways a sameness of writing'. What is being suggested here, it appears, is a conception of criticism as paraliterature, enabling and maybe

20 Ibid., pp. 9, 6.

consisting in a procedural merging of critic and text, 'an act of figurative identification'.[21] And completing the scene of critical judgement, then, is a figure fit to accompany Wood's teeming metaphors: the protean character known as *we/us*, *one* or *the reader*.

The so-called 'authorial we', its equivalents included, is a familiar device of reader management, formally presumptuous or manipulative, even if more often than not a dead letter. But readers coming to *Serious Noticing* will find themselves pre-empted—spoken for—at every turn by a subject as ontologically slippery as Wood's 'lifeness'. This pronominal character doesn't only 'think' and 'believe' and 'feel' in the ordinary way. It 'laughs', sometimes coming close to weeping; it has 'the urge to blow a Flann O'Brien–size raspberry', or 'realizes, with a shock, that Bellow has taught one how to see and hear, has opened the senses'.[22] It sometimes appeals for confirmation ('don't we?'), which at other times can be taken as read ('All of us want . . .').[23] There is an intermittent narrative of reading experience in these little episodes, which may or may not in fact be 'ours', that is, yours or mine. They are instances of 'unverifiable self-projection'— which is the charge laid against George Orwell, as it happens, by one James Wood. 'How can he really know this?' he asks, and now the question is returned to himself.[24] He can't, except in so far as he 'makes' us, much as he says Smith has 'made' Irie Jones, the self-effacing tendentious subject of the writing recruiting the heterogeneous us who are reading into an imaginary concerted *we* for whom the desiderated 'experience' has already occurred.

This one-sided bonding completes a literary-critical process whose master-tendency is identification: of critic and literary text; of critic and readers; and thus, ideally, of reader and text in a new critical appropriation. The tendency is no more than that, however strong, and this may be just as well, for its general consummation would be a scarcely imaginable post-linguistic condition, of which

21   Ibid., p. 10.
22   Ibid., pp. 102–6, 140, 78.
23   Ibid., pp. 210, 335.
24   Ibid., p. 195.

Wood leaves his readers with a foretaste. One case is Virginia Woolf's account of a moment towards the close of a public lecture in central London in which her friend the art critic Roger Fry had been talking about a long slide sequence ranging from Poussin to Cézanne. 'And finally', Woolf reports,

> the lecturer, after looking long through his spectacles, came to a pause. He was pointing to a late work by Cézanne, and he was baffled. It went, he said, far beyond any analysis of which he was capable. And so instead of saying, 'Next slide,' he bowed, and the audience emptied itself into Langham Place

—beginning, Wood continues, 'to experience what Fry saw'.

The lecturer's 'wordless humility' and the audience's suppositious response are outward signs of an 'abeyance' of 'understanding'. This is an affirmative meaning of silence in Wood's lexicon, and it is striking, moreover, how often his essays move towards closing ideas of silence or stillness as though towards a default state of rest. Silence as wonder or as acknowledgement, as the experience of sublimity or of emptiness: in that recurring word and its clustered meanings the trace of a childhood formation in a devout Evangelical family—to which Wood the unbelieving writer has returned so often—is still visible. The contraries, varying from one occasion to the next, are familiar; they include adventitious 'themes', 'problem-solving', compulsive activity and stasis alike, the stock impediments to life's creative flow. The paradox of criticism in the Woodsian manner is, then, that for all its rhetorical energy and analytic skill, the end-state it inscribes in its charter is post-verbal silence. The closing sentence of the review of Marilynne Robinson's *Home* enacts the process at an advanced stage: 'So luminous are this book's final scenes, so affecting, that it is all the critic can do not to catch from it . . . the contagion of ceaseless quotation, a fond mumbling.'[25]

2021

---

25   Ibid., p. 457.

A Party of Latecomers

A magazine, if it is not doctrinaire, should have a character rather than a programme—so wrote Roberto Schwarz in 1967, launching a new publishing initiative for the left in Brazil. His preferred comparison was 'a good essay', something both surefooted and unexpected, clearing an uncertain path by the light of interest and strict reasoning, and certainly not without guiding convictions.[1] Recall of this prospectus is prompted by the record of the New York–based *n+1* in its first ten years of publication as a magazine devoted, in its own phrasing, to 'literature, culture and politics', establishing itself in that time as a distinctive presence on the intellectual left, in the United States and beyond. It is not only convention that suggests the interest and value of a provisional assessment of the project—or more aptly perhaps, an appraisal of its 'character'.

An outline description of the practical ensemble called *n+1* gives a first indication of the unfolding scope and spirit of the undertaking and at the same time suggests the necessary modesty of a small-scale account of it. The magazine itself is dual-platform, combining a print publication that has so far seen more than twenty book-length issues, and an online supplement that expands and also diversifies editorial capacity, creating space for special subject streams, accommodating

---

1 Roberto Schwarz, 'Apresentaçao', *Teoria e Prática*, 1, 1967; reprinted in *Praga: Revista de Estudos Marxistas*, 1, 1996, p. 79.

shorter or more time-sensitive contributions, and in all ways enhancing the ability to manoeuvre. *N+1* has spun out a book series under the same name, some but not all of the material originating in its pages, and also publishes a sister magazine, *Paper Monument*, devoted to contemporary art. These print and online manifestations take on immediate, face-to-face form in occasional panel discussions, public launch parties and other convivial events—all this miniaturized, as it were, if only for a time, in a Tumblr-based personal ads service. More than a publication, *n+1* is a microculture, a whole way of intellectual life.

For all that, the magazine, including its online supplement, amounting to an archive of texts in the high hundreds, will be the main reference here. More programmatic ventures, being more tightly focused and (inevitably) more repetitious, offer interpretive economies. Here, the case is otherwise: in *n+1*, the essay has been foremost, and even paradigmatic, with all that implies of mobility and surprise—and for a reader, the counterpart risks of reductive generalization.

1

However, 'programmatic' is not the last word that comes to mind in a survey of *n+1*'s first six or seven numbers, which appeared over the four years from summer 2004 to fall 2008. The inaugural issue struck an immediately combative note. 'Negations' was its headline theme and it opened with a statement of disaffection: if not quite a manifesto then a warning of mutiny:

> We are living in an era of demented self-censorship. The old private matters—the functions of the body, the chase after love and money, the unhappiness of the family—are now the commonest stuff of public life ... But try saying that the act we call 'war' would more properly be termed a massacre, and that the state we call 'occupation' would more properly be termed a war; that the conspiracy theories, here and abroad, which have not yet been proved true by Seymour Hersh or the General Accounting Office

are probably, nonetheless, true; or that the political freedoms so cherished and, really, so necessary, are also the mask of a more pervasive, insidious repression—try saying all this, or any of it, and see how far you get. Then try saying it in a complex way, at some length, expressing as you do so an actual human personality.

We are living in a time when Nabokov and Henry James are read in Tehran but we have pornography and publicity at home . . . In the future, it will be seen as the time when some of the best people in our intellectual class gave their 'critical support' to a hubristic, suicidal adventure in Iraq.

The problem is hardly a lack of magazines, even literary magazines. Culture can expand now to fill the superstore. But civilization is the dream of advance—to find the new, or take what we know from the past and say it with the care that only the living can claim. 'One must have been in exile and in the wilds to appreciate a new periodical,' said Alexander Herzen, founder of the mighty *Bell*. Perhaps you live in the city or the town, and in the safety of your own country. But you have known the exile, and are acquainted with the wilds.[2]

The grounds of disaffection were both literary and political, and pervasively cultural. As one of the founding editors, Marco Roth, put it, in the Letters columns that soon became a standing feature of the magazine:

At a time when Americans seemed to have lost faith in both progressive politics and the possibility of individual improvement, in literature and thought, without the aid of capitalism . . . we chose *n+1* as the working title of our journal. For us it was a metaphor for the possibility of progress, the infinitely open set.[3]

---

2 'Editorial Statement', *n+1*, 1: *Negations,* summer 2004. Subsequent first references follow this form but omit the title of the magazine.
3 Marco Roth, 'Letters: '(*n*+1)x2', 5: *Decivilizing Process,* winter 2007. Roth was replying to an editor of an Italian Marxist journal of longer standing called *n+1*.

If these terms of diagnosis had an old-fashioned ring, they were not to be mistaken for signs of fogeyism. They were one illustration of a commitment to a change of intellectual ethos, a move beyond the compulsive, enfeebling ironism of the postmodern 1990s. Or in the words of Roth's co-founder Keith Gessen, as he signed off the launch issue with a renewed address to the reader: 'There are better ways to embarrass yourself. It is time to say what you mean.'[4]

Of the twenty-two items that made up the first issue, more than two-thirds were written by five founding editors, either under their own names or in their collective capacity.[5] These included, most strikingly, Mark Greif's 'Against Exercise', a sustained critical examination of the culture of gym and jogging in its symptomatic relations with capitalist work technologies—the first in a long series of critiques of everyday life at the millennium and since. Revulsion at the Anglo-US invasion of Iraq was pronounced in the magazine at this time, and Greif contributed a further two essays prompted by it, one a study in contemporary war-making ending with a call for the moral self-revaluation, the process of 'public self-discovery' that the war should properly bring in its wake;[6] the other an exercise in the high prophetic manner on the subject of the abuses of Abu Ghraib and their source in the cultural pathologies of the homeland:

> Because of the way we live, the American mind fills up with the sexual use of other people. Even on the subway and in the street, porn-i-color daydreams issue through our mental viewfinders . . . You can escape our bombing maybe, but you can't escape our fun.[7]

---

4 Keith Gessen, 'End-notes', 1.

5 Keith Gessen, Mark Greif, Chad Harbach, Benjamin Kunkel and Marco Roth. The sixth founder was Allison Lorentzen. This was a male-heavy line-up, with a first contents page to match. Women's presence in the magazine grew steadily in the next few years, as did the imprint of sexual politics—which had been evident in its critical repertoire from the beginning. Editorial restructuring in 2012 rejuvenated the core group and rebalanced its gender ratio (13: *Awkward Age*, summer 2012).

6 Mark Greif, 'Mogadishu, Baghdad, Troy', 1.

7 Mark Greif, 'A Bunch of Nobodies', 1.

Greif's essay on warfare, with its unabashed interpretive dependence on the Homeric prototype of heroic combat, was one earnest of the attempt to open lines of communication between literary and political values. Benjamin Kunkel offered a second approach in 'Horse Mountain', a story in which an old man reflects on the manifold frictions of a long and strong but difficult marriage, with its recurring clashes over religion and Palestinian rights, but also on the ambiguities of his own contemplative righteousness—political commitment without entailments, judgements without reparative action. The Middle East crisis returned in the unlikely form of a proposal from Greif and Roth for the incorporation of the West Bank and Gaza as the fifty-first state of the Union.[8] Cool and clever in its exposition, this, as Roth explained to the Israeli newspaper *Haaretz* years later, was a piece of 'political surrealism' written in mock-conformity with the conventional demand to take a position on the question.[9] In truth not inclined to make any political statement—'what could we say that hadn't already been said at that point?'—the authors tendered a literary simulacrum.

In the general field of literary and cultural criticism, on the other hand, the appetite for concerted intervention was immediately evident. Under the heading 'The Intellectual Situation', *n+1* opened a 'Diary', a record of critical encounters and engagements giving body to the Sartrean suggestion of the rubric, in which 'The Editors' collectively traversed the institutions, forms and practices of the old and new media, beginning with three centres of literary-cultural evaluation: the long-established *New Republic*; the new literary pacemakers flocking around Dave Eggers's *McSweeney's* magazine and its offspring the *Believer*; and the neo-conservative *Weekly Standard*.[10]

Written in a rapid, unbuttoned, aphoristic prose, these polemics were 'negations' by which to capture something of the positive characteristics of properly critical thought. In the books pages of *The New*

---

8   Mark Greif and Marco Roth, 'Palestine, the 51st State', 1.

9   Cit. Ariel Krill, 'Take a Page from This: How One Magazine Reinvigorated American Intellectual Life', *Haaretz*, 28 September 2013.

10   Founded, respectively, 1914; 1998 and 2003; 1995.

Republic, the editors of *n+1* perceived a degeneration of normative discourse on literature (the historic 'defence of standards') into 'a new vulgarity'. Taste was now confused with 'sniffing out the tasteless', as judgement hardened into censoriousness. Authority, fetishized as 'intelligence', was taking the place of thought:

> The moral responsibility is not to be intelligent. It's to *think*. An attribute, self-satisfied and fixed, gets confused with an action, thinking, which revalues old ideas as well as defends them. Thought adds something new to the world; simple intelligence wields hardened truth like a bludgeon.[11]

The case of *McSweeney's* and the *Believer* was quite the opposite. That the 'Eggersards' were in important respects an avant-garde phenomenon *n+1* was ready to grant. Their leader, the author of *A Heartbreaking Work of Staggering Genius*, had a proven flair for 'creating institutions of a less elitist literary culture', and if his 'movement' should prove capable of restarting 'the engine of literary innovation and strife', then it would have 'performed a real historic service'. But this seemed unlikely: the peculiarity of avant-gardism Eggers-style was its regressive impulse, a return 'to the claims of childhood': 'Transcendence would not figure in [Eggersard] thought. Intellect did not interest them, but kids did.' In keeping with this, the reappropriation in *McSweeney's* of the design and tonal departures of earlier periods went on unburdened by the concern for truth that had been their historic point. The *Believer* would later be launched as the main vehicle of the Eggersards, taking forward 'their version of thinking—as an antidote to mainstream criticism, which they call snarkiness'. But 'mere belief is hostile to the whole idea of thinking'. The magazine's series of philosophical profiles 'confused philosophers with white-haired dispensers of truth. That is not a thinker: that's Santa Claus.'[12] Supervised in the name of a petrified authority or sentimentalized and swaddled to the point of inanity, either way

---

11   The Editors, 'Designated Haters', 1.
12   The Editors, 'A Regressive Avant-Garde', 1.

literary culture risked estrangement from the necessary freedoms and disciplines of critical thought.

To these twin cautions, the 'pomo neo-cons' of the *Weekly Standard* added a third, of a different kind. Now the danger was not the mock-critical posture of an authoritarian liberalism or the faux-democratic enthusiasms of the Eggersards but the complacency of the left in a time of regular intellectual cross-dressing on the hard right. The *Standard* was 'a parallel universe' with the emphasis precisely on the parallel, not the otherness. An article celebrating Mickey Mouse as the great American optimist borrows its procedural inspiration from the *marxisant* '"cultstuds" . . . now available at a discount in most universities'. Another repurposes Foucauldian themes to describe and lament the coming discursive exclusion of those for whom 'gay marriage' is a contradiction in terms—the ordinary guy who believes in 'Adam and Eve, not Adam and Steve', the truly oppressed of his time. Such are the 'advanced methods' that 'too many of us with left-wing prejudices' thought sufficient to 'change the world'. Their successful reappropriation by the right was proof that 'learning to think strategically about symbolic forms doesn't necessitate any particular substantive politics.' Indeed, they had been requisitioned for a strategy that allows 'those from elite backgrounds to pretend to speak like the philistine middle class'. The culturalization of political discourse had long been a key stratagem of the right.[13]

N+1's approach to popular culture was different. The last of the launch editorials turned from writing to sport and from intuitions of value to strict measurement, noting and reflecting on the relentless increase in the average height and weight of professional basketball and baseball players, to the point where the games themselves were altered and compromised. 'Forget the fact that the basket is too low, no longer commensurate with our capacity for jumping; there's not even space on the court to accommodate all the bodies.' At once knowledgeable and unsparing in the way of true fans, the editors offered the most general conclusions, which were not of the kind to flatter the ordinary guy:

---

13   The Editors, 'PoMo NeoCons',1.

As the athletes became less human, they could also have become less meaningful. Instead, the entire culture has bulked up, and the American male body has become, in effect, a miniature version of the economy—for each, 'health' has come to be defined by accelerating rates of production and consumption, regardless of the long-term effects . . . So perhaps it doesn't matter how absurdly huge our athletes become; they are fungible commodities that can be broken down into numbers and swapped accordingly.[14]

2

The subject that spoke in this passage was the formative presence in the new magazine. It was given to hybridation and modal displacement as procedures of writing and critical resources. Thus the editorials that have been so important a part of the contents are not 'editorials' but a self-styled 'Diary', which in this case—the first of many such—turns out to consist of four short essays presented as waystations in the picaresque narrative of a cultural starveling—a small, unresolved fable of arid times. The scope of reviewing is similarly reimagined. In Nicholas Dames's hands, the usual novel round-up has become a form of genre study.[15] What looks, to start with, like a very late review of the movie *Avatar* develops into a sustained critical-historical discussion of stereoscopic art, with a range of reference extending from Baudelaire to Werner Herzog.[16] Similarly, framing decisions can be playful and at times perverse. Lawrence Jackson's 'Slickheads' tells a story (his own) of growing up black in north-west Baltimore, in a text that is easily taken for fiction although framed as an 'essay'—and might well be taken so, with some reason, were it presented cold.[17] Kristin Dombek's 'How to Quit', is another 'essay' that might be a fiction, this one centrally

---

14   The Editors, 'Human, Not Too Human', 1.
15   See his 'The Theory Generation', 14: *The Awkward Age*, summer 2012, and 'Seventies Throwback Fiction', 21: *Throwback*, winter 2015.
16   Moira Weigel, 'Cinema of Disillusionment', 14.
17   Lawrence Jackson, 'Slickheads', 15: *Amnesty*, winter 2013.

focused on the addictive appeal of the addicted, and tagged 'Money
and Power' and 'Urban Planning'. More recent essays by her form a
serio-comic advice column, in which her fictional agony aunt writes
a sequence of what might be—what?—short essays, now tagged 'My
Life and Times'.[18] Redolent of the postmodern years, no doubt, such
tactics are better viewed, overall, in the perspective of two other features of *n+1* that were visible here, a strong attachment to critical
cultural theory (of differing kinds) and unbending resistance to the
logic of the market: they have been part of a general effort to renew
the reach of the literary, in conditions where, as its founders believed,
'literature was being increasingly marginalized, particularly by the
people who were doing it.'[19]

In the same way, however, attachment to 'theory' was now not
quite what it had been in the last quarter of the twentieth century.
Then, thanks to the dual abdication of philosophy and the novel,
European theory had been taken up as the only available means by
which to think the crises that harrowed US culture and society from
the late sixties onwards. Theory was now 'dead', the editors declared:
inevitably, since it had been an import culture that could not long
survive the actual deaths of its great exponents. 'But the big mistake
right now would be to fail to keep faith with what theory once meant
to us'—not all the sometime critics of the sign now worked in advertising. 'An opening has emerged, in the novel and in intellect. What
to do with it?'[20] In respect of the novel, that question remained, for now,
a gesture, notwithstanding a passing salute to Jonathan Franzen's
The Corrections, hailed by the editors as 'a monumental renewal of

---

18   Kristin Dombek, 'How to Quit', 15; see also 'The Help Desk', 19: *Real
Estate*, spring 2014.

19   Krill, 'Take a Page from This', *Haaretz*. See Gessen's long account of
Dave Eggers's tireless and increasingly manipulative self-marketing, also in
the first issue. His lens, appropriately, was the activity of Gary Baum, the
teenage creator of *FoE! Log*, perhaps the most disobliging fan initiative a self-
made celebrity ever had to cope with. ('Eggers, Teen Idol', 1. *FoE* is an acronym
for 'Friends of Eggers'.)

20   The Editors, 'Theory: Death Is Not the End', 2: *Happiness*, winter
2005.

the critical social novel', the thinking novel of life after theory.[21] The sheer miscellaneity of the short fiction published in *n+1* and its uncertain priority in the editorial scheme—for all the pervasive literariness of the magazine—did not encourage strong inferences. The role of 'intellect', in contrast, had already been signalled, and quickly materialized in a steady, versatile flow of cultural criticism. Inflected sometimes towards a Foucauldian ontology of the present, sometimes towards Bourdieusian constructions of the literary field, often recalling the Adorno of *Minima Moralia*, though usually with a dash of mockery to enliven his gallows humour, this has been the central practice and distinction of *n+1*.

It went without saying that the institutions and practices of the literary and wider journalistic culture would be first in line for critical assessment. The editorials against *The New Republic* and the *Believer* were opening shots, to be followed by a report from inside the *Wall Street Journal*, mordant commentaries on the *Atlantic Monthly* and *Harper's*, for their obdurate sexism, and—hilariously—the *Paris Review*, 'for disproving the prejudice that blurb-writing can't extend over thousands of words'.[22] Core issues and practices of book culture were appraised one after another. The panic over a supposed 'reading crisis' was denounced as a 'con' reducing reading itself to a shallow bookstore 'event' and serving to discourage and invalidate the free and responsible exercise of critical judgement.[23] The function of book reviewing was assessed for reconstruction, public readings for abolition.[24] The New York Review Books Classics

---

21   Compare Nicholas Dames, reviewing a wave of 'Theory-wise' novels (six and more in two years) and modifying Henry James's advice for the present: 'Forget the hermeneutics of suspicion. Remember what you've suspected all along—what, looking around you, you can hardly avoid suspecting. Be one of those on whom nothing, not even Theory, is lost.' ('The Theory Generation', p. 14: *The Awkward Age*, summer 2012.)

22   Philip Connors, 'My Life and Times in American Journalism', 4: *Reconstruction*, spring 2006; The Editors, 'The Intellectual Situation', 15.

23   The Editors, 'The Reading Crisis', 3: *Reality Principle*, fall 2005,.

24   The Editors, 'Book Review Nation', 6: *Mainstream*, winter 2008; 'Literary Readings: Cancel Them', 2.

library—'a cosmopolitan minor literature'—prompted a broad reflective survey of the role of book series in canon-formation, while a companion piece explored the functioning of 'the hype cycle' as 'the emotional life of capitalism, an internalized stock market of aesthetic calls and puts [testifying] to the power and then, almost as soon, to the impotence of mere culture'.[25] In a landmark piece subsequently developed as an *n+1* book, Chad Harbach discussed the ubiquitous and widely deprecated university writing programme in its imagined and real relations with the other world of New York publishing. Himself an alumnus of 'the Programme' and a novelist then only months away from a best-selling New York debut, Harbach profiled the contrasting ecologies of the two systems, their respective economic states—the academic flourishing, the commercial nervy and embattled—and divergent canonical priorities, the short story versus the big novel. Stock polarizations of the two were mistaken, he maintained: the illusions and introversion of the burgeoning university writing culture were no less a hazard than the middle-brow pressures of Manhattan publishing.[26]

The greatest challenge to the familiar book world came with the electronic re-equipping of retail and the creation of new computerized systems for writing and publishing, in a period of ascendant neo-liberalism. Between the arrival of the World Wide Web and Amazon in the early 1990s and the advent of personal e-reading hardware and the new social media a decade later, every aspect of book and periodical publishing came under notice of more or less radical restructuring. The gestation of *n+1* belongs to this period and was in part conditioned by it. One characterization of the project—Greif's—suggested an ark of sorts, 'a long print archive in an era of

25   Respectively, The Editors, 'The Hype Cycle', and 'The Spirit of Revival', 6.

26   'MFA vs. NYC', 10: *Self-Improvement*, fall 2010. Originally signed 'The Editors', this became the opening text in a book edited by Harbach: *MFA vs NYC: The Two Cultures of American Fiction*, New York 2014. MFA stands for Master of Fine Arts. In 1975, Harbach reported, there were seventy-nine such programmes in the United States; by 2010 the number had risen to 854.

the short sound bite'.[27] This was apt in its way, but conveyed little of the energy with which the editors would appraise the emergent forms, practices and ethos of the new communication technologies.

The winter 2007 number, headlined 'Decivilizing Process', devoted its Diary to email, cell phones and blogging. These editorials are beyond simple paraphrase in their literariness, and compellingly— impractically—quotable. They range in attitude from high-minded disbelief to knowing desolation. The point about these critics is that they are intimate with the degradations they lament. The rhetorical manner rises to the high epigrammatic—

Alexander [the Great] started the silent era of the West; Nokia will finish it.

—digresses into the learned fanciful—

The email, like the Petrarchan sonnet, is properly a seduction device.

—and modulates at times into a rapid, button-holing style of address we might call Stand-Up:

When writing first developed, ancient philosophers feared it would destroy human memory; to write anything down was to put yourself in the position of that guy in the movie Memento. And this wasn't totally wrong. Also, letters: they had a funny way of getting lost or opened by the wrong people.[28]

And so on. But through all the spirited play there is a steady vision of history progressing by its bad side. Email is an epitome of

---

27   Reported by Susan Hodara, 'Intellectual Entrepreneurs', *Harvard Magazine*, January–February 2010.

28   Respectively, the Editors, 'Whatever Minutes', 'Against Email' and 'The Blog Reflex', 5: *Decivilizing Process*, winter 2007 respectively. Alexander's soldiers are said to have marvelled at his ability to read silently.

uncontrollable, unusable overproduction. Blogging is, for the most part, a travesty of the more democratic public sphere the development of the weblog seemed to promise. Cell phone use nurtures a public behaviour compelling you to talk to someone, anyone, but not the person sitting beside you. Except in emergencies, these debased tendencies prevail. 'The benevolent uses of the phone, the internet, the weblog, email, and so forth, ride like bits of cork on a great tide of waste', a 'decivilizing process' that 'will undo our thoughts, our speech, our fantasies. That's an emergency, too. Only who do you call about it?' [29]

3

The acknowledgement of those bits of cork was more than a rhetorical concession of the familiar kind. At times, indeed, dialectical ingenuity could pass over into wishfulness, as it did a few years later, when Twitter, deplored by some for its intensive cultivation of narcissistic nullity, was salvaged as the new antidote to 'blogorrhea', revaluing the classical literary values of 'terseness and impersonality' in a time of pandemic slackness and self-indulgence. But the more usual emphasis was that struck by Roth, when he denounced 'the faux-democratic, but really "mass-cult" effects of blogging which have reduced news to gossip, critique to fandom, and transmuted taste into mere regional and class preferences.'[30]

Such prose was vulnerable to the charge of 'elitism', not least in a magazine so killjoy that it could turn even a simple tweet into a high-cultural mission. And as the editors perceived, the currency of the charge was a topic in itself, not to be reduced to a description that might or might not be accurate. Their 'Revolt of the Elites' was a piece of reverse engineering designed to elucidate the problem to which the populist commonplace of 'elitism' was a solution of a kind.

---

29   The Editors, 'Decivilizing Process'. The allusion in the title is to Norbert Elias, *The Civilizing Process* (1939).

30   Respectively, the Editors, 'Please RT', 14; and online only, Marco Roth, 'Blog Bound', 29 October 2009.

In its given form, this was already the work of a displacement from politics to culture, in which the most powerful agencies of state and society—once, but no longer, dubbed 'the power elite'—were always-already above suspicion. College education was a central means of collective self-reproduction for America's monied classes and only secondarily an egalitarian resource; but even so it was not a general marker of 'elite' membership. That distinction was reserved for highly educated individuals—very often but not invariably formed in a privileged liberal-arts environment—who appeared indifferent to the 'money-making mandate' that 'real Americans' were supposed to fulfil, whether by succeeding or in failing by the book.

These compatriots were instinctive Bourdieusians, $n+1$ argued, convinced that displays of cultural distinction were no more than badges of class identity: refusing such bad faith, real Americans admitted their real, shared preferences. However, there was an alternative anthropogy of moral difference, which the editors upheld as an attainable, though distant, standard: this was José Ortega y Gasset's inter-war classic, *The Revolt of the Masses*. 'The beautiful blindness of Ortega's analysis', as they understood it, 'was to ignore social distinctions in favour of existential differentiations. Aristocratic and mass man were . . . not social categories at all but separate dispositions.'[31]

This was a naive reading of a rhetorical sublimation that has been commonplace in the high tradition of cultural criticism for two centuries or more.[32] But credulity here enabled a strange misprision, such that Ortega's aristocrats became those who are 'superior' to others only by virtue of believing themselves inferior to what they are capable of becoming. '*Self-improvement*, for all that it smacks of the self-help shelf at Barnes & Noble'—and much else that Don José and

---

31   The Editors, 'Revolt of the Elites', 10: *Self-Improvement*, fall 2010, p. 16.

32   In fact, this gambit was an instance of the culturalist displacement of politics that the editors began by challenging. Ortega's theme was the over-running of 'liberal democracy'—by which he meant a system in which rival elites competed for the votes of the electorate—by 'hyper-democracy', in which the popular classes claimed the right to active political participation. (José Ortega y Gasset, *The Revolt of the Masses* [1930], New York 1932.)

like-minded thinkers despised—is also, in this way, the rallying cry of the only kind of elite worth having. Language use is the ground on which the issue is most tensely staged, for there, in 'the verbosphere', the contradiction between universal capability and minority competence is played out all the time. So it is that 'educated speech and egalitarian ideas', above all when combined, provoke the most powerful 'anti-elitist' reactions. They are reminders that things could be otherwise and better. *The struggle for equality isn't over, we still have a cultural elite.* In this perfectly ambiguous construction, *n+1* countered the reactionary populism of the right, literally word for word, by raising the standard of a responsible critical left.[33]

<h1 style="text-align:center">4</h1>

This was the most concentrated stream of critical engagement in *n+1*'s first years. There was nothing comparable to show for politics. Coming into being at the time of George W. Bush's re-election, the magazine not surprisingly gave space to the man himself, the stifling discourse of the two-party political order that nurtured him and the voting arrangements that helped him home—mixed mockery and yearning in three articles signed by individual editors.[34] Abroad, along with Palestine and Iraq, Bolivia, India and South Africa featured under the rubric of politics.[35] Fundamental matters of policy such as the oil economy and global warming were discussed. Yet for all the varied interest of individual items, this was a miscellany, in which

33 The editors went on to unpack their point: 'This could mean either that the lingering existence of a cultural elite testifies to the persistence of class privilege—or else that today the cultural elite is the only thing standing between us and the full spectrum dominance of the power elite. Both notions are true, but the latter truth has gone unadvertised.' (The Editors, 'Revolt of the Elites', 10, pp. 17–18.)

34 Respectively, Mark Greif, 'W.', 1; Benjamin Kunkel, 'Shhh . . . Swing Voters Are Listening', 2; Marco Roth, 'Lower the Voting Age!', 6: *Mainstream*, winter 2008.

35 Daniel Alarcón, 'Note from La Paz', 4; Johannes Türk, 'The Trouble with Being German', 4.

the clear purpose of politicizing cultural analysis was matched by a less-well-defined aspiration to bring literature in the broad sense into fertile communication with politics. Amidst all this, Mark Greif pointed towards a distinctive order of political engagement in his essay on 'Gut-Level Legislation, or Redistribution', in which he dismissed the pseudo-responsible posturing of commentators, maintaining 'that politics could be served by thinking about problems and principles, rather than rehearsing strategy—a notion that 'leaves them not so much bemused as furious'. The corresponding practice he approved would be 'political surrealism', or

> asking for what is at present impossible, in order to get at last, by indirection or implausible directness, the principles that would underlie the world we'd want rather than the one we have.[36]

As things turned out, opportunities came soon enough.

Looking back from late 2005 to the years around the turn of the century and the drama of boom and bust in the dot-com economy, the editors had dwelt on the generational subjectivity of the time, speaking of the 'mortgaged ease' of their contemporaries—a typically culturalist inflection. By then, a far greater crisis was already beginning. Within months, the US housing market bubble burst, detonating the liquidity crisis of 2007–8 that led to the deepest international recession since the 1930s. Soon, as Gessen later reported, they felt they were 'increasingly turning into a group of autodidact economists'.[37] An interview with David Harvey, carried in the fall of 2008, was synoptic and illuminating. However another feature, begun at the same time and continuing for three years, was more in the house style of the unexpected: a free-ranging tutorial with an unnamed Manhattan hedge fund manager. Beginning with mortgages and the arcana of speculative finance, the series ran to seven interviews and extended to commentary on the worsening crisis of

---

36 Mark Greif, 'Gut-Level Legislation, or Redistribution', 4.
37 Interviewed by Sofia Groopman, 'Keith Gessen and Diary of a Very Bad Year', *The Daily* (blog of *The Paris Review*), 3 August 2010.

the global financial order and the subjectivity of denial so wide-spread at every level.[38] The next issue of the magazine, headlined 'Recessional', called for the development of 'a red and green Marxism as the way out of the crisis'.[39]

Kunkel's article on full (that is, *full*) employment and Christopher Glazek's passionate arguments for the abolition of the US prison system—even at the cost of an increased rate of death sentencing—were examples of Greif's calculated impossibilism.[40] By late 2011, when Glazek's essay appeared, such flights of political imagining had found a tangible, activist context, in the Occupy Wall Street campaign and associated initiatives across America. *N+1*'s first, institutional response was the launch of *Occupy!*, a crowd-funded 'irregular tabloid' gazette published online and in print, from and for the militants of Zuccotti Park and beyond.[41] Editors of the magazine made individual contributions to the debates, in *n+1* online or in the gazette. Roth's 'Letters of Resignation from the American Dream' and Kunkel's 'The Politics of the Poor', co-written with Charles Petersen for *Occupy!*, were early versions of the editorial statement that formed the core of

---

38   Keith Gessen, 'Anonymous Hedge Fund Manager', published as three separate items, transcripts of three meetings in the twelve months beginning summer 2007, appeared in 7: *Correction*, fall 2008. A fourth part appeared in the next issue, as 'Conversations with HFM, December 2008– July 2009' (8: *Recessional*, fall 2009). The interviews appeared in book form, as *Diary of a Very Bad Year: Confessions of an Anonymous Hedge Fund Manager* (2010). See also, online, 'Who Spent the Money', 21 June 2010; and 'HFM Redux', in two parts, 15–16 December 2010.

39   8: *Recessional*, fall 2009; see in particular the editorials 'On Your Marx' and 'Growth Outgrown'.

40   Benjamin Kunkel, 'Full Employment', 9: *Bad Money*, spring 2010; Christopher Glazek, 'Raise the Crime Rate', 13: *Machine Politics*, winter 2012.

41   'Read Our New Gazette', *n+1* online announcement, 21 October 2011, a month after the first demonstration on 17 September. See also Emily Witt, '*n+1* Raises Funds for Occupy Wall Street–Inspired Gazette', *New York Observer*, 20 October 2011. Four more issues appeared at rough monthly intervals. The paper was revived in May 2014 for a special issue devoted to the trial of an OWS activist.

the magazine's main reflection on the OWS experience, 'A Left Populism'.[42]

Set between two personal narratives of uncertain documentary status, 'A Left Populism' took as its focus the celebrated slogan of Occupy, *We are the 99 per cent*. In this, the Editors wrote, there lay a challenge that could not simply be understood by analogies with the radical reforming movements of the middle and later twentieth century: it was 'nothing less than to build a [political force] capable of rescuing the country in the name of the people by and for whom it's allegedly governed', or 'the *active recreation* of American democracy'. The Occupiers had unveiled the features of a new social majority, insecure, under- or unemployed, over-educated, and 'clinging precariously to an idea of middle-classness that seems more and more a chimera'. It could be that the testimony of the self-declared 99 per cent was no more than a record of defeat, were it not that their declarations had performative value, 'actually creating class consciousness for themselves and those around them'. The visual style of that consciousness was captured in the image of the homeless—'the vanguard of contemporary America'. To acknowledge this was to pose the difficult questions of social identification—for it was this, not sympathy, that the slogan demanded. The difficulty was one of personal culture and experience, to begin with, but there was also a fundamental issue of campaigning policy hidden away in the reassuringly simple arithmetic of the slogan. The idea that the income of the 1 per cent could be taxed to any great equalizing effect was an illusion. A far wider fiscal front would have to be opened. But if, as reported in 2000, nearly two-fifths of Americans believed themselves to be either existing or prospective members of the 1 per cent, what were the chances for a redistributive programme attacking the net incomes of as much as 20 per cent of taxpayers? At the same time, however, openness to fundamental political reform was now greater than at any time in recent American history, and here the left might 'begin to contemplate a return from the wilderness'. A new populism was in prospect,

---

42   Marco Roth, online only, 24 October 2011; Benjamin Kunkel and Charles Petersen, *Occupy!* online, 31 October 2011; the Editors, 'A Left Populism', 13.

a 'reconstitution of the American "people" as a progressive force bringing about a society that's just, sustainable and free'.

The word *union* occurred just once in this editorial, and then in the grammatical negative: the new majority was, among other demoralizing things, 'non-unionized'. But what organized labour might have to contribute to the new politics was left unexplored. In fact, trade unions were already contributing to the occupations in material ways, as Nikil Saval reported in a telling online companion piece, but on terms that he summarized in a wounding comparison: the Occupiers viewed them in the same way the Democratic Party did, 'as a source of bodies and money, a mere service that tends to be thanked and repudiated in the same breath'.[43] The historic value of 'solidarity' had been reduced to a matter of discretionary approval. 'People can endlessly rehearse to themselves the failures of traditional trade unionism, or they can try to change the one available form of organization that promises to deliver the things they want.' Movements normally take their names from what they are for or against, Saval noted, and

> the 'Occupy Movement', which, when it lets its guard down, admits that it wants equality, might do worse than submitting to a name that represents the struggle for it in the past, and call itself a 'labour movement'.

5

Occupy marked a high-point of direct political engagement for *n+1*. It was, the editors said, 'the first serious political hope—not less serious for its fragility—that many of us have been able to entertain about our country in our few years or decades of adult life'.[44]

Just who that 'us' encompassed, now as in other moments of high tension, was unclear. What did seem clear was that the engagement

---

43   Nikil Saval, online only, 17 November 2011. Saval, Petersen and Glazek were all associate editors of the magazine at this time.

44   The Editors, 'A Left Populism', 13, p. 10.

was not an uncomplicated embrace. Saval's impatience with the stock anti-union animus on show among the Occupiers was evident— reaching an unforgettable high in his evocation of 'startup hackers skateboarding through picket lines' in San Francisco.[45] (An account of the resistance to the union-busting state governor of Wisconsin had appeared in *n+1* earlier in the year.[46]) Kunkel, writing elsewhere, challenged Slavoj Žižek's claim that for OWS the principal enemy was capitalism as such, and also expressed concern that traditional anarchist norms of unmediated, prefigurative practice might 'stifle, rather than inspire' the development of an adequate programme for the left.[47] The epiphanies of Zuccotti Square fell some way short of the political synthesis that the vision of a capable 'left populism' implied. The call—the editors' own—to 'occupy the future' was stirring but also obscure.

The imprint of the financial crisis was more lasting and various. The writing in Kunkel's *Utopia or Bust,* published in 2014 in association with the militant socialist *Jacobin* magazine, came after the collapse of Lehman Brothers—and for the greater part predated Occupy—and showed a wider concern with the patterns of the capitalist economy since the 1970s. In 2011 came the launch of 'City by City', a diverse series of reports, memoirs and analyses from bigger and smaller population centres around the US, attempting to capture the textures of everyday life at the exposed ends of economic crisis, in a necessary complement and contrast to the view from the Manhattan hedge funds or bohemian Brooklyn.[48] In another vein, the achievements of Wal-Mart's women workers in a long-running class action over equal pay prompted a reconsideration of the old

---

45   Nikil Saval, 'A Labor Movement', *Occupy!,* 17 November 2011.

46   Eli S. Evans, 'The Battle of Wisconsin', 11: *Dual Power,* spring 2011.

47   Benjamin Kunkel, *Utopia or Bust: A Guide to the Present Crisis,* New York and London 2014, pp. 133–4, 140. Nonetheless, Kunkel is committed to a strategy including the elaboration of concrete institutional alternatives. See his contribution to The Editors, 'Election Preview', online only, 5 November 2012.

48   And as the editors made plain in an elaborately literary introduction to the new feature, it was also a specifically cultural intervention against the historic ruralism of US culture, aimed at restoring the city to its real centrality.

notion of 'sex class'.[49] Saval pursued his interest in workplace relations into his magazine's home territory, publishing, organizing a symposium on 'Labor and Letters', including testimony from employees of the *New Yorker* and *Harper's* but also the left monthly *Dissent*, and ending, fittingly, with a short, candid history of working conditions at *n+1* itself.[50] The politics and culture of race have continued to be a feature of the magazine, notably in a number whose special focus is police violence against black Americans.[51]

In literary matters, the sense of a project to elucidate, if not a programme, remained palpable. Jonathan Franzen remained a privileged reference for the editors, who devoted a symposium to his 2010 novel, *Freedom,* in which they saw a triumph of immersive realism and a benchmark for future writing.[52] The editorial 'World Lite' concluded a long, impressively well-read ramble through the conceptual and empirical history descending from Goethe's *Weltliteratur* to the late-Rushdian Davos of Global Lit, with a call for a renewed literary 'internationalism', a commitment to 'project' rather than 'product', and to 'truth' over the prevailing canon of 'the literary'.[53]

In 'Cultural Revolution', published two years ago, *n+1* presented its most systematic survey ever of the general situation and prospects. Again not quite a programme, nevertheless it showed something of the necessary, clarifying schematism of the genre, in its review of options

---

49   Dayna Tortorici, 'Sex Class Action', 14. A year later, Tortorici took a leading part in organizing a print and online memorial for Shulamith Firestone, the pioneering feminist, who had just died. See Ti-Grace Atkinson and many others, 'On Shulamith Firestone', 15; Dayna Tortorici, 'On Firestone', and Jennifer Baumgardner and others, 'On Firestone, Part 2', online only, both 26 September 2012.

50   21: *Throwback*, winter 2015.

51   22: Conviction, spring 2015.

52   Keith Gessen, Mark Greif, Benjamin Kunkel and Marco Roth, 'Four Responses to *Freedom*', 10.

53   The Editors, 'World Lite', 17: *The Evil Issue,* fall 2013. Dissenting from this programmatic approach, associated with Kunkel and her fellow editor Saval, Carla Blumenkrantz declared her preference for a less 'project-oriented' formula in fiction editing, with a stress on 'exploration' rather than 'rigour'. (See Krill, 'Take a Page from This'.)

for left intellectuals such as those gathered around the magazine. Looking back over the decades since the political reflux of the left in the '70s, and beyond that to the heyday of Western Marxism, the editors recalled the anxiety that haunted much cultural theorizing and analysis. Could it be, as Marcuse had suggested in the 1930s, that culture was largely affirmative, with little or no remaining power of negation? That, as Bourdieusians came to hold, in a later period, 'more and more the social purpose and deep content of all culture [including that of the intellectual left] has seemed one identical substance: the content is capital and its purpose is to reproduce capitalism'?[54]

Or might it not be that the deteriorating conditions of intellectual work, whether in (or not quite in) the academy or in an increasingly pinched commercial publishing sector, are now opening up new possibilities for left intellectuals? Not all of these are welcome. One, the worst of all, is that there will be a new social rarefaction of autonomous culture—and, with that, a loss of critical charge—as rising talents decide that the probable costs are too high, the chances of a reasonable living too remote. At the ideal opposite, there lies the path towards cultural revolution and the human transformation heralded by Trotsky in the closing pages of *Literature and Revolution*.[55] The declassing of intellectuals currently in progress might sharpen the edge of a critical culture and enhance the social credibility of those who labour to produce it in visibly unprivileged circumstances. In this, and the creation of independent and accessible institutions of popular learning, were preconditions for the emergence of truly organic intellectuals of the working class and 'a ProBo challenge' to the cultural fatalism of 'the BoBo consensus'. The third possibility saw the return of an old metaphor, now rewritten. This would mean 'the confinement of important varieties of culture . . . to demographic archipelagos amid rising seas of mass corporate product'. There would be no expectation of making a living from serious artistic pursuits, which would be financed by 'uninspiring and ill-paid day jobs'. Such 'cosily disappointed existence, streaked with fear of

---

54   The Editors, 'Cultural Revolution',16: *Double Bind*, spring 2013.
55   Leon Trotsky, *Literature and Revolution* (1924), Ann Arbor 1960.

unemployment', was already familiar as the decivilizing formula of the present.

These, in outline, were the historic options, the unresolved stakes in the 'intellectual situation' considered in the most general terms. The editors concluded:

> We're trying to figure what to do from an unstable position amid crumbling institutions and generalized crisis. More than one variety of brave and honest, necessarily incomplete response to the dilemma can surely be offered, and still more varieties of evasive bullshit: a good ear will know the difference. We can't bring ourselves to cheer the failure of institutions that have sustained us—but we can at least be grateful that the collapsing structures are carrying out a sort of structural rescue of meaningful individual choice, in politics and culture. Bobo or ProBo? Siege mentality ('We writers are in this together!') or sorties beyond the walls: 'We're in this with almost everyone!'? Reform existing institutions, or replace them, or cultivate your own garden, or retire to your Unabomber cabin? . . . What counts is history asking us a question—about our content or purpose in a society of accelerating insecurity, including our own—that one way or another we need to formulate as sharply as possible, since we answer it with our lives.[56]

6

The existential turn of the closing lines is characteristic—a term of judgement that itself looks back to Schwarz's advice but perhaps with a sharpened sense of the associated meanings of the word. 'Who is *n+1*?' is an apt question to ask about a magazine that not only *has* a character but arguably *is* one. That this character bears a close resemblance to persons that the founding editors are or were, and to all or some of their collaborators, does not alter the fact that it is an invention occupying a different order of reality from that of passports and

---

56   The Editors, 'Cultural Revolution', 16.

driver's licences. It is a fiction—a virtuous one, let it be said at the outset. The character is a writer, of course, but one who wants to 'be a writer', and the reason why self-evident achievement seems in this way never quite to fulfil the aspiration is that this writer is young and insecure, and, being a fiction, can never grow older or become settled. *Bildung* is the common label for narratives featuring a protagonist of this kind, and also the master-trope of *n+1*. Three of the magazine's founders—Gessen, Harbach and Kunkel—have published first novels in this category and a fourth—Roth—has written a memoir of his family.[57] (Gessen has also written an account of the *Bildung* of Harbach as novelist.)[58] The trope recurs throughout the archive. Essays as different as Lawrence Jackson's account of Baltimore and Jedediah Purdy's discussion of neo-liberalism as discourse are structured as coming-of-age narratives.[59] The editors visit the occupation in Lower Manhattan and 'the only people we see', besides friends, are young hopefuls, interns from all over publishing.[60] Precarity—high rents, low pay, self-exploitation and a poor outlook—is a constant in reports from the industry. In more recent times, the magazine's personnel roster has been listing some of its creators twice: once in respect of their current roles and a second time, as an unvarying (invariable) group, the 'Founding Editors'. It is as though in a part of their being they will always be that thirtyish bunch of friends with an idea for a magazine.

7

The rhetoric of generation is as marked in *n+1* as it commonly is in the public discourse of the US, and in this case the governing feeling is one of belatedness. It is too late for Theory, too late for postmodern

57   Benjamin Kunkel, *Indecision*, New York 2005; Keith Gessen, *All the Sad Young Literary Men*, New York 2008; Chad Harbach, *The Art of Fielding*, New York 2011; Marco Roth, *The Scientists: A Family Romance*, New York 2012.

58   Keith Gessen, *How a Book Is Born: The Making of the Art of Fielding*, an expanded version of 'The Book on Publishing', *Vanity Fair*, October 2011.

59   Lawrence Jackson, 'Slickheads', 15; 'The Accidental Neoliberal', 19.

60   Verb tense altered for context.

style, too late for the comforts of aestheticism in the Eggers vein, and far too late for illusions in the American imperium and the presumption that comes with a high-end education. Even growing up is not what it once was, as privileged and parlous life circumstances combine to prolong the twenties past thirty. But as Gessen wrote, 'It is time to say what you mean.' Or in Roth's 'shameless', punning retrospect, 'if I'm late to the party, I can start a party of latecomers'.[61] The sense of an ending did not imply general disconnection, which would have been paralysing. There were supporting precedents, both close in time and further back, for critically engaged writing: in the *Baffler* and *Hermenaut*, for instance, but above all in the early *Partisan Review*, with its exemplary combination of independent leftist politics and modernist cultural sympathies, and free-floating metropolitan demeanour. 'The greatest of magazines' in its heyday, in Gessen's judgement, *Partisan Review* was a vivid historical image rather than a template. *N+1*'s interweaving of culture and politics is more intricate than *Partisan Review*'s was, and its range is more extensive across media and national borders—though more haphazard too, in the latter respect. Time will tell whether its talent-spotting skills have been comparable. The spirit of *Partisan Review* and its milieu is perhaps best caught in the tenor of the magazine's essays, including very notably the editorial 'Diary', which has a recognizable ancestry in the older magazine's successive forms of commentary.[62] The address is serious, though not cultivating gravitas. The style is lay, not academic, as in what used to be called the higher journalism. It is flexible in register to a degree that could not have been contemplated in the 1940s, when the proprieties of diction were far stricter, and in that, the comparison must be limited. But the combined seriousness and conversational ease of *n+1*, with its wide variation of

---

61 Jesse Montgomery, 'Young Critics: Marco Roth', *Full Stop*, 22 June 2011. See also Roth, *The Scientists*, p. 174.

62 At different times and in different shapes in the first decade, 'Ripostes', 'This Quarter' and 'Variety'. See for one illuminating instance, 'Variety', 15, 6, 1948, consisting of Lionel Trilling, 'The Repressive Impulse' and Anatole Broyard, 'A Portrait of the Hipster'. This was the most significant of several borrowings from *Partisan Review*'s editorial design.

feeling and ready access to the language of the street and campus, are reminiscent of the manner that John Hollander called New York Baroque.[63]

This should not be mistaken for an instance of the putative post-modern collapse of high into low culture, for all the superficial resemblance there is, and even if that period atmosphere was a form-ative condition of what was now taking shape. It was rather, we might say, that the logic of belatedness released its enabling potential, so that a group of young writers deeply schooled in the intellectual and artistic currents of the 1990s but finding them already failing as responses to the political and cultural conditions of the new century, was driven to look for orientation further back, in the traditions of the 1930s.

8

Partisan Review was the glowing icon of a usable past for this party of latecomers, but the sense of the *n+1* initiative can be captured in more general historical and conceptual terms. For much of the twen-tieth century, in the metropolitan zone, high discourse on culture was dominated by a narrative that pitted traditional values, a minor-ity commitment, against a modern mass civilization that threatened to extinguish them. This *Kulturkritik*, as it was named in its German homeland, developed a Marxist strain in Frankfurt Critical Theory. Then, emerging some sixty years ago, new perceptions and valua-tions of majority culture—'mass' or 'popular', depending on the case and the emphasis of the argument—rose to challenge the conven-tional accounts of the modern landscape of meaning, most influentially in the institutional form of Cultural Studies. This too was conceived as a critical discourse, not less so because of its unam-biguous positioning on the left, though it tended at times to settle into a reflex egalitarian defence of majority culture against the elites of *Kulturkritik* and their alter ego, a remote, uncomprehending 'left',

---

63   Hollander was referring to the milieu of 'the New York intellectuals' as a whole, not just *Partisan Review*.

and in some incarnations became notorious for its wishful political transvaluations of popular cultural experience.

In the perspective of *Kulturkritik*, this was a necessary fulfilment: cultural studies as the final collapse of inherited standards in the face of market populism. On the left, relations between the two discursive strains have seldom been better than watchful. Both are present in *n+1*, in the iconic figures of Adorno and Bourdieu, but what is remarkable is that here, for all the differences there must finally be between them, they cooperate in a loose-limbed critical discourse on contemporary culture in which the familiar binaries, while not lost from view, have lost their power of intellectual inhibition. In the space so opened, critical judgement can be exercised freely and knowledgeably in every register of the culture, in recognizable evaluative idioms both old and new, and in perspectives defined primarily by the aspirations of direct cultural producers and their lay audiences. Trails of money, real estate and educational privilege—the stuff of 'sociological' placeholders where there is no real 'value' to judge, as some say—are followed from the backstairs rooms where publishers' interns devil away in the hope of better things to the heights of the literary novel and the concert hall.

If belatedness was the main condition of this breakthrough, another, in contrast, was an accident of synchrony. The founding editors are exactly contemporary with the digital remodelling of culture that defined the 1990s and the first decade of the new century: college students in the early days of Mosaic and Amazon, new graduates when Google arrived, editors of a new magazine in 2004, the year of Facebook.[64] Young enough to have native fluency in the new technologies but sufficiently formed in a predecessor culture to be able to appraise their emergent behavioural syndromes at a cool distance, they were gifted a whole field of critical opportunity in the form of the blank 'revolution' they were quick to identify and satirize as 'webism'.[65] In all, the result has been a continuous stream of

64   Kunkel, born 1972; Roth, 1974; Gessen, Greif and Harbach, all 1975.
65   The Editors, 'Internet as Social Movement', 9.

commentary on culture today, uniting evaluative, interpretive and explanatory modes, across media, institutions, registers and forms, appraising corporate practice and mass-individual habitus with the same aplomb: a concentration of work without precedent or equal in the US or anywhere else.

9

The defining moment of this unlikely discursive confluence is *n+1*'s Ortega Paradox, as it might be dubbed: the move in which a self-defined elite of the left appropriates a reactionary, fatalistic appeal to inherited prerogatives, rewriting it as a mobilization of retrievable or discoverable cultural standards, in the name of a real equality still to be won. At this point, cultural commentary inevitably takes a political turn. The shared limitation of *Kulturkritik* and cultural studies was their discursive evacuation of politics as a mode of social authority. This logic was more fully worked through in the case of conservative-liberal *Kulturkritik*, where established positions and interests could more easily be sublimated as heritage and standards—the feint that *n+1* missed, or creatively misread. On the left, outcomes have been less predictable, and potentially more misleading. In *n+1*, on the whole, as in *Partisan Review* before it, this culturalist dissolution-effect has not operated. It too has expressly rejected the moralism to which *Kulturkritik* has always been constitutionally prone:

> If human rights are to be reclaimed they must first be restored to the realm of politics. Not the realm of morality, which is always and ever a discussion of good versus evil, but politics.[66]

However, this is not to say that the articulation of politics in the multivocal discourse of the magazine is a simple matter. Politics is a

---

66 Introduction to The Editors, 'A Solution from Hell', 12: *Conversion Experience*, fall 2011. Compare, for example, William Phillips on Ignazio Silone's *The Seed Beneath the Snow*: 'The Spiritual Underground', *Partisan Review*, 9, 6, 1942.

pervasive inflection in its contents, yet some of the work published under that formal rubric seems to have little connection with politics in any ordinary sense, even where the substance is a familiar heading in public discourse, and political commentary overall, especially on the home front, has been relatively scant. Obama passed his first term unscathed in *n+1* and still commanded a majority of votes in the editorial preview of his bid for re-election, even if the enthusiasts were a minority; the abstentionist position was noted—critically— but not voiced.[67] The *New York Times* has attracted more criticism for its incoherent response to the decline of its historic publishing model than for its policy orientations.[68] There are strictly political considerations at work in such judgements, of course. But it seems safe to add, for this case in particular, that the literary ethos of the magazine has not always assisted the development of its political voice. The Poundian injunction to 'make it new' seems ideally suited to a vision of socialist transformation, yet in one key respect it may be not at all well matched. The modern valorization of the negative implies a discursive rule of non-repetition, a constant practice of innovation and departure, that is in tension with the conditions of political discourse, in which repetition is a fundamental resource and necessity. 'What could we say that hadn't already been said?', Roth asked rhetorically, explaining the surrealist proposal for Gaza and the West Bank.[69] That is not the point, and he could hardly have chosen a less favourable illustration of his case. No political position is the worse for having been stated more than once; what counts is whether it is valid or not, according to the calculus of rights and interests in play. And so long as a pressing demand goes unmet, it has to be reiterated.

---

67   The Editors, 'Election Preview', 5 November 2012. The assassination of Osama bin Laden prompted another exercise in displaced politics in the shape of a piece of participant observation of the celebrating crowds at Ground Zero. There was no mention of the politics of the event, either the regressive, sports-sodden nationalism of the revellers or the small matter of premeditated executive murder in an allied foreign jurisdiction.

68   The Editors, 'Addled', 9.

69   Roth, quoted in Krill, 'Take a Page from This', *Haaretz*.

Partisan Review now appears in a contrastive light. In the years after its refoundation in 1937, the magazine was intensely focused, politically, by the great issues of the Russian Revolution and its aftermath: the meaning and direction of Stalinism, the struggle against counter-revolution in Europe, the class character of the imminent world war. The editors of *n+1*, like others before them and since, have made comparisons with the Revolution in their account of the internet transformations of their own time, but with an air of fluctuating conviction that should perhaps be read as a stand-in for due scepticism. The stricter comparisons are with earlier communications technologies such as rail and television, which had myriad social effects while remaining, like the political leaflets in the editors' parable of webist street agitation, blank. They were not, in the relevant sense, revolutions at all. Politically, the greater emphasis must fall on the contrasts, which at this date mark a difference of epoch.

Partisan Review made the Russian Revolution integral to its project . . . Indeed, but there is another way of seeing this connection, to use a word that is itself deficient for the purpose. *Partisan Review* belongs organically to the history of the Revolution, in the sense that it was one of the many embodiments of the surge of hope and energy released by the events of October, at first and mainly in the international workers movement and the parties of the new, Communist International. The lines of transmission were both organizational and biographical. The magazine was initiated as an organ of the Communist John Reed Clubs, edited by two party members, Ukrainian Jews by birth and upbringing (Philip Rahv) or parentage (William Phillips). In the refounded *Partisan Review* the political continuities with October were direct, in the persons of Trotsky, who wrote in the early numbers, and Victor Serge, who contributed both fiction and theoretical-political writing, debating with the editors and members of the New York circle over the class character of the Soviet Union. That political engagement, just as much as the programmatic modernism and philo-Europeanism of its cultural orientation, is what powered *Partisan Review* in its great, early years. The magazine continued for some years in this vein, but editorial departures (over the politics of the war) and incipient Cold War pressures were debilitating. A principled anti-Stalinist communism was soon metamorphosing into anti-Communism, full stop. The ten-year retrospective published in 1946 left few traces of the revolutionary contentions of the early years, and it was given to the literary critic Lionel Trilling, rather than anyone more central to the *Partisan Review* of the thirties, to preside over the volume with a lulling, or prophylactic, invocation of politics 'united with the imagination and subject to the criticism of mind'[70]—a sweet Arnoldian phrase, faultless in its abstraction, with a compromised future ahead of it in the Cold War decades.[71]

Forty years later, that conflict had been concluded in the interests of capital. The Communist regimes had fallen or remade themselves, and the historic movement from which they had emerged did not long survive them. The major formations of the left, Communist or social-democratic, surrendered to the gravitational pull of the new strategic dominant of neo-liberalism, leaving the work of fundamental opposition to an ever more diverse array of political agencies. There was no doubting the militant energies that such agencies could tap, as the many movements of the 1990s and after attested. But equally there was no denying that the imaginative world of *Partisan Review* had ended. This historic closure defined the political horizon within which *n+1* took shape, entrenching a further cause and condition of belatedness in the founding group—a fading of communication with the high tradition of revolutionary thought. The turn to the critique of political economy—Marx and his inheritors in our own time—is admirable, but there have been fewer signs of focused interest in the canon of socialist political theory. In a left culture in which the

---

70   Lionel Trilling, 'Introduction', Williams Phillips and Philip Rahv, eds, *The Partisan Reader: Ten Years of Partisan Review 1934–1944: An Anthology*, New York 1946, p. xvi.

71   *Partisan Review* benefited from covert CIA funding at various times in the 1950s and '60s, as a significant locus of the 'Non-Communist Left' activity the agency sought to cultivate throughout the capitalist world—a fact rather too cryptically acknowledged by Mark Greif in his recent homage to the magazine, 'What's Wrong with Public Intellectuals', *The Chronicle of Higher Education*, 13 February 2015.

foremost oppositional slogan of recent times—*We are the 99 per cent!*—is a demagogic evasion of social reality, the critical considerations of classical Marxist politics are hardly at a discount. Yet Lenin appears, when he does, as a half-seen figure in the distance, a stock reminder of what is not to be done,[72] and Trotsky's visionary conclusions in *Literature and Revolution* are no substitute for his elaboration of the theory of united fronts or critique of bureaucracy.

But after all, the homage to Trotsky comes in a text devoted to the theme of cultural revolution, reminding us of what *n+1*'s essential, justifying work has been, in its first decade. Not politics, with all qualifications made one way or another, even though its atmosphere has been political throughout; and not literature, oddly, except in the old meaning of the word that encompasses far more than the arts of literary fiction; but criticism, sustained, radical, formally resourceful critical commentary on the high and popular cultures of the times, broad in sympathy but quick to judgement, moving in a clearing beyond *Kulturkritik* and Cultural Studies. The magazine has been exemplary in this, illustrating the old wisdom that looks among latecomers for the unexpected novelty.

Postscript 2023

So things stood as *n+1* entered its second decade of life. How do they appear now, at the start of a third? The signs of continuity and growth have been plain to see. The masthead, which has come to list up to four degrees of editorship, is a mix of familiar and newer names reaching back to the start while demonstrating a necessary capacity for renewal. The contents pages, likewise, normally feature both first-time and returning authors, in a ratio of perhaps three to one overall. The magazine remains as free-ranging in its coverage as it set out to be—with a more extensive international sweep, now touching every continent—and as little inhibited in its movement through rhetorical

---

72 But see Kunkel's comments on 'democratic dictatorship', and the general Gramscian inspiration, in his contribution to the 2012 'Election Preview'.

space, with essays that might be fictions and fictions that might be essays, a 'help desk' that might be either of these, or even neither; obituaries that might in one case be a conventional post-mortem appreciation but in another mutate into an exchange of letters. The contents of issue number 20, section by section, coming ten years in and headlined, as it happened, *Survival*, give the flavour at its most piquant.[73] First, as usual, 'The Intellectual Situation: A Diary', or the editorial, this one discussing the question of payment for writing and then the relation between 'privilege discourse' and the return of 'class', with some consideration of Piketty, Bourdieu, and Laclau and Mouffe en route; next, 'Politics', or a care-worker's vocation and lot as a nurse in these times, as narrated by her daughter, a writer. We move on, then, to 'Fiction', two texts, one an excerpt from a forthcoming novel, *The Wallcreeper*, the author's first, the other a story, also by a first-time novelist. The pieces that make up the fourth section, subtitled 'Essays', include a historical account of 'race trouble' in the New York avant-garde in 1979, another centred in the pop music business and titled 'Justin Timberlake Has a Cold'; a study of the ethos of violence in old-style ice hockey, and the story, translated from Alejandro Almazán's Spanish, of 'a no luck narco'. 'Reviews' are represented on this occasion by a thirty-page account and affirmation of the novelist Tao Lin, hailed here as 'the first great male Asian author of American descent', and a round-up of recent writing on political economy after the crash of 2008. The letters that close the issue deal with net neutrality, language death, and bathroom design.

The dominant in this miscellany, its shaping personality trait, is as Roberto Schwarz imagined it. The character *n+1* is above all an essayist, a writer who ranges widely, judging freely and flatly, without ever quite abandoning the ground of personal observation and experience. The keyword here is *writer*. It is hard, in scanning the forty-plus issues of the magazine, to overlook the number of contributors belonging to the category 'a writer living in New York'—or, once in a while, somewhere else. The information is dependably accurate, and surely, on reflection, not so surprising. But the statement is not

---

73   Number 20: *Survival*, fall 2014.

of the same kind as 'X is a professor of Y at the University of Z'. In its sheer abstraction, its spareness of expression, it suggests both euphoric weightlessness and personal exposure in engagements without miti-gation—a romance of writing. The reality is not so stark. The magazine's 'Acknowledgements' have grown from a couple of lines to as many pages, listing public and corporate sources as well as private support. Here, with due allowance made for mixed motives, is clear evidence of esteem, and in this sense there is some ground for the judgement that '*n+1*, more than a decade on, has gone from upstart to institution'.[74] But this is a well-worn figure of commentary that makes light of an evident ambiguity, support offering validation and a measure of practical shelter but also presupposing elemental need. Upstarts such as this one are unlikely to survive the rigours of the open market.

Now completing its second decennium, *n+1* has remained very much the entity launched in 2004, at the centre of a whole institutional complex since extended to include a dedicated online book reviews section, *N1BR*. Most of the founding editors have continued to be active, though in shifting capacities, following a template that varies only for special occasions:[75] the intellectual situation, politics, fiction (and drama), essays, reviews, letters, in that order. The central concern with the state of high and mass culture has been pursued in studies of publishing in the 2010s, and the signs of deepening malaise in reviewing; podcasting, the constraints and affordances of the new net-based reading environment and the 'depressing' revival in op-ed writing. Another cultural register is explored in an essay on the sexual pathology of frat-boy misogyny. Where the magazine most visibly differs from its earlier self is in its increased concentration on politics. In this respect, the layout of contents can be misleading, for just as 'politics' has often accommodated material not obviously political, so politics in its narrower senses can be found under any of

---

74   Gideon Lewis-Kraus, 'Oh, the Humanities: The Cultural Criticism of Mark Greif', *Bookforum*, September-November 2016.

75   Such as those on police violence, or new Russian political poets (respectively 22: *Conviction*, spring 2015, and 26: *Dirty Work*, fall 2016).

the half-dozen set headings: in 'The Intellectual Situation', for example, where Nikil Saval writes about canvassing for Bernie Sanders in Philadelphia, Namara Smith discusses Sanders and Clinton (Hillary), with their comparable limitations in the critical policy zone of women and welfare, while an unsigned editorial arraigns the *'soi-disant* socialist' from Vermont for his 'tepid' commitments in foreign affairs.[76] In 'Politics', naturally, where Greg Afinogenov argues for the abolition of Trump's Immigration and Customs Enforcement agency, the infamous ICE.[77] Or in 'Essays', where Gabriel Winant assesses the state of the US labour movement ('Who Works for the Workers?'), and Jacob Burns records his year-long experience on the front line in Gaza.[78] Here is a handful of cases taken to stand for an editorial investment ranging from fine points of door-to-door mobilizing or the strategic value of an ethos of mutual care in the circles of a beleaguered opposition, to philosophical questions of subjectivity and agency—and including a line in defence of politics as a necessary social mode, in opposition to the economistic and culturalist strains in post-political advocacy today.

Tim Barker's 'The Bleak Left', a review of the file of the left-communist journal *Endnotes,* is chastened, if in the end unrepentant:

> Every political writer must balance groundless hope against deflating realism. *Endnotes* excels at the latter because it transfers all hope to a distant future . . . They offer the rest of us, who I believe are correct to place our hopes in programmes and transitions, challenges that will not be answered easily. Perhaps, despite its cunning and erudition, the politics of *Endnotes* is no more serious than glib forms of anarchism. But on what grounds are our 'realistic' politics any less fanciful?[79]

76   'The Intellectual Situation', 26; the Editors, 'Bernie's World', 25: *Slow Burn*, spring 2016.

77   Greg Afinogenov, 'Society as Checkpoint', 32: *Bad Faith*, fall 2018.

78   Gabriel Winant, 'Who Works for the Workers?', 26; and Jacob Burns, 'Take Me with You', 37: *Transmission*, spring 2020.

79   Tim Barker, 'On *Endnotes*', 28: *Half-Life,* spring 2017.